The Anthro~~~ ~~~riter

THE ANTHROPOLOGIST AS WRITER
Genres and Contexts in the Twenty-First Century

Edited by
Helena Wulff

berghahn
NEW YORK · OXFORD
www.berghahnbooks.com

First edition published in 2016 by
Berghahn Books
www.berghahnbooks.com

Library of Congress Cataloging-in-Publication Data

Names: Wulff, Helena, editor.
Title: The anthropologist as writer : genres and contexts in the twenty-first century
/ edited by Helena Wulff.
Description: New York : Berghahn Books, [2016] | Includes bibliographical
references and index.
Identifiers: LCCN 2015034312| ISBN 9781785330186 (hardback : alk. paper) |
ISBN 9781785337420 (paperback) | ISBN 9781785330193 (ebook)
Subjects: LCSH: Ethnology—Authorship. | Communication in ethnology. |
Literature and anthropology.
Classification: LCC GN307.7 .A56 2016 | DDC 305.8/00723—dc23
LC record available at http://lccn.loc.gov/2015034312

British Library Cataloguing in Publication Data

A catalogue record for this book is available from the British Library

ISBN 978-1-78533-018-6 (hardback)
ISBN 978-1-78533-742-0 (paperback)
ISBN 978-1-78533-019-3 (ebook)

Contents

Tables

Acknowledgments

This volume originates from the fifth Stockholm Anthropology Roundtable, which I organized at Stockholm University. The Stockholm Anthropology Roundtable is an annual forum for international discussion of current and emergent issues in the discipline.

I am grateful to all speakers for thoughtful presentations that developed into inspiring discussion. In particular, I am grateful to those speakers who turned their presentations into chapters for this volume. They constitute the bulk of the volume. Later, I invited some additional contributors. I owe them special thanks.

My greatest debt is to Marion Berghahn for her splendid support and extraordinary efficiency. It is always a true delight to work with her. It has also been a great joy to work with Molly Mosher, Duncan Ramslem, and Jessica Murphy, editorial and production assistants at Berghahn Books. I am very grateful to Kinga Jankus for compiling the index. Many thanks to my niece, Victoria Wulff, for taking the cover picture.

The fifth Stockholm Anthropology Roundtable was funded by Henrik Granholm Foundation, Stockholm University.

Stockholm, February 2015
Helena Wulff

Introducing the Anthropologist as Writer
Across and Within Genres

Helena Wulff

There you are: facing the computer screen. Your "field," whatever that was, is some distance away, at least for now. You have worked through the materials you collected there, and think you have them in a promising order. Time for the next step: to write. You may not get away from the screen any time soon—not really get away.

Then at some later point, you are there again in front of the screen, checking your emails. Has that publisher or editor you had in mind been in touch yet, responding to your proposal, or even to that entire manuscript you sent? If so, expect—at best—a period in front of the screen again, reviewing, rewriting, perhaps reorganizing.

Anthropologists have mostly celebrated the field experience in all its variety. Yet in fact, they are likely to spend as much time sitting in front of the computer screen. Once it has begun, writing is in one way a very solitary activity, but in another way, it is not: you may be in interaction with an imagined audience of colleagues, students, as well as people in your field, perhaps general readers, and, increasingly, the representatives of academic audit culture.

For some time now, anthropologists have understood that they are also writers, and have engaged in scrutinizing the implications of this fact. Clifford Geertz, in his influential book *The Interpretation of Cultures* (1973: 19), famously asked (in the idiom of the time): "What does the ethnographer do?—He writes." Taking existing conversations on writing in anthropology as a point of departure, the mission of this volume is twofold: first, to identify different writing genres anthropologists actually engage with; and second, to argue for the usefulness and necessity for anthropologists of taking writing as a craft seriously *and* of writing across and within genres in new ways. This introduction will contextualize writing in anthropology historically and theoretically, move on to my own experience of writing dance journalism as one instance of broadening anthropological writing, and conclude by offering an overview of ways of writing anthropology as discussed in the following chapters.

What writing genres are anthropologists expected, in various contexts, to master in the twenty-first century? Anthropological writing is a timely topic as it shapes the intellectual content of the discipline, as well as careers and institutional profiles. Academic scholarly writing is obviously the primary genre for anthropologists, and the recent debate has had its center of gravity here. Yet anthropologists also do much writing in many styles and genres other than academic scholarly writing. Writing for various administrative contexts, which includes not one but a number of changing genres, is—because of their control over academic values—regarded as an expanding problem by many, if not most, anthropologists with intellectual drives. Sooner or later most anthropologists find themselves writing academic administrative texts, filling in extensive forms, and filing reports (Brenneis 2009). With increasing demand, many anthropologists also develop a capacity to write reports commissioned by development agencies, municipalities, and business corporations. But there is also significant cultural, social, and political critique communicated through anthropological writings (Gusterson and Besteman 2010). There are anthropologists who write memoirs (Narayan 2007; Stoller 2008; Collins and Gallinat 2010), and fiction, as commented on by Ruth Behar in the book chapter "Believing in Anthropology as Literature" (2009). Anthropologists have taken an interest in writing novels (Stoller 1999), poetry (Tedlock 2002), and even crime novels (White 2007) inspired by ethnography. The fact that anthropologists also are engaged readers of detective stories has been examined by Regina Bendix (2012). Ulf Hannerz (2013) has written about a legendary Swedish detective story writer, Stieg Trenter (whose idiosyncratic spelling of his first name most likely influenced Stieg Larsson of the globally best-selling "Millennium Trilogy" when he changed his name from Stig to Stieg), pointing out similarities between anthropologists and detective story writers. Travel writing, especially that describing dark sides such as violence and security issues, is examined by Skinner (2012).

CONTEXTUALIZING WRITING IN ANTHROPOLOGY

Writing and writers have attracted anthropological attention for quite some time. Clifford Geertz (1988) analyzed the anthropologist as author (particularly Malinowski, Benedict, Evans-Pritchard, and Lévi-Strauss), and in the 1990s, Eduardo Archetti edited the volume *Exploring the Written* (1994a), which applies an anthropological perspective to texts ranging from fiction and songs to letters and newspapers. As Archetti (1994b: 13) argued, "a literary product is not only a substantive part of the real world but also a key element in the configuration of the world itself." And the volume *Anthropology off the Shelf: Anthropologists on Writing (2000),* edited by Alisse Waterston and Maria D. Vesperi, elaborates on anthropological writing for a general audience, especially on questions of racism, sexism, and ethics. An anthropological inquiry into writing is not limited to the anthropology of writing, text (Barber 2007), reading (Boyarin 1993; Reed 2011), and cultural literacy (Street 1997), but includes ideas from literature that have been a frequent source for anthropologists. Writing as a way of life is one of Michael Jackson's recurrent themes as in *The Other Shore* (2012). Kristen Ghodsee presents an original experimental ethnographic writing form when she includes some ethnographic fiction chapters in the third person among other ethnographic chapters in the first person in *Lost in Transition: Ethnographies of Everyday Life after Communism* (2011), her monograph about the collapse of communism in Bulgaria.

One of the enduring impacts of the "writing culture" debate during the 1980s is that it made anthropologists sharpen their writing tools. There was the critique of what was conceptualized as narcissism, with focus on the fieldworker at the expense of the people of the study, which was mostly articulated in British anthropology by, for example, Dawson, Hockey, and James (1997), while the volumes by Barton and Papen (2010) and Zenker and Kumoll (2010) testify to the influence of the debate on "writing culture" two decades after it first came about. So does the issue of *Cultural Anthropology* (Orin 2012) celebrating the twenty-fifth anniversary of the publication of *Writing Culture* (1989) edited by James Clifford and George Marcus. In that anniversary issue of *Cultural Anthropology* there is an interview entitled "Anthropology and Fiction" where Damien Stankiewics (2012: 536–537) talks to Amitav Ghosh, the Indian writer who has a Ph.D. in social anthropology from University of Oxford and is quoted by a number of contributors here. When asked about his writing anthropology versus writing fiction, and his novel *In an Antique Land* (1992), Ghosh replies by first praising his anthropological training:

> But after I finished my dissertation I was left with a nagging sense of dissatisfaction: I felt that everything that was important about my time in Egypt had been left unsaid. To describe this as a "nagging sense of dissatisfaction" is perhaps inadequate. Like many who've spent a long time alone in a foreign circumstance, I was haunted by my experiences. This was one of the reasons why it became so important to write the book. While living in Egypt, I did two kinds of writing. I

kept field notes and I also wrote a set of diaries. In my mind the field notes were the "anthropological" part of my work; the diaries were more literary. My dissertation was based almost entirely on my field notes; similarly the first-person narrative in *Antique Land* is based on my diaries.

A sense of being constrained by the academic form of dissertation writing has thus produced fiction from the field, but also, in line with the argument of this volume, kept developing experimental ethnographic writing and new genres.

In fact, the affiliation between anthropology and literature goes a long way back. With his literary interest, Victor Turner (1976: 77–78) regarded African ritual and Western literature as "mutually elucidating." Richard Handler and Daniel Segal (1990) looked at Jane Austen as an ethnographer of marriage and kinship in her time and class in England, which showed contrasting social realities. And when Nigel Rapport (1994) did fieldwork in the village Wanet in England, he made the writer E.M. Forster his companion ethnographer by considering Forster's literary writings parallel to his own findings in the village. Among the volumes juxtaposing anthropology and literature are Dennis and Aycock (1989), Benson (1993), Daniel and Peck (1996), and De Angelis (2002). In *Novel Approaches to Anthropology* (2013), Marilyn Cohen and her contributors discuss the role of historical as well as contemporary novels in anthropology. Writing about the relationship between fiction and anthropology, Archetti (1994b: 16) distinguished three categories of fiction: "The realistic historical novel that attempts to 'reconstruct' a given period in a given society; the totally imagined story set in a historical period; and the essays devoted to an interpretation of a nation, its characteristics and creed." As Archetti (1994: 16–17) pointed out, "some kind of historical and sociological knowledge is important in fiction," which is where the process of writing fiction is similar to that of writing anthropology. But when Archetti says that he does not believe that novelists are really aware that they make use of cultural topics, he seems to be thinking more of novelists who situate their work in their own culture rather than in foreign places. For Archetti, as for many literary anthropologists, fiction around cultural topics is "ethnographic raw material, not … authoritative statements about, or interpretations of, a particular society."

A TALE OF TWO TRANSLATIONS

"So you're a writer—why don't you write about us in the paper?" one dancer after another kept asking me when I was doing fieldwork in the transnational ballet world in Stockholm, London, New York, and Frankfurt am Main (e.g., Wulff 1998, 2008a).[1] The people I was studying seemed to suggest that I make myself useful by writing about them in the newspaper, and also, they told me, in dance magazines, international and national. In order to give something back to the people that had allowed me access to the closed world of ballet, I thus set out on my first piece of cultural journalism (Wulff 1994) for *Svenska Dagbladet,* a Swedish newspaper that features daily essays on topics of culture, history, and politics by academics, freelance writers, and journalists.

Cultural journalism is a feature of outreach activities at many universities. In the framework of Swedish university life, the activities of communicating and collaborating with groups and audiences outside the university is summed up by the term *tredje uppgiften,* the third task, the other two being teaching and research. Not least among anthropologists, disseminating research results to a wider audience is regarded as a question of democracy, even a matter of ethics; this is also supported by the argument that "scholars live on taxpayers' money." It is also the case that the Swedish Research Council requires a popular article as a part of the final reporting of funded projects. It is remarkable, and somewhat contradictory, that the call to disseminate research to a wider audience is not reflected in academic ranking and citation indices. Nonetheless, cultural journalism contributes to the reputation of the discipline, and not only to that of the individual anthropologist who writes in newspapers and speaks on radio or television. As to the actual writing this is a tale of two translations: from data to academic text, and from academic text to popular text. One crucial point in relation to reputation and ranking is that cultural journalism by anthropologists tends to be performed in the national language of the anthropologist, such as Swedish, Norwegian, German, or French, even though international academic publications are primarily in English. Cultural journalism is thus on the whole unnoticed by colleagues in other countries.

The translation I had to perform when I did my first journalistic essay entailed a different type of translation than the academic one I was trained for. As anthropologists we can be said to translate our fields into academic conceptualizations. Doing journalism, I had to make my anthropological findings not only accessible, but also attractive to a wider readership familiar with culture and the arts, but not necessarily with anthropology. Writing my essay for *Svenska Dagbladet,* I was aware that dancers and other people in the ballet world I was still studying, and thus depended on for my continued research, would also read it. They were more likely to read this relatively short essay rather than my forthcoming academic book (Wulff 1998) (which eventually turned out to be the case) as most dancers are not voracious readers. But it was not difficult to keep their trust. They knew I was not a critic, and that is why they had allowed me back stage for so long, even into intimate situations. I could have been critical in my essay about certain conditions in the ballet world, such as the lack of long-term contracts in some companies, the use of drugs to enhance dancing capacity, the prevalence of anorexia, or wealthy fathers giving large sums of money to ballet companies in exchange for their daughters getting leading roles at the expense of better dancers. But this was not the place for that. Writing my essay, I also had to organize the text differently than I normally did when I wrote academically. The standard academic format provides more space, which allows for an introduction, perhaps in the form of an ethnographic vignette; an articulated aim, followed by ethnographic evidence related to a theoretical discussion; and a conclusion, which shows how this ethnography has contributed to theoretical development. Writing my newspaper essay, I had to stick to no more than 1,800 words, much shorter than academic articles in journals and volumes tend to be. I also had to start with the essence of the essay, rather than building up an argument toward it as in academic texts. And just like on stage in the theater, entrance is essential. In order to capture the general reader of a newspaper—remember, I was writing about ballet, which most people think of as elitist, old-fashioned, and artificial—the entrance of an essay has to be striking. Slightly provocative or seemingly contradictory beginnings often work—something that gets the attention of even the reluctant reader. Next I had to make my sentences short and clear. There is no time for complicated arguments or efforts to impress colleagues with theoretical ideas. In journalism, captivating ethnographic cases are useful as a way to indicate a wider circumstance. This is the same technique as in poetry where a few lines can crystallize a long life or a country's contested history. And just like in the theater, again, exits are important for how and whether a piece is remembered afterward, They should also be carefully crafted. In contrast with academic writing, in journalism it is important to stop in time—otherwise the editor will do it, which often means cutting from the end, raising the risk that concluding points disappear. With newspapers you cannot negotiate about word count. Essays can in fact end on the climax, or with a question. It is common that they end by connecting to the opening, thereby forming a circle. The end can also be used as a contrast, turning everything that has been said previously around without warning, which can be one way of making an argument. In my experience, more often than not, endings appear during the writing process; they do not always end up they way I have planned.

When I posted my first essay in a yellow mailbox one sunny late summer day in southern Sweden, which you did in 1994 (this was before email),

I knew that if the essay was accepted, the editor would do the headline. This is common practice in journalism, and I would not have any influence over it. He would also write a short introduction summarizing the essay. It was thus not until the very morning the essay appeared in the newspaper that I learned that the title of it was "Ballet–a language everyone can understand." Had I been allowed to do my title, I would never have come up with a title that general, but it was fine. The editor obviously knew what he was doing, and I was still learning to relate to a wider readership not only outside academia but also outside the ballet world. The essay was a success. I was suddenly surfing on fame–as long as it lasted, which was for about a week. After all there is a new essay every day in this newspaper. But friends and family, of course, and also colleagues, acquaintances, and people I did not know–such as a ballet fan who wrote a fan letter to me(!)–praised my essay. I even heard from my primary school teacher, whom I had not seen in about thirty years. I got a sense that "everyone" had read my essay, also from the knowledge that this newspaper is printed in hundreds of thousands of copies. This quick major impact is quite different from what happens in the academic world, where publications not only take much longer to write, but also reach a considerably smaller readership. Academic publications may also last much longer, though, while newspaper essays are in most cases forgotten after a while. Even in this era of Internet publication, books and journals are still cherished and kept in collections. Newspapers are thrown away or used for packing things.

What I had not expected with my first essay was that it would become a part of my fieldwork in two ways. First, the dancers did read it, and to my great relief they liked it. And I realized that part of the reason that they liked it was that I had managed to verbalize what mattered the most to them about their dancing life. Contrary to many media reports of the ballet world, my essay was a positive portrait. Dancers are vulnerable; they often feel misrepresented in the media, and see themselves as different from other people. They are trained to express themselves through their dance, not through words. Second, as I mentioned above, by using materials in the form of field notes, for a general readership, I discovered new data, circumstances, and connections in my materials that later would enrich my academic writing.

Since then I have continued to write cultural journalism once a year or so. I keep meeting colleagues who have an interest in writing in this genre, but do not know how to get a piece into a newspaper. There seems to be an assumption that academics can also write popularly without any coaching. To write anthropological journalism requires training. This has to be taken seriously, and it should be provided for students and young scholars. Certain anthropologists who would like to write journalism now and then make the mistake of not adhering to the rules and conditions of journalism. This is surprising in light of the fact that seeing the "native's point of view" is supposedly our expertise. We have to learn to switch into a less academic, meaning more straightforward, tone, and of course to adjust to the very compressed time and space frames, at least with newspapers. This, again, is different from what we are used to in academia.

Since my first journalistic essay, my cultural journalism has consisted of essays on my ongoing research, review articles on books relating to my research, and feature articles on choreographers and composers. I occasionally write for the Swedish daily, the Swedish dance magazine, and British or European dance magazines. Like any writer, I have had rejections, but after one or more attempts found another publication for rejected articles. With time, I have learned that cultural journalism, not least dance journalism, has to be hinged on current events. Timing is central.

I have had commissions for dance journalism. One was for a German art magazine *Parallax,* for which I was asked to write about the fact that dancers have two careers, as they stop dancing early and then move on to a second career. I wrote in English and the essay was translated into German, which meant that I could read it but with effort (Wulff 1997–98). Another commission was for a Swedish magazine, *Axess,* which publishes popular scholarship. I wrote about a dance photographer and his work. Even though I had submitted images, the editor added more images and made the essay into what he referred to as a "photo essay"; it was like a gallery illustrating my text (Wulff 2003). Unsurprisingly, my early essays were more edited by the editors than the more recent ones. I also get higher fees now than I did in the beginning. This is not only because fees are higher for all freelance writers, but because I am now known in some circles as a scholar who sometimes does cultural journalism. With time and articles published, you acquire a reputation in your field of journalism. All this also applies to fellow anthropologists such as Andre Gingrich in Vienna, Thomas Hylland Eriksen in Oslo, and Dan Rabinowitz in Tel Aviv, who write anthropological journalism now and then.

Going back now to the issue of translation: already Evans-Pritchard (1965) identified anthropology as cultural translation, a notion that has been influential in the discipline, as well as debated. For what is it exactly that is translated? Cultural conceptualization can obviously get lost in translation, or be misunderstood. There is a risk that we look for cultural units that are actually incomparable. What does a dance anthropologist, for example, study in a culture where there is no word for dance? Anthropologists are acutely aware of this problem. Yet things may also be *found* in translation: call it understanding, interest in a different way of life. The classical insight in anthropology is, of course, that learning about difference is a way to learn about yourself. The debate on cultural translation in anthropology has generated insights into the relationships between interpretation, understanding, and authenticity. As Hannerz (1993: 45) suggests, there are "two main ideas of the translator's role, when we think of translation in its ordinary sense": the first type of translator is expected to convey the meaning of a language in an exact, literal way, "impartial," official, while the second type is allowed more creativity as this translation is "to be responded to in aesthetic and intellectual terms both as a reflection of the original work and as a work in its own right." It is obviously the latter type of translation that anthropologists are aiming for. And it can be taken further to a second translation, from academic findings into cultural journalism, as an instance of one anthropological genre.

WAYS OF WRITING ANTHROPOLOGY

Cultural journalism is thus one way of writing anthropology. The following chapters offer a variety of ways of writing anthropology: in relation to the making of an anthropological career, ethnographic writing, journalistic and popular writing, and writing across genres.

Dominic Boyer argues most convincingly in the opening chapter for the necessity of being a writer in anthropology today. Despite the fact that the discipline depends on engaging teaching for its survival and reproduction, and that teaching can be said to be the discipline's oxygen, it is as Boyer points out nevertheless "the knot of writing, peer review and publishing" that defines an academic career. In a neoliberal perspective of academic audit, ranking, and impact factors, teaching is losing its prestige. Instead, a central concern is writing and publishing in relation to careers and academic organization. This is an elusive area as criteria keep changing: what one cohort of anthropologists was trained for is bound to be different once they begin being exposed to assessment. To what extent is the quality of academic writing tailored to research assessments and evaluation formats, and what are the intellectual consequences of this? Don Brenneis has done extensive ethnographic work on scholarly publication, research funding, assessment exercises, and the construction of scholarly knowledge. As he reports on its limitations, he is not convinced about the efficacy of peer review. In his chapter he investigates "writing to be ranked" as well as different types of "reading for ranking." With his scholarly approach, Brenneis sheds new light on the idea of managerial accountability in the academic world. Research applications for funding form a special genre, one genre within the genre of writing to be ranked. Sverker Finnström's chapter details the clash between academic values and administrative values in research funding. In order to write a successful research application, Finnström learned to streamline his text, which lead to what he experienced as intellectual corruption. Applying Maurice Bloch's (1977) idea of "the long conversation" for a long-term relationship to the field, Finnström also discovered, did not fit with the rhythms and realities of European academic life. Eventually, he was awarded a major research grant and landed a lectureship. Now that he finds himself on the other side, so to speak, with requests to evaluate research applications, Finnström has developed the dual capacity of performing assessment work in accordance with administrative requirements while keeping his intellectual integrity alive.

In that part of the global scholarly landscape where English is the natural choice of language, alternatives are hardly ever explicitly discussed. In Máiréad Nic Craith's chapter, the dominance of the English language in academic publishing and ranking is problematized. Writing in English means a larger readership, at least potentially, but the size of the readership might depend on the publisher's reach. As Nic Craith says, the focus on English excludes many scholars and institutions, but there is an expanding drive to learn to operate academically in English as a second language. Translation, both literal and cultural, is a dilemma here, including the fact that things get lost in translation. Despite efforts to acknowledge other world languages as well as small languages, Nic Craith is not very hopeful that this will change the position of the English language in the academic world. Still, as she concludes, in light of the nature of anthropology as a discipline for human diversity, it makes sense, not only academically but also ethically, to sometimes publish in other languages than English.

The acclaimed Irish writer Roddy Doyle had his breakthrough with the novel *The Commitments* (1987), which describes a group of unemployed young people in working class Dublin who form a soul band. It has also been made into a film. Interviewing Doyle for my study of the social world of Irish writers (Wulff 2008b, 2012a, 2012b, 2013), I asked him about his writing routine. He then talked about self-discipline, and how he writes Monday to Friday between 8:30 in the morning until about 6 in the evening, divided into two-hour sessions. He spends one of his daily breaks, he spends "looking at the BBC football page." As to the actual writing, Doyle prefers filling pages rather than worrying over the quality of the first draft. This is why editing is key. "When I edit, I'm a bit obsessed!" Only editing can make him work into the night or on a Saturday morning.

In his chapter in this volume, Brian Moeran considers the craft of editing anthropological texts. This is clearly an underestimated craft, despite the fact that it is key also for writing academic texts. Editing requires training, and it is possibly useful with a bit of talent to start with. Admittedly, some people seem to have a natural flair for editing (and some for proofreading, as they spot errors more easily than others). Moeran identifies self-editing as a process of making choices. It has to do, basically, with what to include and exclude, how to pitch the texts theoretically, the role of the ethnography, and—following Van Maanen (1988)—what style to chose: realistic, confessional, or impressionistic. Moeran applies Howard Becker's (1982: 198) notion of "editorial moments" to these situations in which choices are made, both in editing one's own texts and those of colleagues. This is where editing from the perspective of the publisher's editor, as well as from that of the desk editor, comes in. Moeran does not want editing to be conflated with writing. They are different activities: writing means striving to get into a flow, while editing means stopping the flow in order to think about structure.

Alma Gottlieb, Paul Stoller, and Kirin Narayan have long offered authoritative approaches to ethnographic writing. For Alma Gottlieb writing an engaged anthropology for a wider readership and teaching ethnographic writing to students are paramount. Having already been a fine writer in high school, Gottlieb joins Amitav Ghosh in his frustration over the constraints of the academic writing format. Gottlieb confesses in her chapter that while adhering to the expected academic writing style and publication outlets first as a Ph.D. student, and later when she was on her tenure track, she began clandestine writing. Together with Philip Graham, the fiction writer, Gottlieb wrote what was going to be published as *Parallel Worlds* (1993), a popular account in which the anthropologist and the writer each commented on their shared experiences of Côte d'Ivoire. As there was a risk that this book might jeopardize Gottlieb's application for tenure, she kept it separate from the university world. This worked until the book was awarded the Victor Turner Prize in Ethnographic Writing. Since then it has been used extensively in teaching. Paul Stoller likewise found the academic format limiting as a young anthropologist. In his chapter he spins the story of how he (together with Cheryl Olkes) wrote the experimental ethnography *In Sorcery's Shadow* (1987), which, despite a number of early institutional setbacks, became a classic in anthropology. The book builds on Stoller's time as an apprentice sorcerer. It was his teacher, the sorcerer Adamu Jenitongo, who put him on the path to experimental writing that eventually would release his writing powers. The sorcerer urged Stoller to write a story that would be remembered, a story from which younger generations could learn about "the truth of being." As Stoller rightly says, good stories are not only effective for making points, they also tend to remain. Therefore, anthropologists should write for the future. For Narmala Halstead, the process was the reverse. She had written novels, plays, poems, and short stories in the past, but her Ph.D. work put an end to that kind of writing, she explains in her chapter. As a committed Ph.D. student, she did not find time for writing fiction. She also notes that she had to accommodate her writing style to an academic one. Still, her experience as a fiction writer, as well as a journalist later on, did contribute to the way she conceptualizes anthropology. Halstead shows how a life history of writing in different genres fuses into a notion of *life-writing* that is a conduit for both personal and professional writing experiences. In *Alive in the Writing: Crafting Ethnography in the Company of Chekhov* (2012), Kirin Narayan merges her experience of ethnographic writing with that of Anton Chekhov, playwright and short story writer, as he reported on Sakhalin Island, the Russian penal colony. And it is around Chekhov, as her ethnographic muse, that Narayan's chapter revolves. She considers letters about Chekhov's journey to Sakhalin, his own reflections on his research, and the actual act of writing about this, which resulted in his most substantial nonfiction work. It enticed Narayan to rethink her engagement with ethnography in terms of "a golden thread of continuity" as she gathered different topics and texts into her book. She also learned how an ethnographic sensibility structures not only Chekov's ethnographic work, but much of his literary *oeuvre.*

To the problem of negotiating between scientific study and engaging storytelling belongs the desire to share one's work with as broad an audience as possible. In the spirit of Amitav Ghosh, Anette Nyqvist wrote a popular account parallel to writing her doctoral dissertation. She explains in her chapter that she did not feel held back by the academic form, but with her background in journalism she found that writing a popular version of her dissertation was most beneficial for her academic writing. Interestingly, she introduces the notion of *cross-writing* as a way to improve a text in one genre by imports from another one and to keep the flow going. Oscar Hemer identifies himself as a writer, a literary writer but also a journalist. His doctoral research in anthropology was on fiction and truth in the transition processes in South Africa and Argentina (Hemer 2012). In his chapter Hemer mentions the "like-sided triangle" (Hemer 2005) covering the three writing practices—academic, journalistic, and literary—that are distinguished by different traditions and genre conventions. Hemer's preferred writing style is a discursive text that makes room for literature and journalism, as well as aspects of reportage, essay, and memoir. His literary case is Jorge Luis Borges's (1974) short story "The Ethnographer" about a doctoral student who eloped from the field.

Again, usually when you sit there in front of your computer screen, you are alone at your keyboard. At their keyboards, pianists sometimes sit next to one another, making music together. Something like that may now occur increasingly often in anthropology as well.

The recent upsurge in different forms of collaboration shape writing styles, intellectual contents, and careers. This is evident in the multi-authored chapter written by anthropologist Eva-Maria Hardtmann, activist-scholar-lawyer Vincent Manoharan, feminist Urmila Devi, Jussi Eskola with an M.A. in religion, and activist-drummer Swarna Sabrina Francis. It describes how the writing process emanated from a workshop of the Global Justice Movement in Kathmandu attended by scholars and activists. In order to include their various personal styles in the same text, they agreed to write in a dialogical form. This went very well, as everyone felt their voice came through. But when they tried to write a collaborative text with a single voice, their different writing styles and political and intellectual approaches made it a conflictual endeavor.

As to writing across genres, in his chapter Nigel Rapport draws inspiration from the novelist E.M. Forster when he declares his belief in the individual rather than in "the people." Rapport's twinning of anthropology and literature has the form of a Kantian cosmopolitan vision of anthropology that entails "a bringing together in a dialectical tension two poles of human existence": all of humanity and the individual. Rapport outlines his notion of fiction and anthropological understanding around "fiction as local practice," and makes clear that what he refers to as anthropology's fictional truth goes back to the discipline's humanistic origin. Mattias Viktorin's chapter is framed by a literary case from a novella by Andrei Volos (2005) about a woman who at times struggles to convey her thoughts into words, to "wrap them into words." To her, ideas seem to change in the process, and what comes out is not her sparkling thoughts but flat statements that fall apart. With Hanna Arendt's notion of emergence, Viktorin goes on to show how anthropologists are able to address processes of rending visible the "not yet," also using examples from the painter Paul Klee.

A notable current development relevant to the volume, which urges for writing across genres, is the growth of new media forms, in large part connected to the Internet. Blogs, social media, and open access now also have their part in the shaping of anthropological writing, raising urgent questions about how technology impacts on writing skills, collaboration, and communication (Kelty et al. 2008; Balakian 2011; SavageMinds.org). Drawing on her experiences of writing the monograph *Digital Drama: Teaching and Learning Art and Media in Tanzania* (2012), Paula Uimonen discusses the three formats it took: a printed book, a website (http://www.innovativeethnographies .net/digitaldrama), and a hyperlinked e-book, as well as the relationships between them. For one thing, the website had to tell its own tale, through many visuals and videos with some short texts. In designing the website, Uimonen's intention was not only to make it into a colorful illustration of the book for readers who wanted to learn more; even more importantly, the idea was to present the website as a trailer for the book for those who had not yet read it.

In contrast with many writers of fiction, scholars tend to develop a writing style that follows a set structure, and then stick to that style. While aware of both intellectual challenge and academic audit requirements, Ulf Hannerz, in the final chapter of this volume, suggests two possibilities to further writing styles, as well as careers, in anthropology. The first possibility is to continue to do field research, which might entail different types of field studies than the traditional one year away. The second possibility, which is his main concern in this chapter, is "a plea for experimenting with greater diversity in styles of writing, more ways of using anthropological ideas and materials, perhaps developing new genres." Rather than pursuing the widespread "me and my fieldwork" approach when writing, Hannerz suggests an openness to "writing otherwise." Among other things, this would entail making more use of ethnography that colleagues have collected and analyzed, especially in terms of comparison and synthesis.

Before concluding, let me note that the development of creative writing in university programs and workshops, and the process of teaching writing, is beginning to be analyzed anthropologically (Wulff 2012a). A sibling genre to creative writing, which has come forth especially among anthropologists in the United States, is creative nonfiction (Cheney 2001). Going back to New Journalism in the late 1960s, this literary genre features real events in a fictional form (Narayan 2007). Connected to this is a growing concern in anthropology with having its reporting and its social and cultural understandings reach a wider public (Eriksen 2006). The particular task of anthropological writing naturally has much to do with the emphasis on understanding social and cultural diversity, in local and national society but not least globally. Some of the deliberations over the forms and techniques of writing relate to parallels and contrasts with journalism and other reportage as shown by Boyer and Hannerz (2006).

Prefiguring chapters on different ways of writing anthropology, I have made the case for the advantage of writing across and within genres in new ways. This is especially captured by Anette Nyqvist's concept of *cross-writing* and Ulf Hannerz's call to *writing otherwise*. Geertz's (1980) notion of blurred genres might seem like an obvious backdrop here, but my aim has been to show the importance for anthropologists of constantly developing their writing skills in distinct genres. One advantage of writing across genres is the possibility of taking inspiration from another genre, in style and structure as well as content. Rather than blurring genres, this is actually an efficient way to keep developing the character of one genre.

It is clear that anthropologists have a lot to gain from honing the capacity to operate in different genres ranging from academic writing to journalistic writing, even fiction. By cultivating flexible writing, new possibilities for expression and conveyance spring up. This is beneficial for anthropological knowledge production, not least as such writing might reveal different aspects of social and cultural life than traditional anthropological writing can do.

Helena Wulff is Professor of Social Anthropology, Stockholm University. Her research is in the anthropology of communication and aesthetics based on a wide range of studies of the social worlds of literary production, dance, and visual culture, and recently on writing and contemporary literature in Ireland. Among her publications are the monographs *Ballet across Borders: Career and Culture in the World of Dancers* (1998) and *Dancing at the Crossroads: Memory and Mobility in Ireland* (2007), as well as the edited volumes *The Emotions* (2007), and *Ethnographic Practice in the Present* (with Marit Melhuus and Jon P. Mitchell, 2010).

NOTES

1. Some paragraphs in this section first appeared in Helena Wulff. 2011. "Cultural Journalism and Anthropology: A Tale of Two Translations." *Archivio Antropologico Mediterraneo online* 12/13, 13, no. 1: 27–33.

REFERENCES

Archetti, Eduardo P., ed. 1994a. *Exploring the Written: Anthropology and the Multiplicity of Writing.* Oslo: Scandinavian University Press.

——. 1994b. "Introduction." In *Exploring the Written: Anthropology and the Multiplicity of Writing.* Oslo: Scandinavian University Press.

Balakian, Sophia. 2011. "Mapping a Lost Friend: Technology and Tracing a Transnational Life." Paper presented in session on "Writing Ethnography: Experimenting on Paper, Experimenting Online" at the American Anthropological Association, Montreal, 16–20 November, 2011.

Barber, Karin. 2007. *The Anthropology of Texts, Persons and Publics: Oral and Written Culture in Africa and Beyond.* Cambridge: Cambridge University Press.

Barton, David, and Uta Papen, eds. 2010. *The Anthropology of Writing: Understanding Textually-Mediated Worlds.* London: Continuum.

Becker, Howard S. 1982. *Art Worlds*. Berkeley: University of California Press.

Becker, Howard S. 1998. *Tricks of the Trade: How to Think about Your Research while Doing It*. Chicago: University of Chicago Press.

Behar, Ruth. 2009. "Believing in Anthropology as Literature." In *Anthropology off the Shelf: Anthropologists on Writing*, ed. Alisse Waterston and Maria D. Vesperi. Oxford: Wiley-Blackwell.

Bendix, Regina. 2012. "'Tatorte'—or: Why Do Anthropologists Love Mysteries?" Paper for the Symposium for Andre Gingrich's 60th Birthday, University of Vienna.

Benson, Paul, ed. 1993. *Anthropology and Literature*. Urbana: University of Illinois Press.

Bloch, Maurice. 1977. "The Past and the Present in the Present." *Man* 12, no. 2: 278–292.

Borges, Jorge Luis. 1998. "The Ethnographer." In *Collected Fictions*. London: Penguin.

Boyarin, Jonathan, ed. 1993. *The Ethnography of Reading*. Berkeley: University of California Press.

Boyer, Dominic, and Ulf Hannerz. 2006. "Introduction: Worlds of Journalism." *Ethnography* 7, no. 1: 5–17.

Brenneis, Don. 2009. "Anthropology in and of the Academy: Globalization, Assessment and our Field's Future." *Social Anthropology* 17, no. 3: 261–275.

Cheney, Theodore A. Rees. 2001. *Writing Creative Nonfiction: Fiction Techniques for Crafting Great Nonfiction*. Berkeley: Ten Speed.

Clifford, James, and George E. Marcus, eds. 1986. *Writing Culture: The Poetics and Politics of Ethnography*. Berkeley: University of California Press.

Cohen, Marilyn, ed. 2013. *Novel Approaches to Anthropology: Contributions to Literary Anthropology*. New York: Lexington Books.

Collins, Peter, and Anselma Gallinat, eds. 2010. *The Ethnographic Self as Resource: Writing, Memory and Experience into Ethnography*. Oxford: Berghahn Books.

Daniel, Valentine, and Jeffrey M. Peck, eds. 1996. *Culture/Contexture: Anthropology and Literary Studies*. Berkeley: University of California Press.

Dawson, Andrew, Jenny Hockey, and Allison James, eds. 1997. *After Writing Culture: Epistemology and Praxis in Contemporary Anthropology*. London: Routledge.

De Angelis, Rose, ed. 2002. *Between Anthropology and Literature: Interdisciplinary Discourse*. London: Routledge.

Dennis, Philip A., and Wendell Aycock, eds. 1989. *Literature and Anthropology*. Lubbock: Texas Tech University Press.

Doyle, Roddy. 1987. *The Commitments*. London: Vintage.

Eriksen, Thomas Hylland. 2006. *Engaging Anthropology: The Case for a Public Presence*. Oxford: Berg.

Evans-Pritchard, EE. 1965. *Theories of Primitive Religion*. Oxford: Clarendon Press.

Geertz, Clifford. 1973. *The Interpretation of Cultures*. New York: Basic Books.

———. 1980. "Blurred Genres: The Refiguration of Social Thought." *American Scholar* 49, no. 2: 165–179.

———. 1988. *Works and Lives: The Anthropologist as Author*. Stanford, CA: Stanford University Press.

Ghodsee, Kristen. 2011. *Lost in Transition: Ethnographies of Everyday Life after Communism.* Durham: Duke University Press.

Ghosh, Amitav. 1992. *In an Antique Land.* New York: Vintage.

Gottlieb, Alma, and Philip Graham. 1993. *Parallel Worlds: An Anthropologist and a Writer Encounter Africa.* Chicago: University of Chicago Press.

Gusterson, Hugh, and Catherine Besteman, eds. 2010. *The Insecure American: How We Got Here and What We Should Do about It.* Berkeley: University of California Press.

Handler, Richard, and Daniel Segal. 1990. *Jane Austen and the Fiction of Culture.* Tucson: University of Arizona Press.

Hannerz Ulf. 1993. "Mediations in the Global Ecumene." In *Beyond Boundaries,* ed. Gísli Pálsson. Berg: Oxford.

———. 2013. "A Detective Story Writer: Exploring Stockholm as It Once Was." *City and Society* 26, no. 2: 260–270.

Hemer, Oscar. 2005. "Writing the World." In *Media and Global Change,* ed. Oscar Hemer and Thomas Tufte. Göteborg: Nordicom.

———. 2012. *Fiction and Truth in Transition: Writing the Present Past in South Africa and Argentina.* Berlin: LIT Verlag.

Jackson, Michael. 2012. *The Other Shore: Essays on Writers and Writing.* Berkeley: University of California Press.

Kelty, Christopher M., et al. 2008. "Anthropology of/in Circulation: The Future of Open Access and Scholarly Societies." *Cultural Anthropology* 23, no. 3: 559–558.

Marcus, George E., and Michael MJ Fischer. 1986. *Anthropology as Cultural Critique: An Experimental Moment in the Human Sciences.* Chicago: University of Chicago Press.

Miller, Daniel., ed. 2009. *Anthropology and the Individual: A Material Culture Approach.* Oxford: Berg.

Narayan, Kirin. 2007. *My Family and Other Saints.* Chicago: University of Chicago Press.

———. 2012. *Alive in the Writing: Crafting Ethnography in the Company of Chekhov.* Chicago: University of Chicago Press.

Orin, Starn, ed. 2012. *Current Anthropology* 27, no. 3, special issue on 25th anniversary of *Writing Culture.*

Rapport, Nigel. 1994. *The Prose and the Passion: Anthropology, Literature and the Writing of E. M. Forster.* Manchester: Manchester University Press.

———. 1997. *Transcendent Individual: Towards a Literary and Liberal Anthropology.* London: Routledge.

Reed, Adam. 2011. *Literature and Agency in English Fiction Reading: A Study of Henry Williamson Society.* Manchester: Manchester University Press & University of Toronto.

Routledge Innovative Ethnographies Series InnovativeEthnographies.net/digital drama.

Savage Minds: Notes and Queries in Anthropology SavageMinds.org.

Skinner, Jonathan, ed. 2012. *Writing the Dark Side of Travel.* Oxford: Berghahn Books.

Stankiewicz, Damien. 2012. "Anthropology and Fiction: An Interview with Amitav Ghosh." *Cultural Anthropology* 27, no. 3: 535–541.

Stoller, Paul. 1999. *Jaguar: A Story of Africans in America.* Chicago: University of Chicago Press.

———. 2008. *The Power of the Between: An Anthropological Odyssey.* Chicago: University of Chicago Press.

Stoller, Paul, and Cheryl Olkes. 1987. *In Sorcery's Shadow: A Memoir of Apprenticeship among the Songhay of Niger.* Chicago: University of Chicago Press.

Street, Brian V. 1997. *Cross-Cultural Approaches to Literacy.* Cambridge: Cambridge University Press.

Tedlock, Dennis. 2002. Electronic Center Poetry. Buffalo, NY. epc.buffalo.edu/authors/tedlock/.

Turner, Victor. 1976. "African Ritual and Western Literature: Is a Comparative Symbology Possible?" In *The Literature of Fact,* ed. Angus Fletcher. New York: Columbia University Press.

Uimonen, Paula. 2012. *Digital Drama: Teaching and Learning Art and Media in Tanzania.* London: Routledge.

Van Maanen, John. 1988. *Tales of the Field: On Writing Ethnography.* Chicago: University of Chicago Press.

Volos, Andrei. 2005. "Ivachev's arv." In *Hurramabad.* Uppsala: Ruin.

Waterston, Alisse, and Maria D. Vesperi, eds. 2009. *Anthropology off the Shelf: Anthropologists on Writing.* Oxford: Wiley-Blackwell.

White, Jenny. 2007. *The Sultan's Seal.* New York: WW Norton & Company.

Wulff, Helena. 1994. "Balett – ett språk som alla kan förstå." *Svenska Dagladet.* 5 September.

———. 1997–98. "Das Leben nach dem Tanz: Der Wechsel zur zweiten Karriere." *Parallax* December/January 5: 8–15.

———. 1998. *Ballet across Borders: Career and Culture in the World of Dancers.* London: Berg/Bloomsbury.

———. 2003. "Frusna rörelser." *Axess* 5, no. 2: 36–40.

———. 2008a. "Ethereal Expression: Paradoxes of Ballet as a Global Physical Culture." *Ethnography* 9, no. 4: 519–536.

———. 2008b. "Literary Readings as Performance: On the Career of Contemporary Writers in the New Ireland." *Anthropological Journal of European Cultures* 17: 98–113.

———. 2012a."An Anthropological Perspective on Literary Arts in Ireland." In *Blackwell Companion to the Anthropology of Europe,* ed. Ullrich Kockel, Máiréad Nic Craith, and Jonas Frykman. Oxford: Wiley-Blackwell.

———. 2012b. "Instances of Inspiration: Interviewing Dancers and Writers." In *The Interview: An Ethnographic Approach,* ed. Jonathan Skinner. London: Berg/Bloomsbury.

———. 2013. "Ethnografiction and Reality in Contemporary Irish Literature." In *Novel Approaches to Anthropology: Contributions to Literary Anthropology,* ed. Marilyn Cohen. New York City: Lexington Books.

Zenker, Olaf, and Karsten Kumoll, eds. 2010. *Beyond Writing Culture: Current Intersections of Epistemologies and Representational Practices.* Oxford: Berghahn Books.

I.

The Role of Writing in Anthropological Careers

Chapter 1

The Necessity of Being a Writer in Anthropology Today

Dominic Boyer

On the phone, staring down at the gunmetal blankness of a desk that is only sometimes my own, I have just received the news of a tenure-track job offer from a prestigious American research university. And now the Department Chair is going down his checklist. There are many artful pleasantries, flirtations, and flatteries involved in faculty recruitment. But, at some point, as in any relationship where marriage is on the table, seduction verges into contract: "Of course, we hire tenure-track faculty with every expectation that they will be able to achieve tenure…"

Tenure. It must certainly be one of the most overdetermined words in a young American academic's life, a locus of fantasy, aspiration, and anxiety throughout the early phases of professionalization. Tenure is the scepter of class distinction in the US academy. The elite passport to sovereign professional power and security so rare in the oceanic era of neoliberalism, where labor protections (not least in the world of higher education) have everywhere become like heavy fog, vapor in the guise of substance. Nothing seemed more paradoxical at that moment then the Chair's earnest informational mission contrasted with how I was burning. To be invited to join the "tenure track" juxtaposed the bright thrill of recognition with the dizzying realization that the scepter would now have "to be achieved."

Unsteady, holding on to that timeless desk for support, I listened as the Chair continued with an air of routine authority. For him this was, above all, the end of a long day. It was also his last semester as Chair and he was undoubtedly hoping that this would be the last such call he would ever have to make. He was thus efficient to the point of bluntness, "… To get tenure at Cornell, we expect you to be a first-rate scholar, and you will need to publish a book with a respected academic publisher and six or seven articles in major peer-reviewed journals. You need to be a *good* teacher…" He lengthened that word *good* in a way that said to me, "adequate," not too many complaints. "… And the Department expects that you will do your collegial share of administrative and committee work, the details of which you will work out with the new Chair…"

Another sentence or two may have followed, but not much more. I had my map to the grail and a hierarchy of values to orient me in the event the map failed. To be a successful professional academic anthropologist meant, in this case, excellence in research and publishing, solid but unspectacular pedagogy, and functional, collegial administrative assistance. A department would be immensely grateful to a colleague who went above and beyond the call of duty in teaching, mentoring, and committee work, but such an investment would only make sense if one's record of research and publication was already sterling. An administrator at another elite university in the United States once confessed to me that he would never put forward an untenured faculty member for a teaching award, "because it could easily backfire and the senior colleagues might begin to doubt whether this junior colleague really had his or her priorities in order." Recognition of teaching excellence could thus, seemingly paradoxically, exert negative influence over a tenure case, at least at some research universities. My Chair had sent the same message in less dramatic terms. What he had communicated with his *good* was simply the warning that being an excellent teacher and/or departmental citizen would not save me come tenure evaluation time were I judged to have failed in my scholarly responsibilities.

The social truth (if not the ethical validity) of this value hierarchy concerning forms of academic activity has been proven to me many times during my career. I have seen careers demolished where young scholars did not or could not respect the logic of research- and publication-oriented professionalism; I have participated in acts of demolition myself in which my colleagues and I justified our actions by gesturing to the obviousness of the criteria by which our profession and our institutions of higher education judge who can stay and who will go. Inevitably, blame comes to rest on an individual's lack of wisdom to set priorities or to manage time. In most instances, confidence, health, and training failed rejected candidates for contract renewal or tenure. But in all cases that I have experienced, the root problem was a matter of what Bourdieu describes as "academic habitus" (1988), the capacity to absorb the normative range of professional practices, values, and signs in a given field of knowledge. Imagine the trouble that could result from something as simple as the inability to discern what was really meant by the word *good* during a phone call. Because, as Bourdieu also observed many times, power and discretion move hand in hand. It would be impolite and disrespectful to the organizations that employ us to openly suggest that teaching labor (which they value and market) and service labor (which helps them remain operational) do not matter. So, by the time one is offered a job at an elite university in the United States, it is assumed as a matter of course that the candidate has internalized an unspoken understanding that teaching and service matter very little to the profession and to its dominant modes of evaluating professional performance.

Nevertheless, failed careers are embarrassments for colleges and colleagues and the preferred institutional response in the United States has become the development of mentoring programs within faculties. These programs are concerned above all, both for reasons of law and conscience, with establishing the transparency of tenure review criteria and with planning intermediate goals to help junior colleagues achieve the greater goal of a tenure-worthy résumé. In many instances mentoring relationships do offer useful guidance and counsel to anxious junior colleagues, but they also do not routinely question the value hierarchy that ranks different modes of professional activity. Quite the contrary, mentoring typically tattoos junior colleagues with the message that research productivity is the necessary condition of both survival and success as a professional anthropologist. If all goes well, at some point, the experience of professionalization is normalized and naturalized enough that the lexical chrysalis of "professional" disappears from self-characterization. Then, it simply becomes the case that to be a successful *anthropologist* means being a scholar who does fascinating research and who publishes brilliantly and prolifically.

Lest we imagine this has always been the way the value of being an anthropologist has been determined, let me share one more memory. I had a senior colleague in my first years at Cornell, a wonderful, modest, and gentle man. Each month, he read voraciously and carefully all the major anthropological journals and he loved to be invited to talk about something he had just read. If you did so, he proved to be an exceptionally and generous interlocutor, someone who loved to tell stories about his fieldwork and about his past conversations with other anthropologists. Indeed, in the days before AnthroSource and Google Books, he was a walking, talking, searchable database of anthropological citations and ideas. And, as one might imagine, students loved him because he gave his time to them and to all of us very generously, never checking his watch or yawning or significantly mentioning the writing deadline he was scrambling to meet. He was smart and thoughtful, very erudite, and a great storyteller. But he had not done research for many years and had never been much of a writer. He accepted this condition without apology. But one of the sadder but also most instructive moments of my young professional life was to hear him thank his colleagues past and present at his retirement conference with the words, "I am something of an anachronism in today's academic world. I've not published much, I've never even published a book. So I'm glad I was an anthropologist when I was. I don't know if I'd be allowed to become an anthropologist now."

I share these memories to put our joy of anthropological writing in context. This volume contains a great wealth of testimony to the pleasures, the privileges, the responsibilities of the anthropologist as writer. It is a book by writers for writers, a confirmation of the power, beauty, complexity, and purpose of our shared craft. It contains contributions from some of the most talented ethnographers in the world and I am proud to be linked to them. I do not consider my work as exemplary of the finest writing anthropology has on offer, but writing really is an exquisite joy for me nonetheless; it is what I look forward to doing every morning and one of the many reasons why I believe myself to have what Stanley Aronowitz once aptly described as "the last good job in America" (1998). Also, in full disclosure, I feel entirely at ease in a professionalism centered on research and writing. That is, I am not (or, rather, no longer) afraid of the social valuation of written productivity. I do not personally find it arduous to achieve contemporary performance standards. But, of course, this relative ease was the end result of a great deal of effort and not a little self-torment. And I have always been one of the lucky ones. Not only did I begin my career with every imaginable advantage in terms of social and educational "capital" (an academic family; high quality secondary, collegiate, and postcollegiate education; a white straight male subject position), but I have now had over a decade of stable, well-compensated professorial life in elite universities through which to further hone my habitus of research productivity.

So, this volume speaks very comfortably to me. But I wonder how it might be read by someone at the beginning of her or his anthropological career, a graduate student perhaps. Could all our confidence and obvious faith in our writerly craft not also come across as somewhat aggressive? One could hear in my sincere description of my love of writing an injunction: Be a writer! Not just because it is a fine way to spend one's time but also because there is no place for you in this profession if you are not already a writer or capable of becoming one.

That graduate student would not be imagining things. Indeed, I now feel ethically compelled to inform our entering graduate students at Rice of just this social fact. I make the point less bluntly, euphemism and conditionality being of course other effective strategies for the naturalization of inequality. I say that there is *probably* a general recognition that to be a good anthropologist means developing a wide range of skills and identities. If called upon to produce a list, I would mention being a good fieldworker, reader, thinker, critic, interlocutor, mentor, colleague, even storyteller. But, above all, I tell them that one must be a writer; this is the one quality that is no longer an option but a necessity. One's professional survival depends on the capacity to communicate in writing. A generation or two ago, as my example above indicates, it was still possible to survive and thrive professionally, even at a research university, as a critic or a teacher. But these are no longer primary identifications in academic anthropology: "pure" critics and teachers are on the path to becoming endangered species in our discipline as in other disciplines. Today, to try to become an academic anthropologist without at the same time trying to become a writer is to not only to risk dismissal but also to deny oneself full professional selfhood.

Yet, to recognize and reproduce a value hierarchy of modes of professional activity is not necessarily to understand the logic of that hierarchy. In order to fairly assess whether the current primacy of writing among professional practices is legitimate, we need first to understand why writing (or, more specifically, the knotted practices of writing, editing, review, and publishing) has become such a central measure of professional worth. What, in other words, has changed over the past half century that could explain why writing has become so central to professional legitimacy in anthropology?

This is, as one might imagine, a complex question. However, a good place to search for answers is within the dramatic demographic shifts of the second half of the twentieth century. Here we see, as elsewhere in anthropological research, how the mysterious valuation of certain forms of productivity is linked closely to the intimacies, anxieties, and necessities associated with modes of *re*productivity.

Taking again the case of the United States, the case that I know best, anthropology completed the first half of the twentieth century much as it had begun it, a community of researchers that could be measured in the hundreds, focused mainly upon the study of North American indigenous peoples, dominated intellectually and politically by the work of Franz Boas and his students. Academic anthropology had experienced slow growth throughout the first half of the twentieth century but its ranks literally exploded from 1945 to 1975, a transformation directly driven by new educational opportunities created through the G.I. Bill of 1944,[1] by the expansion of universities and colleges to accommodate a new political emphasis on mass higher education across the world, and by new political attention to internationalism (in the academic form of "area studies") associated with both Cold War geopolitics and decolonization. In 1945, the American Anthropological Association had 678 members. Only three years later, its membership had increased over 150 percent to 1,723. By 1960, the AAA's membership had reached 3,174 and by 1967 it was 4,678. The vast majority of growth in the 1940s and 1950s (97 percent) came from male students on the G.I. Bill, which helped cement gender inequality and hierarchy in the discipline for decades thereafter (Patterson 2001: 107).

As one might imagine, the septupling of AAA membership between 1945 and 1965 was directly connected to greater student demand for courses and degrees in anthropology across the country. The demand for new instructors was immense. Yet, supply was initially rather limited given that, in 1950, there were still only eleven Ph.D.-granting anthropology departments in the United States (Berkeley, Catholic, Chicago, Columbia, Harvard, Michigan, Minnesota, Northwestern, Pennsylvania, Wisconsin, and Yale), which together produced only twenty-two doctorates that year (Hurlbert 1976). To meet new demand, "old growth" departments expanded their graduate programs and their Ph.D.s were heavily mined to support the composition of sixty-three new doctorate-granting programs in the United States over the next twenty-five years. In 1975, the AAA estimated that there were 381 Ph.D.s, 1,063 M.A. degrees, and 6,239 B.A. degrees awarded in all the subfields of anthropology in the United States, approximately a twenty-fold increase over similar rates in 1950.

It is thus easy to see why the period between the late 1940s and the early 1970s represented something of a golden age for the discipline, at least in the United States. Demographic growth at all levels was strong and steady, which engendered optimism not only regarding the future of the discipline but about the importance of its expertise and the solidity of its authority. Anthropologists enjoyed significant research support from the US government and frequent access to political and public spotlights especially when it came to assessing events and conditions in faraway places. And, perhaps most basically, academic jobs were plentiful and career paths were multiple. The first need, after all, was teaching and mentoring power to meet the swelling ranks of students at all levels. As part of an external review process, I recently did oral histories with a few faculty emeriti of my current department (founded in 1970). One of them, Fred Gamst, recalled his "job search," such as it was: "I returned from my fieldwork in Ethiopia in 1965 to some eighteen offers for a faculty position [that] came to me through the mail, not 'feelers' but genuine offers. Persons tendering offers did not care who I was or what I had done; only my warm and cognitively functioning body was required. Burgeoning college classes must be met." When I shared this anecdote with our current graduate students, they were incredulous that employers pursued doctoral candidates rather than other way around. And, yet, as recently as the 1970s, in other words just two academic generations ago, such tales were not uncommon. Another former senior colleague used to share a story of how he had been first hired in the early 1960s after his graduate program's Chair had received a call from a friend in need, "So, who can you send us?" Although no one has, to the best of my knowledge, done extensive historical research on faculty hiring practices in anthropology in the 1950s and 1960s, anecdotal evidence suggests that they were largely organized through patron-client relations and through graduate program networks rather than through a "job market" in the contemporary sense of the term.

Boom periods never last. But the end of this particular boom had little to do with anthropology specifically or with the academy generally. The global economic crisis of the 1970s derailed the postwar "economic miracles" of the countries to which we now refer as the Global North and high growth rates were never to return no matter what economic philosophy or policy package was applied to resurrect them (Duménil and Lévy 2011). Keynesianism proved incapable of solving the riddle of the 1970s and the subsequent neoliberal revolution achieved little more than concentrating elite wealth and generating conditions of increasing instability and misery for everyone else (Harvey 2007). The most persuasive explanation I have heard of the failure of philosophy and policy to lead the Global North back from the 1970s crisis is that the fundamental problem of stagnation can be retraced to an emergent energopolitical dilemma. That is, since the 1970s, the fossil fuel supplies upon which the industrialized world came to depend in the first half of the twentieth century have moved increasingly outside the Northern sphere of control (Mitchell 2009). Since the formation of OPEC and the 1973–74 oil embargo, Western imperial control over crucial fuel supplies has never been fully reestablished, making Europe and the United States (other than their transnationally invested elites) vulnerable to other regional powers in ways they had not been for centuries. A parallel argument suggests that low growth since the 1970s is rooted in developments in communication and transportation technology that have allowed industry to escape the constraints of Keynesian contracts in the North and to find more profitable labor conditions in a Global South pressured into liberalization (e.g., Appadurai 1990). In this scenario, the out-migration of industry and employment has essentially deprived Northern states of vital drivers of economic growth and employment. And, more could be said about how the massive post-1970s expansion and leverage of a financial industry predicated on the commodification of insurance against "risk" (that polite way of saying "fear") infiltrated and undermined senses of hope and confidence (LiPuma and Lee 2004). But, again, whatever the ultimate cause or causes, I think it is clear that none of the aforementioned have much to do with the academy (beyond perhaps the work of the Chicago school of economics) and nothing, so far as I can see, with anthropology as a profession.

And, yet, anthropologists quickly learned the truth of what Milton Friedman once termed "neighborhood effects"; as Northern economies stagnated and Keynesianism (and its strong sponsorship of higher education) fell into crisis and disrepute, our professional conditions eroded as well. 1976 to 1983 was the only sustained period since 1945 in which the AAA lost members (going from 8,404 to 6,486). The average annual output of Ph.D.s did remain remarkably steady (oscillating between 360 and 460 per year) between 1974 and 1995. But federal funding of graduate training dropped off dramatically (from 39 percent of doctoral students in 1972 to only 19 percent in 1990) and especially striking was the decline in governmental support for field research funding (from 51 percent of projects in 1972 to only 17 percent in 1988). Most importantly, reproduction became more difficult and uncertain. The percentage of anthropology Ph.D.s who were able to move from doctoral training directly into professorial positions in academic anthropology dropped very significantly from 74 percent in the early 1970s to under 40 percent by the late 1980s. I am quite certain that the current figure, were the AAA to calculate it, would be lower still. Some of this drop is linked to the increasing success of anthropology Ph.D.s at finding academic positions outside of anthropology, but not all of it. Even as the ranks of the professional community of anthropology have swelled (the AAA now has rebounded to over eleven thousand members), it has been hard to avoid a sense of abandonment by former benefactors and anxieties at downward trajectory and growing irrelevance. Not only did a phase of rapid growth end but normative social reproduction (in the form of Ph.D.s finding positions in the field) was undermined as well. Indeed, the difficulty of finding academic employment (either in anthropology or outside of it) has become an unavoidable presence and standard index of "professional crisis" ever since.

Anthropologists continue to place far too much blame on themselves for this condition, as though our expertise has somehow become less publicly relevant. Such an assertion seems preposterous in a world that has only grown more "culturally complex" (Hannerz 1992) over the past three decades. People, practices, and meanings have only become more interknotted in the era of neoliberal globalization and yet the ranks of other professional intellectuals devoted to teasing apart those knots (for example, foreign correspondents) are thinning out. The relevance of our expertise has perhaps never been greater. But we find ourselves caught in the neoliberal double bind that admonishes us to take responsibility for our victimization by forces we do not control in order to find a salvation that is truly beyond our capacity to guarantee.

In this environment of uncertainty and fear for the future, one way of understanding why writing has become so central to professional survival and identity is that it has itself come to serve as a form of risk assessment and insurance. This is especially salient given our vulnerable reproductivity. It seems that there are so many of us and yet so few jobs. All of us know that publications, especially those that appear in "highly selective" journals and presses, are difficult to achieve. They require not only good writing skills but a collegial willingness to work with peer reviewers and editors to adapt the thematic, conceptual, and stylistic nuances of one's own research productivity to those of other scholars. Assuming fair and constructive criticism (which is often if not always the case), one could say that a strong list of publications connotes a potential future colleague's sensitivity to the going norms of anthropological discourse and willingness to bridge one's individual voice to the transindividual communicational norms of the profession. A strong publication record[2] thus becomes a good general yardstick of both professional skills acquisition and professional performance. For those of us anxious about professional and departmental reproductivity and reputation, we can reassure ourselves that a well-published candidate is likely to be a survivor (and one who can help us, in turn, to survive too).

And, yet, risk assessment is only part of the story. There are times when I think that the social valuation of written productivity has no hidden purpose and that it is simply a reflexive response to the scale and complexity of our professional field today. There are tens of thousands of professional anthropologists operating in hundreds of languages across the world. Most national anthropological communities, including those in the United States and Europe, are fairly parochial and insular at their core. But to the extent that we can imagine ourselves as having a shared transnational sense of professional unity, this is only possible through publications that circulate in the world with greater freedom than their authors do. Publications have the potential to communicate ideas and experiences across a vastly complex and compartmentalized professional field. Even though they may appear as beacons of individual achievement, publications are also invitations to connection, reasons to start new relationships with others whose ideas and experiences have moved us. Publications thus mediate our own projects of scale making, operating as mobile forms of connectivity, and they are accorded a certain preeminence on this basis as well. Even in its digital forms, writing has a certain textual tangibility and translocal efficacy that grants it an object-status more elusive to, for example, the local spoken words of teaching and conversation.

Such objectivity can be further manipulated in a variety of ways to produce a value index. I know for a fact, for example, that harried hiring committees very often utilize publications as a filter for paring down an initial pool of hundreds of applicants to a more manageable number whose works can be reviewed with more care. I don't think there is any conspiracy here to privilege writing. It is just that a publications list represents an objective form of distinction (as do competitive grants, as do superb letters of recommendation) that helps to reduce workload for a group of faculty that might rather be spending their time and concentrating their attentions elsewhere. What might seem to the candidate as a normative impulse that writing is a superior form of activity could thus have its roots in a more ambiguous search for efficiencies via performance comparisons.

Still, this sounds perhaps a little too innocent; especially when one bears in mind that there are also fully institutionalized systems of value calculation centered on measuring and rating publications and their "impacts." At public institutions of higher education across the world, for example, neoliberal managerial techniques have been applied to institutions of higher education in the effort to reform them as centers of "knowledge production" (Brenneis, Shore, and Wright 2005). Knowledge here is always imagined as some kind of objective epistemic commodity or capacity that can be made subject to projects of organizational management and made interconvertible with other value systems, notably money. And, as Don Brenneis writes here and elsewhere, increasingly sophisticated services have emerged to measure not only raw publication productivity but also to rationalize intertextual citations as a new index and form of value in their own right (Brenneis 2009). Anthropologists working in institutions of higher education dominated by such "audit culture" (Strathern 2000) find the professional valuation of written productivity further overdetermined by organizational benchmarks and productivity targets, rewarding those who exceed them and punishing those who fail. Even if organizational audit regimes often imitate professional expectations for written productivity, their higher degree of formality and publicity (and more or less latent expectation for the conversion of knowledge into capital) can make them even more consequential in terms of determining professional success and survival.

There is, in short, no simple answer to why it has become necessary to be a writer in anthropology today. But if these remarks help to illuminate some of the hows and whys behind our present condition, then the final issue is: should we maintain this course? Are we satisfied with a profession whose sense of citizenship centers on performance and especially on performance in the forms of research, writing, and publishing? Are we comfortable allowing the teachers, critics, and storytellers to become relics of our golden era? Or is there something to be said for diversifying or rebalancing our criteria of professional belonging now?

I will not answer that series of questions but I will argue that we are capable of answering them. We may not be able to do much to remediate the rotten log of neoliberal modernity in its totality, but a profession is a much smaller and more responsive target. It is, after all, us. And anthropology has always exhibited a healthy degree of self-criticism, even contempt, for its status quo (Hannerz 2010: 163). As a first step, I would advocate that the national anthropology associations of the world create joint task forces on "the standards of legitimacy" in professional anthropology. I would further demand that our professional associations commit themselves to serious and ongoing historical and ethnographic inquiry into the principles, mechanisms, trends, and effects of professionalization in our discipline. With such data in hand, I think we will have the evidentiary basis to take a long, frank look at ourselves, specifically at the conjuncture of our vocational ideals and professional realities in anthropology. Writing is a joy to us here, and for good reason. But it is not the only way to be an anthropologist let alone to engage the world anthropologically. So we must take care not to let writing become another of those neoliberal indulgences enjoyed by the few and acquiesced to by the many.

Dominic Boyer is Professor of Anthropology at Rice University and Founding Director of the Center for Energy and Environmental Research in the Human Sciences (CENHS, culturesofenergy.org). He is an editor of the journal *Cultural Anthropology* (2015–18) and recently authored *The Life Informatic: Newsmaking in the Digital Era* (Cornell University Press, 2013). With James Faubion and George Marcus, he has recently edited *Theory Can Be More than It Used to Be* (2015, Cornell University Press) and with Imre Szeman is preparing *Energy Humanities: A Reader* for Johns Hopkins University Press. His next book project is a collaborative multimedia duograph with Cymene Howe, which will explore the political complexities of wind power development in Southern Mexico.

NOTES

1. The Servicemen Readjustment Act of 1944 (known more colloquially as the "G.I. Bill") was designed to smooth the reentry of Second World War veterans into civilian life. One of the key emphases of the Act was the creation of educational opportunities and it provided tuition and supplementary support to encourage the pursuit of higher education. By the time the original Act expired in 1956, almost eight million veterans had participated in an educational or training program. The Act is still widely viewed today as a watershed in the

expansion of higher education in the United States. In 1945 only 4.6 percent of American citizens had received a bachelors (or higher) degree. By 2006, that figure was estimated by the United States Census Bureau to be 26.0 percent.

2. It is noteworthy that a "strong publication record" at the time of tenure today normally involves at least one monograph, if not more. Although anthropologists have published books since the beginning of the discipline, the expectation of a "book for tenure" is a more recent, post-1960s standard. The relatively Herculean efforts involved in rewriting a dissertation, finding a publisher, surviving peer review, and so forth—all while learning a thousand other professional skills—seem to suggest that the making of the book is treated not only as a measure of intellectual value but also as the ultimate endurance test for the young scholar, the performance that decisively proves one's capacity for professional survival.

REFERENCES

Appadurai, Arjun. 1990. "Disjuncture and Difference in the Global Cultural Economy." *Public Culture* 2, no. 2: 1–24.

Aronowitz, Stanley. 1998. "The Last Good Job in America." In *Chalk Lines: The Politics of Work in the Managed University,* ed. R Martin. Durham, NC: Duke University Press.

Bourdieu, Pierre. 1988. *Homo Academicus.* Trans. P. Collier. Stanford: Stanford University Press.

Brenneis, Don. 2009. "Anthropology in and of the Academy: Globalization, Assessment and Our Field's Future." *Social Anthropology* 17, no. 3: 261–275.

Brenneis, Don, Cris Shore, and Susan Wright. 2005. "Getting the Measure of Academia: Universities and the Politics of Accountability." *Anthropology in Action* 12, no. 1: 1–10.

Duménil, Gérard, and Dominique Lévy. 2011. *The Crisis of Neoliberalism.* Cambridge, MA: Harvard University Press.

Hannerz, Ulf. 1992. *Cultural Complexity: Studies in the Social Organization of Meaning.* New York: Columbia University Press.

———. 2010. *Anthropology's World: Life in a Twenty-First-Century Discipline.* London: Pluto.

Harvey, David. 2007. "Neoliberalism as Creative Destruction." *The ANNALS of the American Academy of Political and Social Science.* 610, March: 22–44.

Hurlbert, Beverley McElligott. 1976. "Status and Exchange in the Profession of Anthropology." *American Anthropologist* 78, no. 2: 272–284.

LiPuma, Edward, and Benjamin Lee. 2004. *Financial Derivatives and the Globalization of Risk.* Durham, NC: Duke University Press.

Mitchell, Timothy. 2009. "Carbon Democracy." *Economy and Society* 38, no. 3: 399–432.

Patterson, Thomas Carl. 2001. *A Social History of Anthropology in the United States.* New York: Berg.

Strathern, Marilyn, ed. 2000. *Audit Cultures: Anthropological Studies in Accountability, Ethics and the Academy.* London: Routledge.

Chapter 2

Reading, Writing, and Recognition in the Emerging Academy

Don Brenneis

INTRODUCTION

In a March 2012 colloquium a Danish colleague visiting our department at UC Santa Cruz presented the introduction to her book manuscript on the complex world of a posttsunami coastal community in Tamilnadu, a textured, multiperspectival account. She prefaced her discussion with several framing remarks, among them the observation that she was, she knew, taking something of a risk as she had deliberately chosen to write a book rather than a series of articles. Why would this be a problem? Key here is the Danish Higher Education Reform Act of several years ago, which, among other things, shaped a model for evaluation in which citation rates are taken as the proxy for quality, and such rates only apply to articles. Further, while a scholar would receive publication credit for a book, the book would only be taken as equivalent to 2.5 articles.

As a second example, that same week I was asked to join a new ad hoc committee under the auspices of our campus academic personnel committee. The purpose of the committee was to focus on new ways of assessing scholarly value in the "book disciplines." Those of us who had finally convinced colleagues from the sciences that many fields are "book" rather than "article" disciplines now face a new need to point to other possible marks of scholarly accomplishment and trajectory, given the increasing financial challenges to book publishing and the near disappearance of some fields from university press lists.

And, just before the Greek election in June 2012, in the context of an on-line committee conversation on the future of journal publishing in anthropology, a very knowledgeable, accomplished, and mildly acerbic participant prefaced her remarks by saying that she wanted to put in her "Two cents (or drachmas, as one senses that professional opinion is less valuable in these digital democratic days)."

What might these three stories suggest about both writing and reading in anthropology? There is currently a great deal of concern and reflection on ongoing transformations in scholarly publishing. Clearly a challenging nexus of new technology, new economic relationships, and personal and institutional consequences is developing, along with new demands for recognition and accountability. In this chapter I focus on the reading of anthropological writing and especially on those at times unexpected, almost invisible, but consequential audiences central to evaluation.

As anthropologists, we very likely have a good sense of how we individually read scholarly work, although the reasons we read it, whether for our own research, for teaching, or for assessment, may shape quite different ways of engaging with the texts. But who else might be reading anthropological writing? How do they read our scholarship, and toward what ends? As we write, what audiences might we imagine, and how do we understand the expectations and practices those audiences might bring to their reading? How, as these other readers figure in increasingly significant ways, might our own reading practices be transformed? And how, finally, do they—and we—attribute value to what has been read? The essay draws upon my ongoing ethnographic study of peer review, scholarly publication, assessment practices, higher education policy, and the shaping of scholarly and scientific knowledge within and beyond anthropology. Here I focus on some aspects of the processes of "writing money," that is, producing such texts as grant proposals and scholarly manuscripts, and of "reading value," how such works are recognized, read, cited, evaluated, compared, acted upon, and taken as central elements in proposal, personnel, and program assessment. These processes take place at the intersections of talk, paper forms and documents, and electronic media, and of peer conversation and formal analytical methods such as citation analysis. They have also come to include a much broader range of engaged respondents through new styles of postpublication peer-to-peer review. In this chapter I'll be exploring three heuristic types of "reading for ranking": traditional expert peer review, formal, often mediated techniques for quantitative evaluation, and emerging crowd-based distributed response.

Before turning to this discussion, I want briefly to introduce several terms that inform my perspective. First is the notion of performance as developed by Bauman in a germinal article on verbal art. He argued that performance "involves on the part of the performer an assumption of accountability to an audience for the way in which communication is carried out, over and above its referential content" (Bauman 1975: 293). Two elements of this definition are relevant here. First, communication is rarely just a matter of meaning; form, style, and the social calibration of one's actions vis-à-vis one's interlocutors are at times even more consequential. The second element is that communicative practice is also always social practice. More particularly, a specific kind of social relationship, one that Bauman terms "accountability," a responsibility not only to provide an account but also to take others' expectations into account, is crucial. "Accountability" is a polysemic term with a complex prehistory. Phillip Agre has noted that

> the word ["accountability"] involves a studied ambiguity between two existing uses. The first use, in business discourse, refers to the reporting relationships through which authority is organized in a company. One is "accountable" (one is usually not "accountable to" anybody but simply "accountable") to the extent that one's activities are, as a practical matter, subject to the broader imperatives of the company as articulated by its management. The second use of "accountability" derives from ethnomethodology… Here the word refers to a broad property of human activity, which roughly speaking is the responsibility to make one's actions intelligible to other people… The management of mutual intelligibility and the moral order that surrounds this process are regarded by ethnomethodologists as the very "glue" of society. (1995: 181)

The third term I want to highlight here is the idea of "entextualization" and the complex consequences of citation and recontextualization that it entails. Bauman and Briggs (1990: 73) use "entextualization" to describe the transformation of chunks of talk or writing into "texts" separable from their original contexts of use and available for situated and often strategic reuse.

READING VALUE

Recently I suggested that, "before one can, to use James Clifford and George Marcus's phrase, 'write culture,' one must first write money and that someone also must "read money" (Brenneis 2011: 3). In my research I initially focused on the writing and reading of grant and fellowship proposals, a consequential nexus in the shaping of contemporary American science and scholarship, and one in which the style and aesthetic coherence with which proposals are shaped make a significant difference. These are classic cases of verbal performance, ones in which the audience's response cannot be

ignored. Beyond research funding, however, the academic world is perme-
ated and sustained by moments in which we, individually and collectively,
make judgments concerning value, whether of pieces of work, scholarly trajectories, departments, or disciplinary directions. Many of us, and especially
senior scholars, are routinely involved in such mutual assessment, hitherto
primarily through deliberative peer review in its multiple forms. It is also
the case that the conditions and possibilities through which we do this work
are changing in crucial ways, a theme to which I'll return. And in many
ways we are less alone or autonomous in such activities than we have been
at times in the past.

Practices of peer consultation and evaluation, activities in many ways
internal to disciplinary communities, are in ongoing and, at times, tense
interaction with those hierarchical, transdisciplinary state organizations
that regulate and support higher education and research. Jointly these two
institutional complexes help define something like a force field, one within
which disciplines have been and are being developed and transformed.
Movement within this field often oscillates between compatible collaboration and reciprocal resistance.

These two poles imply different styles of assessment and comparative
evaluation, styles that involve quite different kinds of readers, readings, and
representation. On the one hand is deliberative peer review; on the other
are some emergent, contrasting, putatively more objective strategies for at-
tributing value. A recent US National Research Council report distinguishes
between "deliberative processes," such as those of "expert review panels,"
and "analytic techniques," which include "bibliometric analysis" (Feller and
Stern 2007: 2). I'll also discuss below a third model of evaluation, "peer-to-
peer" review or "open review." Each of these three styles implies a somewhat
different view of the kind of expertise at play: in classic deliberative peer
review, the expertise is primarily individual, topical, and substantive; in the
case of analytical methods it often has more to do with mastering complex
evaluative technologies; and in the case of open review, it's something more
like distributed expertise, the collective knowledge manifest in respondents'
comments.

My own ethnographic work on research funding and assessment has
pointed to the self-limiting possibilities of even the best intentioned and best
informed peer review practices (Brenneis 1994, 1999, 2006). Peer review is
deeply embedded in and shaped by complex social relationships, in a kind
of shared sociality that often serves, among other things, "to limit what one
might say or how strongly one might say it" (Brenneis 1999: 142). Further, a
range of practices and devices intended to restrain the "subjectivity" often
seen as the key problem with peer review can also work against zealous argu-

ments for the out of the ordinary. Guided by forms and documents, shaped by ongoing sociality, and always informed by the anticipation of subsequent readers and decision makers, as well as being quite time consuming and expensive, peer review is indeed problematic.

Analytical measures and particularly bibliometrics, "using counts of journal articles and their citations" (Evidence 2007: 3), pose a different set of difficulties that I have explored at length elsewhere (Brenneis 2009). Such indicators count instances of citation of one's work by other scholars, which is taken as a proxy for the paper's impact and influence. Only citations of articles are counted; books and essays in edited volumes are not included. And the most commonly used citation index includes only a fraction of journals in print, almost all in English. Generally only those citations within two years of a piece's occurrence are taken into account, a policy that might match the citational practice in some disciplines but decidedly not in others such as anthropology or, perhaps more surprising, mathematics.

Despite many critiques, the indexes central to such bibliometric analysis have been a resource for generating a wide range of consequential artifacts. As one example, a 2008 box score in *Times Higher Education* shows the "[t]op countries in sciences and social sciences based on impact" (cf. Strathern 2008: 19). Such charts appear weekly and without framing comments in a periodical that also routinely critiques the methodologies on which they are based. Remarkably, Switzerland is the leader on the score sheet, considerably ahead of the United States. Perhaps this reflects the Swiss location of CERN, a high degree of intracommunity cross-citation in such large research institutions, and the fact that physics is a field in which citational turnaround is routinely quite rapid.

Citation indexes have also been used to generate more complex artifacts such as the "map of science" featured in a piece by Boyack, Klavans, and Börner (2005). The network map they develop is meant to "represent...the structure of all science, based on journal articles, including both the natural and social sciences, [and to be one that] can be used to visually identify major areas of science, their size, similarity, and interconnectedness" (351). The project is part of a scientific study of the structure of science, clearly a research project in its own right. At the same time the authors want to provide clear and valuable information to managers and decision makers. This added goal provides a fine example of what my colleague Melissa Cefkin (n.d.), an anthropologist at IBM, refers to as "data base determinism:" if you've got it, use it. On this particular map anthropology's closest disciplinary neighbors include neuroscience and paleontology, likely a reflex of how long biological anthropology journals have been available and searchable online and of the generally quick citational turnaround within that subfield.

Artifacts such as this map, especially when framed as guides as well as representations, provide telling examples of what has come to be known as Goodhart's Law, after an economist and Governor of the Bank of England who first made the observation that "Any statistical regularity will tend to collapse once pressure is placed upon it for control purposes," or, in more user-friendly terms from the anthropologist Marilyn Strathern, "When a measure becomes a target, it ceases to be a good measure" (McIntyre 2000; cf. MacKenzie 2006).

A central type of expertise within these new analytical systems is what I would call metaexpertise, a developing specialization in shaping and administering decision making within the academy. Such metaexperts serve as consultants, whether as individuals or in groups, in shaping the new languages and practices of university governance. What's key here is that the subject of such metaexpertise is ultimately translation, or strategies for getting past the need for translation, both across fields and for external, nonspecialist audiences, and that such translation is crucial for the repeated, assumedly transparent, and comparable measurement of value.

Kathleen Fitzpatrick, a recent director of publications for the Modern Language Association, is one of many advocates for an innovative cluster of practices emerging in scholarly publishing: peer-to-peer or open review (Fitzpatrick 2010, 2011; Fitzpatrick and Santo 2012). Such practices, that is, where a manuscript is first put up online and then subjected to critique, revision, and potential removal as determined by online reader response, reverse the usual temporal flow of publication, raise significant questions about the stability of scholarly knowledge, and presume a much more broadly shared and enacted understanding of how knowledge might best be produced. Fitzpatrick (2010, 2011) argues compellingly that the current shift from a context of scarcity in scholarly publishing to a context of abundance (cf. Jensen 2007) has led to a situation in which time, attention, and searchability have become the scarce resources. This transforming publications scene makes it both possible and desirable to move to assumedly more democratic and fairer practices of review and publication. Central to the success of such a change is the development of a critical mass of community participation, one characterized by the ongoing exchange of reviewing and being reviewed, and one that minimizes or gets rid of altogether the gatekeeping role of editors. "Trust," Fitzpatrick argues (2010: 172), serves as the currency in this system of what I'd call "distributed expertise." In many ways this is an attractive model, but, apart from the potential resistance from personnel committees to such emergent genres and evaluative processes, the system of trust she proposes depends explicitly on the ongoing reviewing of reviewers as well as of the publications themselves.

The expanded ambit of evaluation to include the assessment of scholarly interlocutors, indexed rather than laid out in Fitzpatrick's arguments, is advocated much more fully in a significant article by Michael Jensen from the US National Academies. His position is that, with the shift from scarcity to abundance in terms of the availability of scholarship, and with the rise of open access, peer-to-peer publications, the critical challenge of finding relevant, useful, and authoritative work will be met in part by the development of what he calls "trust" (2007: 302), "value" (302), or "reputation-and-authority metrics" (307). Drawing upon emerging practices in social media, such metrics "are different models for computed analysis of user-generated authority, many of which are based on algorithmic analysis of participatory engagement" (Jensen 2007: 303). Peer-to-peer review indeed might prefigure an emergent digital democracy, one dependent on new understandings of expertise and on new forms of consultation, but it also may end up relying on forms of automatized judgments of trust and value, judgments based on a systems of at times quite problematic proxies, much along the lines of bibliometrics.

ABSTRACT KNOWLEDGE

I want to turn now to a slightly different question concerning evaluative reading practices: what is it that actually gets read? Perhaps surprisingly, article abstracts figure centrally here, and especially what have come to be called "structured abstracts," that is, article abstracts that are organized so that "key aspects of purpose, methods, and results are reported with a partly controlled vocabulary, and in a standardized format" (Ad Hoc Working Group 1987: 598). The original impetus for such abstracts came from a recognition that practicing physicians attempting to keep up with relevant and useful research in their specialties were faced with a highly daunting challenge: how in the welter of the then all-print medical journals could practitioners with only a few free hours a week locate the most pertinent research? Somewhat surprisingly, abstracts were a relatively recent addition to medical publications, not widespread until the late 1960s. Over the following two decades a number of committees recommended standardizing abstract formats as a partial solution to the complexities of information retrieval. Search and retrieval have become critical. The recommendations of one group advocating structured abstracts in medical publications list such key elements as objectives, designs, setting, patients or participants, interventions, measurement and results, and conclusions (Ad Hoc Working Group 1987: 599). There is a complex relationship between the assumptions underlying how such abstracts should be structured and the epistemic assumptions of different disciplines. Some styles of research lend themselves more easily to systematic abstraction. An article along evidence-based medicine lines, for example, would more easily fit the model suggested above than a detailed ethnographic case study.

Such abstracts, structured or not, have some surprising effects, two of which I'll highlight here. First, abstracts are effectively prefabricated for entextualization. They are structurally separable, intended to capture the core of an article's argument in miniature, and in combination with a title, an assumed synecdoche for the larger work. In interviews with program officers at NSF and NEH, several stated that one of the most difficult but necessary tasks they had to pursue was to convince authors of proposals they recommended for funding that they should change their project titles and abstracts so as not to provide easy targets for subsequent congressional audiences. Older American scholars vividly remember Senator Proxmire's "golden fleece awards," given annually to projects, known to him and his staff solely through titles and abstracts, that seemed silly, self-indulgent, or of little value. This is a bipartisan pursuit. In April 2011 Senator Tom Coburn, M.D., R-Oklahoma, released *The National Science Foundation: Under the Microscope* (Coburn 2011), a report sharply critiquing what he considered the unworthiness of much of the research funded by NSF.[1] What is particularly important here is that his staff's research for this very problematic and ultimately well-rebutted report consisted primarily of titles and abstracts for funded projects and/or press releases from those institutions where the grants are based. The short version may be all that is read and may well be put to uses other than those the author intends. Entextualization does not guarantee automatic authority.

I want to turn to a further particularly important, if opaque, complication of abstracts. I'm indebted to Oona Schmid, the AAA's publications director, for pointing out that, over the last fifteen years, machinic rather than human readers have become increasingly significant (Schmid 2008), especially in regard to scanning journal article abstracts for topical relevance in the context of large-scale search engines (cf. Introna and Nissenbaum 2000; Grimmelmann 2007a, 2007b; Origgi 2008). Again, search and retrieval, especially in the context of the abundance of publications, matter. Such machine readers attend not only to expected elements like key words but also to the discursive form of the abstracts themselves. According to Schmid, the better the fit with expected forms of argument, however abstracted, the higher the chances of a strong relevance ranking. The more automated the scanning process, and the less the possibility of human scrutiny, the lower the chances of the quirky, idiosyncratic, or slightly untranslatable article finding its way to the top of the search outcome list, and what is that likely to do for anthropology or others among the humanities and interpretive social sciences? There is an odd resonance here with Bauman's definition of "performance"; form matters, above and beyond the actual message conveyed. The elements of automation, formal recognition, speed, and the absence of deliberation may well figure in our own field's future within the broader research sphere.

Our Danish colleague's challenge, the institutional nonrecognition of a genre of scholarly writing she sees as critical to her epistemic and representational commitments, derives in large part from the new conditions posed by a particular emergent analytical regime, one devised and operationalized by metaexperts of the kind I suggest above. "Book disciplines" are challenged by the vortex of new technology, the restructuring and unpredictable trajectory of scholarly publishing, increasing demands for assessment, and shifts in senses of collegial responsibility. Finally, my other colleague's "two drachmas" remark speaks to understandable pressures for a deeply transformed system of producing and valuing scholarly knowledge, one in which gatekeeping and older forms of specialized, professional expertise are deliberately circumvented.

CONCLUSION

In closing, I want briefly to make two broader observations. The first has to do with time and temporality. At one level, it is apparent that there has been a dramatic acceleration in expectations for publication. Marilyn Strathern (1997), among others, has written eloquently of the dramatic erosion of time to think under this regime and of the challenge to good, well-cooked, and innovative scholarship and science posed by this loss. But, I'd argue, another temporal change is also in process. In earlier decades the fact of an article, for example, appearing in print in a peer-reviewed journal was pivotal, not only on one's curriculum vitae but also in terms of fixing the article as a finished product. The article "was" the article. The life histories of manuscripts have gotten considerably more complicated. That such problematic bibliometric measures as impact factors have come, in many circles, to be taken as more salient and telling data than the fact of publication is one dimension of this. But it's not a matter of citation alone. For multiple reasons, including the range of new electronic formats and media, the financial predicaments of scholarly publishing, and the understandable drive toward open access, peer-to-peer models are increasingly coming into play. In contrast to the fixed-form article, there is no necessary end point for publications under such regimes. These new forums for scholarly communication suggest a world very like that depicted by Adrian Johns (1998) in his magisterial history of the book, that is, a time when it was uncertain what a book was—or if and when its form and content might become stable (cf. Fitzpatrick 2011). Certainly there are colleagues in many scholarly associations and on many personnel policy committees trying to wrestle with just such questions and across a wide range of emergent genres. University presses themselves are in a similarly complex situation, with emerging new patterns of aggregation and disaggregation changing the nature of the book.

Second, I've been struck by the transformation of the role and regard of traditional academic expertise in recent years. This has been in the broader context of the erosion of higher education as what economists once, quite recently, wrote about as a "trust market" (Winston 1999), one where outcomes were necessarily long-term, and where self-governance was seen as both feasible and desirable. There could clearly be and were problems with such an at least semi-autonomous realm, but this brings us back to the theme of accountability, or at least its rhetorical and practical invocations within the current academic scene.

The sites and practices associated with peer review provide key contexts for the enactment of expertise as both individual and collective capacity, and new forms of open review hold a similar promise, albeit one requiring considerable institutional transformation to make it work as well as it might. I'd argue that classic deliberative review and practices drawing on distributed expertise contrast strikingly with the rise of a particular kind of managerial accountability, one in which the metaexpertise I've noted above plays a key role. Central here are the questions of to whom, as scholars, researchers, and authors are accountable, and in what ways.

In closing I'd suggest the value of keeping that earlier, performative sense of accountability in mind. The perspective Agre (1995) lays out holds that our obligations vis-à-vis our quite specific interlocutors are situationally grounded, always under negotiation, intelligible but not necessarily wholly clear, ongoing, and perhaps dependent on obliqueness, ambiguity, and a certain degree of trust for their social capacities. In contrast, current usage centers on a kind of responsibility without apparent relationship, that is, being accountable but to no one in particular. In reality there are quite concrete social relationships inherent in contemporary styles of accountability, often highly mediated and translated into highly abstract metalanguages, frequently without identifiable interlocutors, and usually aligned with institutional interests and outcomes. And, as I've discussed at length elsewhere (Brenneis 1994, 1999, 2006), the nature of our own reading—especially in regard to evaluation—may well be transformed through our interaction with the forms and frameworks central to such institutional practices. Writing and reading are practices central to shaping our collective scholarly knowledge of the world and constitute a pattern of ongoing exchange at the core of our intellectual communities, both within and beyond anthropology (Brenneis 2004). Taking into careful account changing patterns in how value is read in and out of our work seems both timely and critical.

ACKNOWLEDGEMENTS

This chapter and the larger project in which it figures have been a long time in the making. I began working on some of the questions central here while a Fellow at the Center for Advanced Studies in the Behavioral Sciences (2007–08) and have written the chapter itself while a Fellow at the Lichtenberg Kolleg, University of Göttingen. I am grateful to these institutions and especially to many colleagues at both for their lively and generative conversation. I first approached the question of new reading practices when invited to participate in the Stockholm Roundtable on writing in anthropology and am deeply grateful to Helena Wulff, both for her invitation to be part of those conversations and for her subsequent patient support as an editor. Various of the arguments made here have been presented at Cambridge University, the University of Chicago, Brown University, the University of Oregon, the Center for Digital Humanities at the University of Göttingen, UCLA, Indiana University, and at the twentieth anniversary meeting of the European Association of Social Anthropologists. I appreciate the invitations, the hospitality, and the discussions. I very much appreciated my colleagues' comments and suggestions, and I was able to talk with and hear several lectures by Kathleen Fitzpatrick, one of the catalytic figures in open review publishing, to whom I give many thanks. Finally, the Lichtenberg Kolleg also supported an interdisciplinary workshop on expertise that I organized along with Regina Bendix, Dorothy Noyes, and Kilian Bizer; many thanks to workshop participants and especially to my generatively collegial coconvenors. Such scholarly exchange—reading, writing, talking—has been invaluable in this long process, and I thank all of those involved for their generosity, imagination, and insight.

Don Brenneis is Professor of Anthropology at the University of California, Santa Cruz, and works at the intersections of communicative practice and social, political, and intellectual life. His research has focused on the ethnography of research funding panels and other key sites in which peer review figures centrally in the ongoing shaping and circulation of knowledge in the social sciences. Most recently he has complemented this work on deliberative review with an exploration of the underlying structure, uses, and consequences of assumed indicators of scholarly and scientific value such as citation analysis within the academy and the research funding world.

NOTES

1. Senator Coburn has been persistent in his critique of NSF and recently figured centrally in a successful attempt to "restrict[] the ability of the NSF to approve any grants involving political science unless the agency can certify them as 'promoting national security or the economic interests of the United States'" (Basken 2013).

REFERENCES

Ad Hoc Working Group for Critical Appraisal of the Medical Literature. 1987. "A Proposal for More Informative Abstracts of Clinical Articles." *Annals of Internal Medicine* 106: 598–604.

Agre, Phillip E. 1995. "From High Tech to Human Tech: Empowerment, Measurement, and Social Studies of Computing." *Computer Supported Cooperative Work (CSCW)* 3: 167–195.

Basken, Paul. 2013. "Senate Moves to Limit NSF Spending on Political Science." *The Chronicle of Higher Education.* 21 March, http://chronicle.com/article/Senate-Moves-to-Limit-NSF/138027/..

Bauman, Richard. 1975. "Verbal Art as Performance." *American Anthropologist* 77, no. 2: 290–311.

Bauman, Richard, and Charles L. Briggs. 1990. "Performance and Poetics as Critical Perspectives on Language and Social Life." *Annual Review of Anthropology* 19: 59–88.

Boyack, Kevin W., Richard Klavans, and Katy Börner. 2005. "Mapping the Backbone of Science." *Scientometrics* 64, no. 3: 351–374.

Brenneis, Don. 1994. "Discourse and Discipline at the National Research Council: A Bureaucratic *Bildungsroman.*" *Cultural Anthropology* 9, no. 1: 23–36.

———. 1999. "New Lexicon, Old Language: Negotiating the 'Global' at the National Science Foundation. In *Critical Anthropology Now,* ed. George E. Marcus. Santa Fe: School of American Research Press.

———. 2004. "A Partial View of Contemporary Anthropology." *American Anthropologist* 106, no. 3: 580–588.

———. 2006. "Reforming Promise." In *Documents: Artifacts of Modern Knowledge,* ed. Annelise Riles. Ann Arbor: University of Michigan Press.

———. 2009. "Anthropology in and of the Academy: Globalization, Assessment, and our Field's Future." *Social Anthropology* 17, no. 3: 261–275.

——. 2011. "Writing–and Reading–Money." *Anthropology News* 52, no. 8: 3–4.

Cefkin, Melissa. 2008. Personal communication (27 April).

Coburn, Tom A. (US Senator, R-Oklahoma). 2011. *The National Science Foundation: Under the Microscope.* April 2011.

Evidence. 2007. *The Use of Bibliometrics to Measure Research Quality in UK Higher Education Institutions.* London: Universities UK.

Feller, Irwin, and Paul C. Stern, eds. 2007. *A Strategy for Assessing Science: Behavioral and Social Research on Aging.* Washington, DC: The National Academies Press.

Fitzpatrick, Kathleen. 2010. "Peer-to-Peer Review and the Future of Scholarly Authority." *Social Epistemology* 24, no. 3: 161–179.

——. 2011. *Planned Obsolescence: Publishing, Technology, and the Future of the Academy.* New York: New York University Press.

Fitzpatrick, Kathleen, and Avi Santo (for the Mellon Open Review Grant Team). 2012. "Open Review: A Study of Contexts and Practices." *Open Review,* http://mediacommons.futureofthebook.org/mcpress/open-review.

Grimmelmann, James. 2007a. "Information Policy for the Library of Babel." *Journal of Business and Technology Law* 3, no. 1: 201–212.

——. 2007b. "The Structure of Search Engine Law." *Iowa Law Review* 93: 1–63.

Introna, Lucas, and Helen Nissenbaum. 2000. "Shaping the Web: Why the Politics of Search Engines Matters." *The Information Society* 16: 169–185.

Jensen, Michael. 2007. "Authority 3.0: Friend or Foe to Scholars?" *Journal of Scholarly Publishing* 39, no. 1: 297–307.

Johns, Adrian. 1998. *The Nature of the Book: Print and Knowledge in the Making.* Chicago: University of Chicago Press.

MacKenzie, Donald. 2006. *An Engine, Not a Camera: How Financial Models Shape Markets.* Cambridge: MIT Press.

McIntyre, Michael. 2000. "Audit, Education, and Goodhart's Law or Taking Rigidity Seriously." http://www.atm.dampt.cam.ac.uk/people/mem.

Origgi, Gloria. 2008. "Designing Wisdom through the Web: The Passion of Ranking." *La Vie des idees.* http://www.laviedesidees.fr.

Schmid, Oona. 2008. Personal communication (9 May).

Strathern, Marilyn. 1997. "From Improvement to Enhancement: An Anthropological Comment on the Audit Culture." (Founder's Memorial Lecture). *Times Higher Education.*

——. 2008. "Top Countries in Sciences and Social Sciences based on Impact." *Times Higher Education* 19. July 17.

Winston, Gordon C. 1999. "Subsidies, Hierarchies, and Peers: The Awkward Economics of Higher Education." *Journal of Economic Perspectives* 13, no. 1: 13–36.

Chapter 3

O Anthropology, Where Art Thou?
An Auto-Ethnography of Proposals

Sverker Finnström

> Unlike Malinowski, when the magician had stopped incanting his spells, they did not stay to watch the canoe building.
>
> —Maurice Bloch, "The Past and the Present in the Present"

In this chapter I revisit the so-called Malinowskian legacy in light of my efforts to raise funds for my own anthropological endeavors. Today's almost habitual dismissal of this legacy as parochial risks missing the fact that the anthropology of Bronislaw Malinowski's days was not simply a colonialist enterprise working under faulty premises. Even if epistemologically ethnocentric, Malinowski's achievements made possible debates that paved the way for an engaged, reflexive, open-minded and open-ended, and indeed global, anthropology. I will sketch some possibilities and potentials for ethnographic writing, but more, forces that tend to corrode the anthropological mind, a kind of control and restriction of the anthropological and academic freedom that I guess Malinowski never had to deal with in his life. As one of those ancestors who still interfere with our daily anthropological lives, I suspect him to be somehow troubled with today's predicament.

Perhaps my intervention more than anything else deals with the question of how to keep *thinking* anthropologically when an ever-increasing intellectual effort must be dedicated to the promoting and selling of the anthropological perspective in the so-called free market of research funding and higher education. I see ethnography as both process and product, and to be able to capture lived moments of global coevalness in places as geographically far apart as Uganda and Sweden, I think of fieldwork and writing-up as intertwined and parallel processes, in which research interlocutors are co-authors, not only in the phrasing of their stories, but more, in the very analysis itself. At the same time, the job of the anthropologist is not to absorb uncritically the stories of his or her informants, neither is it for the anthropologist to impose his or her stories upon the informants. Ultimately anthropology is about the informants' familiarity with the world, not that of the anthropologist. Yet such a goal is not always an easy achievement, as will be illustrated—and paradoxically so—by my auto-ethnographic approach. My aim is to acknowledge the importance of assessing critically our own cultural and symbolic regimes, in academia and beyond. Only then can we realize the potential of ethnography to overcome the legacies of our discipline's colonialist, even torturous, epistemologies (Whitehead 2013; Whitehead and Finnström 2013; Finnström 2015).

Anthropology rests on firm empirical ground, a disciplinary emphasis on fieldwork established by Malinowski and his contemporaries. The ambition today, however, is not really to search for final answers to the equally final questions asked, which would be a kind of parallel with the mapping of the allegedly disappearing cultures so important to Robert Murdock, and indeed, to Franz Boas and his students, notably Margaret Mead and Ruth Benedict. Rather, what anthropologists ought to do is to ask questions that will enable further and, it can be hoped, better informed questions. Such anthropological openness, serendipity, and directionality yet without any preset direction, or a kind of never-ending conversation, does not really pay off with the big research agencies of today. As a matter of fact, all I have said so far goes against the whole idea of "a project," framed by its clear beginning and its even clearer end. Again, as long as we remain uncritical of our own managemental regimes, while we still desperately try to get a piece of the funding cake with applications that we think are catchier than ever before, most projects that we eventually run, framed as they are and must be, will circumscribe the very openness that is ethnography's potential. In other words, if anthropology is coopted by forces whose agendas we not necessarily share, anthropology is again at risk of reproducing its colonialist legacies.

THE LONG CONVERSATION

In 2003 I defended my Ph.D. thesis on a war with northern Uganda as its epicenter, one of Africa's most violent conflicts. After a publishing house in the UK had invited me to submit a manuscript but then withdrew their initial interest, citing a limited market for my suggested book, and one in

Uganda just went silent, I was given a third opportunity to rework the thesis and have it published with Duke University Press. So I did (Finnström 2008). For this accomplishment I am indebted to, among others, my fieldwork co-workers Anthony Odiya-Labol and Otim p'Ojok who took turns to visit Sweden to offer feedback and take part in the rewriting process (see Finnström 2010b). Their visits connected Uganda with Sweden, and my field notes with the interpretations of my research co-workers. It was part of what Maurice Bloch—in an appreciation of Malinowski's keen interest in the everyday, that is, the sacred *and* the profane, the spectacular *and* the mundane—has called "the long conversation view of society" (Bloch 1977: 286; see also Brandström 1990). In the process I sacrificed, or at least postponed indefinitely, the time originally dedicated for writing up a postdoctoral project, but this too I like to view in light of the long conversation.

When I was carrying with me the symbolic capital of a Ph.D., a few articles and a published monograph, a new phase in my academic life started—that of submitting job applications and more, of writing research proposals. True, about halfway through my Ph.D. research, I managed to attract funding needed for finalizing my Ph.D. At one point during my Ph.D. studies, not yet knowing that my proposals would actually land me the necessary research funds, I made a calculation out of frustration, and concluded that I had so far spent six months full-time only writing applications, out of a Ph.D. program that in the Swedish system of higher education is supposed to take no more than four years, fieldwork included. I say supposed to take because there are ways to somehow get around these rules. If nothing else, life itself will intrude on the authoritarian rules, originally designed for strictly regulated research carried out in some kind of natural science laboratory, but universally imposed on the humanities and social sciences as well. This remained a theory of the policy makers, I found out from experience: I was accepted for the Ph.D. program in 1996, went to Uganda for the first time in 1997, got proper funding starting from 1999, and defended my Ph.D. in 2003, making a total of seven years. Yet here I was, about halfway through the Ph.D. program, when my first major application was accepted in late 1998. Besides a salary for the coming four years, it covered traveling and fieldwork costs, even if I was soon to find out that Swedish standards were different from those of some fellow graduates from the UK or the US, who, often under the umbrella of some non-government organization, seemed to have the costs of renting whole houses and four-wheel-drive vehicles covered. I moved around on foot, bicycle, and by public transport, and in 1999 and onward with the help of a small secondhand *BodaBoda* motorbike that constantly had to be sweet-talked with. But with my co-worker Tonny Odiya-Labol as navigator and supervising mechanic, this bike took us all over the place. In the midst of an ongoing war, it was hard work. At times, after long hours on the bike on bad and bumpy rural roads, it was literally a pain in the ass. In a story fit for the *Leatherman Tool Tales* webpage and in using an old bicycle tube, we once tied our multi-tool knife to the broken gear pedal. Deep in war-torn rural Uganda, it saved us when no welding was available. Such experiences, even if most often much less dramatic, kept me in contact with the everyday in the shadows of war, and emerging was a truly holistic fieldwork habitus that could hardly have been outlined in any research proposal. In short, Tonny the social navigator gave life to my proposal and made sure to have me in daily contact with for him urgent Ugandan realities.

When I think back, it somehow reminds me of Jack Goody's story about his receiving of a grant from the Colonial Social Science Research Council to work in Ghana. "The offer of motor transport," writes Goody, "was vetoed by my mentors at Oxford on the grounds I would have less contact with the people with whom I was working and would be unable properly to appreciate their concepts of space and time" (Goody 1995: 153). It was suggested that the mobility that a four-wheel-drive vehicle offers in these parts of the world would make the anthropologist too mobile, moving up and down all the time, and thus less in touch with the lives of the people he or she is supposed to study. For me, it was more a question of money, or rather the lack of it, so the idea of buying a vehicle never really crossed my mind. In retrospect, this was nice. In a war-torn place where white-painted neutral-flagged humanitarian four-wheel drive vehicles were speeding up and down the roads, with the white expatriate always seated next to his African driver, I soon became known in town as the (only) white guy who walked, even if people often complained over what I take to be my non-Ugandan way of goal-oriented walking, more or less straight from A to B, leaving one meeting for another. Embodied as it was, I painstakingly had to unlearn this, if the rumor of me as a US marine was not completely to take root.

BEING SOFT, BEING HARD

Surely the intersubjective encounter, so important in anthropology, becomes difficult if a windscreen—or a questionnaire or a predetermined hypothesis for that matter—seals off the researcher from the informant. I am not objecting to the importance of multi-sited or a more transnational anthropology, indeed important in our times of globalized movements, refugee flows, and increased cosmopolitanism. I think that the fact that I invited Tonny Odiya-Labol and Otim p'Ojok to Sweden testifies to this. Nor am I promoting some kind of colonial nostalgia. Rather I want to be attentive to life's open-ended conversations. I recall a note from rural Tanzania, a hidden piece of advice found in the writings of my supervisor, Per Brandström, beautifully addressed simultaneously to readers and the writing anthropologist:

> In his darker moments the anthropologist often envies his colleagues in those social sciences that boast more sophisticated field techniques. The only time he ever sees them is when they make hit and run visits to the village. They appear early in the morning in their Land-Rover in a cloud of dust. They know what they want, go about their business and are gone long before sunset. Only their field assistants remain behind, and briskly and without wasting time they select their informants according to the sampling schedule, take out their question-naires, and within one or at the most two days these have all been filled in down to the last square with nothing but "hard" data. In the not terribly cool shade of the tree, the anthropologist vows by all that he holds holy to dedicate his next life to the pursuit of only "hard" data and to forget all his ambitions about the "soft" ones. (Brandström 1990: chap 7: 2)

With Brandström's thoughtful mentoring, I eventually completed my Ph.D. And as I decided to try to remain in the academic arena and in my ambition to remain anthropologically sane, continuous conversations with him have always remained essential. While surviving academia by way of temporary teaching contracts, my file of rejected applications and proposals constantly grew. When the serendipity of things in late 2011 did land me a senior lec-tureship in anthropology after some years on the road, which among other things included a spell with Stockholm University, I was tenured at Uppsala University and the very department from where I first set out on my aca-demic journey, a situation that seems all too common in the Swedish uni-versity system. With a job secured, I could also see that the job folder on my computer houses some thirty-seven major applications and proposals, all rejected. In other words, perhaps cursed by Swedish academia eventually to return to Uppsala, it gives my anthropological career, so far, an air of failure, of surrender. I have been moving in a circle, and I realize that my professors were right in an insight for which I silently castigated them back then when I was doing my Ph.D. and that I curse still today: they pointed out that there will never be as much time to dedicate to anthropological research and writ-ing, and indeed, to contemplation, as there is when one is doing one's Ph.D. I wonder if Malinowski felt the same.

I should not only complain. I can also tell that my job folder lists some twenty-seven smaller applications, all successful. Even more, I have to con-fess that this subfolder of supposed success also lists one application for a postdoctoral studentship and one for a senior lectureship, but these two I eventually turned down. Evolving here was not the flow of anthropological serendipity that I was searching for, because generally, it seems to me, in a catch-22-like development one such golden opportunity tends to exclude another, or vice versa. If nothing else, life intervenes. Anyway, the folder mainly consists of applications for traveling and conference grants, a laptop, language editing grants, and grants that made it possible for me to invite Ugandan co-workers, guest lecturers, and visiting professors, despite the fact that I have been without any faculty position.

Some success, I have to admit. Yet there is a question that never seems to fade fully from my anthropological being: what if I could have redirected my attention away from writing all those applications, every single one meticulously formatted according to the specific instructions of the various employers and research agencies? Also, my CV had to be reformatted over and over again, to fit the online computerized and thus completely standardized application forms. In a sense, this is also a form of creative writing, as I always tried to secure at least some little anthropological openness to it all, but in the long run it is also a form of intellectual prostitution that risks shutting down the openness that I struggle to nurture. Anthropological creativity is traded for square-minded creativity, if there is such a thing. For example, in ticking the accurate box of preset focuses listed on the cover sheets of the applications, the very box that assumedly would specify my focus, I was circumscribed. Anthropology was circumscribed. Literarily speaking, I found myself thinking *inside* rather than *outside* the famous box.

THE POLITICS OF REJECTION

What if instead I had spent the time writing the real thing? I am thinking of research articles, scholarly and popular, reflective essays and newspaper opinions, even a second monograph perhaps, basically genres Per Brandström encouraged me to try out. My argument is that all that time I have spent writing proposals, and formatting them according to all kinds of guidelines that do not necessarily have anything anthropological to them, has had profound influence on my anthropological being. Take my 2010 application to the Department of Research Cooperation of the Swedish International Development Cooperation Agency. Among other things, the instructions demanded that I summarize my project's relevance "in accordance with the Swedish Policy for Global Development (PGD)" as well its "relevance as regards gender issues." These motivations, shortened to "PGD and gender" and to be clearly framed in a preformatted box called "Relevance and Gender prespective" were to contain no more than 2,500 characters, blanks included. I am not sure if "prespective" is a misspelling or a new word, prescribed perspective? And what is PGD, if not anthropology reduced and dehumanized to yet another unnecessary acronym (Finnström 2008: 134, 240, 2010a: 223)? Again I was left with the feeling that anthropology was reduced to self-pervasive impression management. And again I was inside a box that was not mine. But more importantly perhaps, such agencies would support knowledge production only if it could translate into policy and then be applied to the benefit of the research subjects, not necessarily in ways that they themselves want but rather in ways defined by the intervention of these very agencies. Anthropology becomes part of the exercise of power yet framed as empowerment or in other positive and allegedly neutral ways (Whitehead 2013: 27–29).

As many times before, I complied and surrendered to the format, but basically I proposed a critical scrutiny of the social and political life of acronyms and other dehumanizing policy devices. My proposal was eventually judged by a fellow academic to be "theoretically innovative." Also "the planned methodology" was described as "innovative and ambitious." The friendly reviewer even opened the review by stating that "the project is ambitious and relevant, innovative and theoretically cutting edge." However, in a situation of little funds available and great competition, research agencies tend to listen more to the critical voices, perhaps in search of an easy way out, a rejection. Thus a second reviewer concluded that "the direct relevance for development processes could be further elaborated upon." Even more, "Gender issues are important for the study and ought to be further elaborated upon in the project description." In the end also this reviewer judged it to be "an innovative project." Yet when it came to my anthropological ambitions, it was simply stated that a scientific assessment was "outside the reviewer's competence." Well, I thought for myself, if this is to be a scientific evaluation of the anthropological contribution, why cannot the agency hire someone who can do such an evaluation?

In the end these two assessments were boiled down to a rejection that, while acknowledging that the proposal as "ambitious and relevant," even "innovative," still stated that "it is not clear how the findings from the project can be transferred into a regional or international context." These were the wordings of a research secretary at the agency. For a desk bureaucrat to summarize the evaluations would be standard procedure. Yet the very meaning of this sentence, critical as it is since it paves the way for a rejection, is not completely clear *to me*. It becomes even more strange since the research secretary, in a situation whereby the agency on its side had imposed harsh limitations on how much applicants were allowed to write, repeated these very words in the sentence following immediately thereafter, replacing only "not clear" with "unclear", and I quote: "Further, it is unclear how the findings from the project can be transferred into a regional or international context." End of rejection. All in all, these two sentences, almost identical and linked together in a rather comic way by help of the word "further," made up more than 50 percent of the short text of the rejection. The individual evaluating statements were sent to me only later, on my explicit request.

In other words, if you do not have anything sensible to say, say it twice. I was perplexed, recalling that a previous application to the same agency was rejected on the grounds that it lacked "more detailed research questions" and was "very argumentative," as a reviewer had put it. A second reader had described this proposal as "daring," with a "political provocativeness" that was "refreshing," concluding that it deserved to be supported. However, also this time the agency had followed the critical voice. These are but the rules of the game, and perhaps I need to surrender to them and also realize that anthropology may gesture toward radical equality while at the same time remaining inherently structured in ways that preclude any such equality.

LOST IN TIME AND SPACE

Somewhere here anthropology was lost to me. With the thirty-seven major applications and proposals filed in my folder of rejected submissions, my anthropological being started to crumble, but I also suspect that the anthropological standards of the colleagues of mine who ended up evaluating my proposals are disintegrating in ways similar to what I experience. When (writing and judging) proposals becomes a genre in itself, it seems to have such a force-multiplying effect of mutual corrosion. We are all participants in the process, it seems, together on the proverbial slippery slope. From experience, I slowly learned what my senior colleagues already knew: this game is not about securing anthropological (or even scientific) standards, since the game is no longer about anthropology. Still we all play the game, because just as in Vegas, there might be a jackpot out there. And such a jackpot, rather than any lengthy monograph, will today be a most important proof of your scientific competence. But the jackpot may be that of the bullet of the Russian roulette, a bullet that kills the anthropology of it. I can no longer imagine a situation whereby my university would offer me enough time to develop without restrictions my anthropological skills to have them materialize in thirty-seven articles and essays rather than thirty-seven proposals.

But no, here was a development that actually promoted the proposal as the product. I found myself being subjected to a sudden death, but paradoxically it was a slow death, so slow that I would most likely not realize it before it was too late. As a Ugandan informant living in the shadows of war once told me, "Do not be surprised if you wake up in the morning only to find your head chopped off" (Finnström 2008: 191). There is no irony here; the old man was dead serious. And his comment was perhaps not that absurd. Indeed, I am also asked to review research proposals. The bullet is coming my way.

At a moment in time when all my research proposals were rejected, I had to focus on teaching. So in a rather dull moment in my brief career as an anthropologist, I turned to the students, the best source of inspiration. And I gave them a reading list with anthropological classics, starting with Malinowski, Mead, Benedict, by way of Evans-Pritchard, Leach, and Lévi-Strauss, to end up with Douglas, Geertz, and Bourdieu. It was truly amazing to see the energy with which they embarked on this old stuff. So, by way of a master course into the history of anthropological theory at Stockholm University I managed to recapture some of my anthropological senses. Even if some students noted that Evans-Pritchard's (1940) *The Nuer: A Description of the Modes of Livelihood and Political Institutions of a Nilotic People* somehow remained a report commissioned by the colonial authorities and directed to their purposes, this very fact offered us a lot to discuss. And it all made me think that Evans-Pritchard's holistic fieldwork ambitions indeed could be regarded as anthropology purposely lacking the fixity of "more detailed research questions." This would however be misdirected and, as the philosopher Paul Feyerabend (1993: 188) has shown, a fundamental misunderstanding of the very basics of Evans-Pritchard's work on the ground, and anthropology more generally. But I also noted that the colonial regime that Evans-Pritchard lived under, and worked for, has been replaced with the development regime of our times, namely, that of "PGD" and other dehumanizing acronyms of the many international development cooperation agencies' research and policy departments. Our present-day regime is perhaps no less imperial than that of Evans-Prichard. And, also, perhaps, Evans-Pritchard's employers tore their hair out when they received his Nuer report on their desks. Indeed, they never contracted him again. Perhaps they too found it unclear how his findings could "be transferred into a regional or international context." I mean, Evans-Pritchard's financers were in the process of conquering the Africans of Sudan, bombing their villages and their cattle, and perhaps the British colonialists too wanted to know why these poor Africans so stubbornly refused the efforts of modernization and development.

When some students rightly said something along the lines of "Gender issues are important for the study and ought to be further elaborated," I could refer them to the sequel, *Kinship and Marriage among the Nuer* (Evans-Pritchard 1951), or even *The Position of Women in Primitive Societies and Other*

Essays in Social Anthropology (Evans-Pritchard 1965). Like an old-time an-thropologist, I have actually produced one monograph of one people, the Acholi. If you like, I hereby embraced a colonial legacy in anthropology. The marketing people of my publishing house even demanded that "north-ern Uganda" be in the subtitle. Evans-Pritchard, for his part, had the time, skills, and anthropological courage to write no less than three books on the Nuer, the northern neighbors of the Acholi. One of my students actually went home to read Evans-Pritchard's book on kinship and marriage.

WHEN LIFE INTERVENES

Malinowski taught us a lot of things, indeed, some of which generations of anthropologists meticulously had to unlearn over the years to come. Yet perhaps his best advice for us was to get "off the veranda." If anthropologists once had been stuck in their armchairs, it was now time for them not only to travel to the so-called field, but also to get their hands dirty. Imagine a research proposal so open that the methods are simply described as an ambition to get off the veranda, leaving the rest in the air, in a sense as it is supposed to be. And what research proposals could be more unfocused than those we can imagine that Evans-Pritchard wrote. He indeed promoted a theoretical and methodological openness that would earn him little money from the research departments of today's international development coop-eration agencies. He sketched this openness in "Some Reminiscences and Reflections on Fieldwork," a text that eventually ended up as an appendix to the 1976 abridged edition of the classic book on Azande witchcraft: "The anthropologist must follow what he finds in the society he has selected for study: the social organization of its people, their values and sentiments and so forth. I illustrate this fact from what happened in my own case. I had no interest in witchcraft when I went to Zandeland, but the Azande had; so I had to let myself be guided by them. I had no particular interest in cows when I went to Nuerland, but the Nuer had, so willy-nilly I had to become cattle-minded too" (Evans-Pritchard 1976: 242). Evans-Pritchard's reflections were put in my hands by my supervisor (see also Brandström 1990: chap. 1: 10f), a silent advice to me that appendices and other sidetrack departures, intellectual as well as social, may contain messages of great anthropological importance. But again, to follow Evans-Pritchard's willy-nilliness is not really what you are supposed to do with your research proposals. I guess it would be deemed as "unscientific." As Paul Stoller, whose anthropological writ-ings I admire greatly, commented on one of my many draft proposals: "The section of methods is very important as well. Here you need to be concrete and pay attention to minute detail: types of interviewing and observation; archival work, analysis of data, if appropriate, and as you have included, a schedule of research activities." But even if one ends up in the field with strict research questions that the informants find highly relevant, the quandary has just begun. The lived realities of the informants will interrupt, and suddenly anthropology, as the intersubjective and dialectical endeavor it is supposed to be, just happens. Again my mentor Per Brandström puts his own thinking into writing, as he contemplates his anthropological being among the Sukuma of Tanzania:

> If he studies ritual he cannot avoid taking part in such prosaic everyday occupations as weeding and harvesting. If he studies land use, he must resign himself to whiling away the hot hours of the day during the dry season sitting with the men under the grass roof of the hut or in the shade of a tree and listening to endless and abstruse palaver that deals with every possible subject under the sun but that which he has painstakingly presented in his project proposal. The chances that he will be able to plan and decide how to spend his time are small. A funeral intervenes, and all work in the village is abandoned for three days (Brandström 1990: chap. 7: 1–2).

NEW BEGINNINGS?

In the end, as mentioned, I landed a senior lectureship. I also did get a major research proposal accepted. And suddenly the serendipity of things allowed me to combine these two anthropological tracks. So here I have two confessions to make. First of all, when I was about to finalize this chapter, I did so from the position of having secured a senior lectureship. Secondly, over the two years that eventually landed me the aforementioned grant, I had been hired by a multidisciplinary research center at Uppsala University, with the principal task of initiating research in the form of proposal writing and networking. I should therefore not complain too much. Time was on my side, and besides composing proposals, I was even able to write some stuff less anthropologically compromised. But my efforts to remain true to my anthropological ideas perhaps just prolonged the painful politics of rejection. Existentially I was at a loss, with the nagging feeling that I no longer had a voice in the marking out of anthropology. Still I tried. For example, I opened early versions of the proposal with a narrative that I naively thought of as a smart way to present a case for an anthropology of global war and transnational (in-)justice, of placements and displacement, and that at the same time was firmly anchored in my long-term commitment to war-torn northern Uganda:

I am sitting in a coffee bar [in Uppsala, Sweden], waiting for Olak, one of my research interlocutors. Over the past two years or so, we have met regularly, at periods almost on a weekly basis. When he finally arrives, he is limping, and he walks only with the assistance of a crutch. I know from our conversations that he has some permanent torture injuries in one of his legs, and the Swedish winter climate seems to worsen the pain in the leg. But more, I can also detect a parallel to the developments on the ground in war-torn Uganda, his native country and the subject of my research since more than ten years. When things seem OK in Uganda, with both fighting parties declaring their dedication to end the war with peaceful means, I notice that his leg is better, and this regardless of the Swedish weather. Sometimes, as when the two parties signed a formal cessation of hostilities agreement, he arrived for one of our meetings on bicycle, without the walking stick. We were both elevated, sharing the news. But eventually the Ugandan government launched new attacks on the Lord's Resistance Army rebels, and we both knew the consequences: a lot of unarmed civilians would now again suffer, even die. And the Lord's Resistance Army would again react as the wounded buffalo, as my Ugandan friends often describe it. Nothing is more dangerous than a wounded buffalo. Like a landmine hidden in the soil in northern Uganda, the wounded buffalo seems to strike without any sense of direction, indiscriminately. My friend Olak would again need his walking stick. And the landmine came from somewhere...

A version of the proposal, I have to admit, landed me some good fieldwork money, but as I was preparing the fully financed project proposal, Paul Stoller again provided straightforward guidance. He advised me to skip the opening story. "The last thing they want to read," he told me point black, "is a kind of narrative, which, they probably think, has no place in a proposal or in an academic text."

So I dropped the opening story. And eventually funds came my way. The research funds allowed me to gather new data, while the lectureship puts me in much-needed contact with new generations of anthropology students. This, so I thought, would allow me to revisit and expand my ethnographic "field," and it would allow me to revisit the writings of Malinowski and other old-time anthropologists as well as those in the making identified by curious and clever-minded students, which then again would force me to reconsider my past readings of my own anthropological heroes. However, I soon realized that less time than ever before was left for my own anthropology and (creative) writing. With the tenure secured, what have I really arrived at, besides a fully booked calendar? There are committees to sign up for, meetings to attend, peer-review work to be done, an ever-increasing mountain of administrative tasks to carry out, and also for me, proposals to evaluate. Robin Wilson summarizes a situation that is, I have to realize, general to academia: "The path to achieving what amounts to higher education's golden ring is well marked and includes guidance from more-experienced peers. But once a professor earns tenure, that guidance disappears, the amount of committee work piles on, and associate professors are often left to figure out how to manage the varying demands of the job—and fit in time for their research—on their own" (Wilson 2012). I am still trying to figure it all out. And somehow anthropology continues to be good to me. Tonny and Otim regularly call from Uganda, and I regularly call them. I try to keep up with my research. So I have no regrets. Yet there are days to come, and I can only hope always to remember advising new generations of students to hang around also when the canoe is being built, when life just happens, in liberation of (or despite) any research proposal. Someday the order of things may change. In the meantime we need to continue the critical assessment of our own managemental systems, as we struggle to find ways to avoid any circumscription of the very openness that is ethnography's potential. If not, and as always, we are at risk of reproducing a legacy of colonialist and even torturous epistemologies still persistent in anthropology.

NOTE/ACKNOWLEDGEMENT

Thanks, Per Brandström, for everything. I first aired the frustrations of my anthropological predicament at the Stockholm Anthropology Roundtable in 2009, then again at the EASA meetings in Paris, 2012; my attendance at these two events generously sponsored by the Department of Social Anthropology, Stockholm University. Eventually my thoughts became a paper and if this chapter sketches my efforts to hold on to some kind of anthropological sanity under circumstances when the future of my professional career was highly uncertain, I also want to formally acknowledge that I took it out from my drawer to finalize it while being based at the Hugo Valentin Centre, Uppsala University, working on a project on global war and transnational (in-)justice, funded by the Bank of Sweden Tercentenary Foundation. But I would not have reopened my drawer in the first place had Helena Wulff not been so persuasive, supportive, and wonderfully patient. Again, here is an example of anthropology as the long conversation. Thanks also to Sam Dubal for joining the conversation.

Sverker Finnström is Associate Professor of Cultural Anthropology at Uppsala University. Starting from 1997, and focusing on young adults coming of age in the shadows of civil war, he has conducted recurrent fieldwork in northern Uganda, where the Lord's Resistance Army and other groups have been fighting the Ugandan government. He is the author of *Living with*

Bad Surroundings: War, History, and Everyday Moments in Northern Uganda (Duke University Press, 2008), for which he was honored with the Margaret Mead Award, and he is co-editor of *Virtual War and Magical Death: Technologies and Imaginaries for Terror and Killing* (Duke University Press, 2013).

REFERENCES

Bloch, Maurice. 1977. "The Past and the Present in the Present." *Man* 12, no. 2: 278–292.

Brandström, Per. 1990. "Boundless Universe: The Culture of Expansion among the Sukuma-Nyamwezi of Tanzania." Ph.D. diss., Uppsala University.

Evans-Pritchard, EE. 1940. *The Nuer: A Description of the Modes of Livelihood and Political Institutions of a Nilotic People.* Oxford: Clarendon Press.

———. 1951. *Kinship and Marriage among the Nuer.* Oxford: Clarendon Press.

———. 1965. *The Position of Women in Primitive Societies and Other Essays in Social Anthropology.* London: Faber and Faber Ltd.

———. 1976. *Witchcraft, Oracles, and Magic among the Azande.* Abridged with an introduction by Eva Gillies. Oxford: Clarendon.

Feyerabend, Paul K. 1993. *Against Method: Outline of an Anarchistic Theory of Knowledge.* Third Edition. London & New York: Verso.

Finnström, Sverker. 2008. *Living with Bad Surroundings: War, History, and Everyday Moments in Northern Uganda.* Durham: Duke University Press.

———. 2010a. "Review Article: Political Bodies, Local Realities and Institutional Structures of (In-)justice." *Social Anthropology/Anthropologie Sociale* 18, no. 2: 220–224.

———. 2010b. "The Tide of War and the Mango Trees of Uganda: On Receiving the 2009 Margaret Mead Award, México, March 2010." *Multiethnica* 32: 17–19.

———. 2015. "War Stories and Troubled Peace: Revisiting Some Secrets of Northern Uganda." *Current Anthropology* 56, no. S12, pp S222–S230.

Goody, Jack. 1995. *The Expansive Moment: Anthropology in Britain and Africa 1918-1970.* Cambridge: Cambridge University Press.

Whitehead, Neil L. 2013. "Ethnography, Knowledge, Torture, and Silence." In *Virtual War and Magical Death: Technologies and Imaginaries for Terror and Killing,* ed. Neil L. Whitehead and Sverker Finnström. Durham: Duke University Press.

Whitehead, Neil L., and Sverker Finnström. 2013. "Introduction: Virtual War and Magical Death." In *Virtual War and Magical Death: Technologies and Imaginaries for Terror and Killing,* ed. Neil L. Whitehead and Sverker Finnström. Durham: Duke University Press.

Wilson, Robin. 2012. "Why Are Associate Professors So Unhappy?" *The Chronicle of Higher Education,* 3 June. http://chronicle.com/article/Why-Are-Associate-Professors/132071.

Chapter 4

The Craft of Editing
Anthropology's Prose and Qualms

Brian Moeran

This chapter describes the editing of both self and others. On the one hand, editing constitutes an essential part of writing and researching in the field. On the other, it makes an undervalued, though enormously important, contribution to the academic world. This chapter weaves together the two activities as it describes and tries to come to terms with what it means for an anthropologist to be both writer and editor.

SELF-EDITING

To edit is to make a choice, or series of choices. Will I write a rough draft of this chapter in longhand, or hammer it out on my computer? If the latter, what font shall I use? Times New Roman, Book Antiqua, or Garamond? Once I get started, what style shall I adopt: realistic, confessional, or impressionistic, or a combination of all three (Van Maanen 1988)? Should I try to impress with "learned scholarship," or should I merely outline in conversational English a few thoughts based on my own experiences?

And once I'm done, what then?

My editor has already made her initial choices when selecting and preparing material for this book, and finding authors for each of its chapters. But will she approve or disapprove of the choices I've made, once she's read my manuscript? Does this text properly reflect her vision of the book? Is its order logical and my writing clear? Have I adhered to the guidelines for the chapter's length? Am I consistent in what I've written? Is my use of language good or beyond remedial care? Do I go into excessive detail over trivial points? Will she ask me to revise what I've written to her, or a reviewer's, satisfaction?

And once she's accepted what I've done, what then?

The publisher's editor has already decided that this volume may be worth putting out in print. First, though, she calls upon reviewers who read the manuscript and comment on its contents. Their remarks on this particular chapter—"simplistic," "unsupported generalizations," "marred by banalities"—suggest that, more than a year after the initial draft was submitted, further editing in the writing is required. How best to pacify anonymous peer reviewers, book editor, and publisher?

If all goes well—the fact that you are reading this suggests that it has—the publisher's editor will then call on the services of a copyeditor, whose task is to ensure that all the chapters in the book, including my own, are "clear, consistent, unambiguous and well organised" (Page, Campbell, and Meadows 1997: 60). Ideally, the copyeditor should change as little as possible of each author's text, but he or she makes her livelihood from *not* leaving things as they are. Manuscripts can—indeed, should—never be perfect!

And, for the most part, they're not. Every writer has her mannerisms. Some consistently misspell certain words; others use the dreaded *nominativus pendens* and the split infinitive (its use now, apparently, sanctified by the *Chicago Manual of Style*). These need to be put right, as do other inconsistencies. A reference is missing in the bibliography; numbers up to twenty, for example, need to be spelled out (Or is that 20? Does "up to" include or exclude that final number?); the contents of a note bear no resemblance to the text; and so on and so forth. More choices and changes are made. And if the author doesn't agree with what the copyeditor does to his text, what then? There will be a bit of to-ing and fro-ing. If matters reach an *impasse* (they rarely do), the publishing editor may be called upon to arbitrate. Sometimes, but by no means always, the author wins his point (appeasement wins the day!). At each stage of production, poor editing can contribute to written work becoming "the death mask of its conception" (Benjamin 1985: 65).

Choices such as these are not necessarily confined to the written word. Having finally opened up a new file in Word, adjusted margins according to instructions, inserted numbers at the bottom of each page, and started to write, I find myself wondering how soon I'm going to stop. What excuse will allow me to press the *Save* button and go downstairs to make some coffee, have a pee, or mow the lawn? What if my editor, who spends the summer in a village not that far away from my own, were to drive over and ask me if my chapter is going to be on time? Will I reassure her with a resounding "yes"?

Or will I merely raise an eyebrow in a noncommittal way, wiggle my ears for effect, and pour her a glass of Irish whiskey to keep her quiet?

Or will I make another choice out of the infinite possibilities available to me?

EDITING RESEARCH

Every time we pause to make choices like these, we find ourselves in what Howard Becker (1982: 198) calls "editorial moments." These moments involve editing of both the self and others. As anthropologists, we are aware that self-editing starts when we are selecting the kind of research we want to do, where we want to do it, and how to go about doing it. Fieldwork is one long series of editorial moments, as we make choices about what is and is not relevant to our observations, participation, and communication. Whom do we speak to, and whom do we ignore? What's the best way to broach a tricky issue like money? What questions are better left unasked? What do we, and what do we not, record? Do we write more than one "record": a "subjective" diary, for example, as well as "objective" field notes? How much do we consign to memory? How much to the tape recorder or video camera?

And when we start to analyze all we've learned, we make more editorial decisions. How are we going to organize our material and structure our results? What sort of theoretical frame should we use? How much detail should we include? What sort of style should we adopt? Who, if anyone, is going to be our audience? What is the sound of one hand clapping?

An answer to one of these questions inevitably has an effect on the answers to others, which in turn may enforce a change in the first. Editorial moments are messy, not least for anthropologists. They do not constitute a neat or logical process, if only because of their variety. In the words of Clifford Geertz (1995: 20):

> One works *ad hoc* and *ad interim,* piecing together thousand-year histories with three-week massacres, international conflicts with municipal ecologies. The economics of rice or olives, the politics of ethnicity or religion, the workings of language or war, must, to some extent, be soldered into the final construction. So must geography, trade, art, and technology. The result, inevitably, is unsatisfactory, lumbering, shaky, and badly formed: a grand contraption. The anthropologist, or at least one who wishes to complicate his contraptions, not close them in upon themselves, is a manic tinkerer adrift with his wits.

My oldest—but, alas, recently departed—friend, David Kennedy, was a sculptor who loved to make such grand contraptions out of numerous lengths of wire, roughly hewn wood in the shape of a guitar, old cutlery, tin plates, papier-mâché figures, a toothbrush, and false teeth. He used to wind a handle like a barrel organ and, with splendid, ear-splitting cacophony, everything moved. One figure clashed symbols with a knife and fork, another strummed the guitar, a third—the singer—had his teeth cleaned between jerking upper body movements and singing into a microphonic spoon. The effect was overwhelming, wondrous, and guaranteed to elicit a smile, even from the most hardened police officer or *apparatchik*.

But grand contraptions, with all their attendant tinkering, were not enough for David, who also sculpted and welded in steel finely wrought forms—of cats and goats in the main, but also delicate figurines of women working in the garden, playing a cello, and dandling a newborn child. It was this blend of styles that, together with more than an occasional jug of *retsina*, used to keep him sane. But what of anthropologists? Do we, too, need to find a balance between these two forms of expression attendant in our monographs and articles? How many qualms accompany our prose?

WRITING AND EDITING

Editing is not writing. The two should be kept separate as activities. When I write, I go with the flow, allowing the words to form their own spaces, to take over from my thinking self, and to express ideas I never knew I had. In writing, words should have a mind of their own. This is the point at which creativity begins. When I edit, I put down anchors that interrupt what the cognitive psychologist, Mihaly Csikszentmihalyi (1996: 118–123), refers to as the merging of action and awareness. It is at this point that my logical mind takes over. I have to be careful, of course, to balance the two activities, the two states of being. The perfectionist is someone who edits all the time and doesn't allow himself to write. This leads to writer's block. Or is it editor's block? Whichever, at that stage it's time to learn a few tricks of the writing trade: using fewer words, and active, rather than passive, tenses; paying attention to syntax; avoiding repetition, metaphors, and abstractions; basic common sense stuff like that (Becker 1986: 68–89).

When writing, we compose, we build, we weave our prose (Benjamin 1985: 61). So, at the beginning at least, writing should exclude editing. This is particularly important for anthropologists, who often have to wrestle with mountains of data that they believe should be theoretically framed. How on earth are we to get started?

When I was in the middle of the second year of fieldwork studying folk art potters in Japan, my supervisor, Rodney Clark, unexpectedly wrote to me, saying that he was coming to Tokyo and that I should send him the first draft of my doctoral dissertation, "with a beginning, a middle, and conclusion, and no loose ends," no later than 15 November that same year. I had exactly three months and two days from the time I received his letter (this was before the era of email) to write my thesis.

Because I was, in spite of appearances maybe, conscientious, I settled down to do as he asked. But because I was in the field, I had no scholarly books to read and rely on for help, and the nearest university library (which, in fact, had few of the works I needed) was more than two hours away from my fieldwork site. This was a blessing in disguise. I had no choice but to write the whole of my thesis on the basis of my copious field notes and nothing else.

I had two sets of notebooks. One was unexpurgated, raw material, consisting of hurriedly jotted field notes made during interviews, making pottery, and *sake* drinking sessions. The other consisted of larger notebooks, in which I had neatly transcribed these jottings in greater detail, and edited them too, according to specific themes such as household organization and community structure, pottery production and distribution, and aesthetics and the Japanese folk art movement.

Beginning is the hardest part.

I remember gazing rather hopelessly at these two sets of notebooks piled on a table temporarily set up on the earthen floor of a storeroom in our house. I remember, too, the harsh symphony of cicadas in the pear orchard outside, and the keyboard of my portable typewriter with a fresh white sheet of A4 paper inserted, straightened and with margins adjusted. Gradually it dawned on me that all I could do was tell a story—a story about the community of potters I'd been studying and how they'd been caught up in an artistic movement that they didn't really understand or appreciate. I would tell the story they had been telling me the past eighteen months.

And so I began to write that story—a long story maybe, but a story nevertheless. I edited it, of course, to fulfill Rodney's criterion that it have a beginning, middle, and conclusion—themselves prerequisites for what constitutes a story. But because the emphasis was on *writing,* and writing a *story,* rather than on trying to fit the details of that story into some kind of theoretical framework, I managed to finish the whole of my thesis two days ahead of the stipulated time.

"Very interesting," Rodney remarked when I went up to Tokyo to hear his judgment on what I'd written. "Now go away and find a theory." It was then that I started editing.[1]

EDITING AND REWRITING

Editing, then, is not writing but rewriting. Already I've made three changes in the sentence you've just read, before moving on to this one. Before I'm through, I may well have made several more, or less, significant changes, or even deleted what I've written altogether. In which case, you will not read any of this paragraph. How do you read a cut without the paste?

Rewriting isn't easy. You have to learn to be tough with yourself. You have to stand back and read what you've written with the eye of another. You have to make sure the theory makes sense, avoid clichés, eliminate *inconsequentia,* check those ingrained habits that lead to the same old spelling or grammatical mistakes, and cut down on all those fascinating snippets of research detail so that they do no more than illustrate a particular point you wish to make. Editing operates at two levels in particular: one at that of grammar and style; the other, of organization. The first demands an experienced love of language; the second, clearheadedness. What you have written must be clear and simple, and it must be organized in such a way that your reader can easily follow your argument. Organization's the key.

So, how do you know when your written work will be judged sufficiently well written to be understood by people potentially interested in what you have to say?

Rodney Clark helped me with this, too. After reading one particularly tortuous theoretical section in the third draft of my thesis (there were six in all before it was ready to be examined), he said: "why don't you read this aloud to your elder son when you go home tonight? See what he makes of it." Poor Alyosha was only thirteen years old at the time. He was bewildered by my account of the intricacies of the Japanese household system and what made it different from a family. Dutifully, though, he managed to ask a question about one of his school friends when it came to my description of how to make pots ("Is Takuchan going to be a potter like his dad?"). But he soon fell asleep night after night as I read aloud extracts from what I'd written.

From this I learned two things: first, how to put a restless child to sleep; second, to write more simply, in such a way that Alyosha—or someone like an intelligent baker in a Greek island village (Moeran 2005a)—could understand what I was communicating, if he put his mind to it.

It's an effective test, or trick of the trade (Becker 1998), but not many of my colleagues seem to have tried it. You can see how people nod off in department seminars as the speaker drones on in what, to a layperson, is pure gobbledygook. It was during the course of reading my second departmental seminar paper that I realized that what I'd written sounded pompous (a common feature of theory), and didn't make sense, even to myself. I stopped in mid-flow and extemporized, speaking to what I'd written. People woke up and smiled encouragingly.

If only we could all learn from our mistakes! I was once invited to attend a workshop on "Advertising and the new middle class in India." Other participants included a dozen or so, mainly American, academics and a handful of representatives from the Bombay (or should I say Mumbai?) advertising industry. Five minutes after one, rather famous, anthropologist had begun reading a prepared paper, littered with obscure phrases about an epistemological this, a postmodern that, and a subaltern other, one of the advertising executives interrupted the speaker: "Excuse me, sir," he said, "But I don't understand a bloody word you're saying. Could you please be speaking in plain English? That's what we have to do in advertising. Get to the point." Alas! The rather famous anthropologist was rooted to his text and was totally unable to engage his audience. We dutifully nodded off.

Don't forget, then. Your audience is an intelligent layperson, not just a colleague.

EDITING OTHERS

Not all editing is self-editing. Editing a book, for example, requires being tough in a different way. You have to be tough with other people, your contributors, as well as with yourself to make sure that you're properly tough with them. Since your contributors are often your colleagues, and sometimes your friends, it can be difficult to be honest about what you think of what they've written. After all, as authors, we're for the most part convinced that nobody has the right to tamper with our thoughts! What we fail to realize is that if our editor, who is, after all, a reasonable and intelligent person, finds something we write to be ambiguous, then it's likely that other readers will be likewise bemused (Powell 1985: 119).

As an editor, then, you need to be sympathetic, yet prepared to say what you dislike or find irrelevant. At the same time, you have to be able to "read" your authors and judge how they may react to criticism (Powell 1985: 120). Too often, though, we let things slide. As a result, we find ourselves reading too much sloppy writing and too many badly edited books. Maybe, after all, publishing editors are right: academics get the books they deserve (Kadushin 1979: 64).

As an editor, you must, first and foremost, have a vision—a vision for a book or a special issue of a journal (or even for a journal itself), it doesn't matter. Second, you must be able to communicate that vision to others: to the publisher whom you wish to take on the manuscript; and to those you ask to contribute to it. Third, you have to know the field of scholarship required. And finally, you need to work, and work long and hard, to ensure that the vision is realized to your satisfaction.

Vision affects both content and form. As an editor, you first map the field that you wish your contributors to cover: writing in anthropology or the social sciences, for example, and the different facets that the topic of writing presents. Then you have to decide how best to put these different facets together into a seamless work. For this you need *flow*.

I've already talked about the need for a flow in writing. But you need to ensure that a written text—whether it be a monograph, journal article, case study, edited volume, or contributing chapter thereto—has an appropriate flow. If you stop to examine other media forms more closely—a television series, for example, or fashion magazine—you will see the same works that draw you to them tend to be characterized by flow. Flow is part of organization.

In an edited book, the editor needs to ensure that each chapter follows on smoothly from the one before it. It must exhibit a certain consistency of style and subject matter, ideally perhaps, through reflecting points made in the book's Introduction. At the same time, each chapter *anchors* itself in a particular topic that is different from those of surrounding chapters, in the same way as advertisements anchor textual matter in our magazines (Moeran 2005b). Anchorage and flow are crucial components of all media productions (Barthes 1977).

The need for flow means that you shouldn't just edit a book on the basis of a set of papers presented at a conference. True, it's not impossible, provided you've organized the conference really well and brought in as many participants as necessary to cover all the topics you envisage are necessary for the volume you wish to edit. But even then, things can go wrong. One of the participants suddenly decides to ignore his abstract and talk about classical music instead of contemporary art. Another fails to turn up, or presents a paper that is so scrappy that its only place is, indeed, on the scrap heap. However well you communicate your vision to your colleagues, one of them will almost always ignore you.

So what do you do? You ask, you cajole, and occasionally, if you're senior enough, you threaten. You may decide at one point that you have to drop one chapter you already have in hand because it doesn't quite fit into your vision. That's a tough decision, especially when its author has been meticulous in delivering various versions of the paper on time. Some colleagues accept your decision; others complain bitterly and become your sworn enemy for life. Editing encourages the biting of backs! Some of us have the scars to prove it.

You may also find yourself seeking new chapters. In a book that I re-cently co-edited, I realized that we needed to commission three new chap-ters, even though the workshop on which the book was based had been meticulously planned. One was needed to plug a gap: we had one chapter on the French *Salon,* another on art biennales, but none on art fairs, even though many of the other chapters were concerned with fairs. A second was needed to help the flow of the book and effect a transition from exhi-bitions to fairs through a focus on auctions. The third was commissioned because, as editors, we were convinced (it turned out, wrongly) that one of our workshop participants would not deliver what we required on time. As a result, the finished volume has—at the risk of editorial *hubris*—a flow that helps the reader move seamlessly from Introduction to Afterword (Moeran and Strandgaard Pedersen 2011).

BEING EDITED

Editing isn't confined to academics, but extends to publishers' editors, who are so called because their task is also to work with authors and turn a man-uscript into a publishable book. These editors have at least two sets of ques-tions that they ask of every manuscript. The first concerns its content. How well written is the manuscript? How much work is it going to need to make it publishable? Is it worthwhile spending time on and, if so, how much time? And does the manuscript make a substantial contribution to scholarship? The second concerns its target audience. Who will the manuscript appeal to? Will it be adopted in courses? Answers to questions like these determine print runs and retail pricing (Powell 1985: 103).

Once upon a time, editors actually read manuscripts and, in close col-laboration with their authors, edited them to whatever extent was needed. They still do in a country like Japan where publishers insist that, ideally again, an editor should be a *kuroko,* a black-robed Bunraku puppeteer, who remains invisible. The lifeblood of a publishing house lies in the trust that is built between author and editor—a trust based on editorial skill and knowledge.

Such trust is rare in the English-speaking world of academic publishing, for two interrelated reasons. One lies in the effect of the changing nature of the trade publishing industry on academic publishing, where editors now tend to move from one publishing house to another with some frequency, and where many of their responsibilities are beginning to be taken over by literary agents (Thompson 2005, 2010). As a result, and this is the second reason for the breakdown of trust, publishing editors of the old school are a dying breed. There is no longer anybody to appreciate us as authors, to stroke and curry us (Powell 1985: 116). Feeling forlorn, we send our next manuscript to any publisher who talks to us encouragingly at a conference bookstand.

Of course, we're being deceived; that's the nature of the game! Nowadays, even more than they did a quarter of a century ago, editors spend almost all their time planning new titles and talking to authors about the possibility of delivering manuscripts down the line (Powell 1985: 11–12). Publishers no longer employ editors to rewrite manuscripts in the way that they used to. It was in the same year as Walter Powell published his book about decision making in academic publishing houses that I last had a publisher (Grant Barnes at Stanford University Press) who took the trouble to read one of my manuscripts carefully, pointing to a grammatical mistake here ("my data reveals that...") and a non sequitur in the argument there ("given that your data have not yet been presented, they cannot 'reveal' anything at this point"). Publishing editors now are not textual editors, but *commissioning* editors (usually under pressure to produce so many [hundred] thousand pounds or dollars' worth of turnover in new books every year). Editing itself is a dying craft.

Not surprisingly, perhaps, publishers aren't that enthusiastic about edited books. They need too much real editing work, especially when many of them are churned out without much regard to vision, flow, or anything else I've talked about here. Too often, edited books are the result of the proceedings of some ill-thought-out or insufficiently theorized conference, on the one hand, and of both editors' and contributors' misguided respect for research ratings, on the other. It's easier to turn a conference paper into a book chapter than to sit down and *think*. What actually needs to be written about that hasn't been put on paper already?

EDITING AND ACADEMIA

As, finally, I accept that I cannot ignore the subject of journal editing, what is there to add? Much of what I've already written here holds true for journal editors. They must have a vision; they should at least be aware of flow; and they should know how to communicate. They cannot hope to be abreast of all the latest developments in all the fields of knowledge covered by their journal, but for this they rely on referees, who assess manuscripts and make editorial judgments about their worth (or lack thereof).

Even so, a journal's editor has to make decisions. Which accepted manuscripts should be placed together with which, and in what order? Should a referee's recommendations be followed to the letter, or should the author be allowed some leeway in revising her manuscript? And what if two referees give totally opposing assessments and recommendations? The editor of one journal to which I submitted my first article on advertising sent the manuscript out to three reviewers. One liked it very much and recommended it for publication as it stood; another thought it lacking in scholarship and rejected it; a third regarded it as a bit like a Curate's egg: good in parts.

I was asked to revise in the light of reviewers' comments. I did so and sent the manuscript back. Unable to make up her mind, the journal editor sent it out to three more reviewers, one of whom liked it, another disliked it, while the third wavered between hot and cold. Since the journal editor still couldn't make up her mind, I sent the manuscript to another journal, together with the six reviewers' assessments. It was published without further ado!

Flexibility, adaptability, and an openness to new ways of doing things are crucial aspects in a journal editor's work. Here we have a classic case of structure versus agency. A journal's name and reputation enforce a particular kind of article to be found therein. This limits editorial choices. But an editor should be able to spot a gap and broaden the field of her journal's inquiry, thereby encouraging the publication of slightly different kinds of articles that still maintain the reputation of the journal's "brand." She should also realize that journal articles generally make very little contribution to scholarship, if she insists on their following a format that includes problem orientation, research question, literature review, and methodology sections before presentation of the actual data.

Digital technology has broadened a journal editor's field of possibilities. In launching a *Journal of Business Anthropology*, Christina Garsten and I were faced with the initial challenge of selection of a publisher. Should we go for Wiley or Blackwell, Routledge, or Taylor & Francis? One of our supporters asked: why not Open Access? Anything to do with computers not being my strong point, I approached my university librarians for advice. Easy, they said; we have all you need. As they showed me some of the other journals that they were running online, I began to realize the possibilities open to us. We didn't *have* to publish just two issues a year. We could also run in parallel case studies, field reports, book reviews, debates, and blogs—all of them developing all the time, as contributions became available. The whole concept of the phrase "academic journal" began to take on new meaning.

But this doesn't mean that editorial work isn't needed. We still have case studies assessed by anonymous reviewers, and, as editors, we select (and edit as appropriate) the field reports sent in. We need to establish topics for debate and to monitor blogs. Because of the so far ill-defined nature of the field of "business anthropology" (what's wrong with "organizational," "economic," or even "enterprise" anthropology?), we can use the reviews section to comment not just on recently published books, but on everything written during the past century or so that has contributed to the anthropological study of businesses. We can, as they say, "configure" the field (Lampel and Mayer 2008). The sheer breadth of publishing opportunities made available by Open Access then allows us to focus on what themes we wish to cover in each issue of the journal and to commission articles (which are then peer reviewed). Things certainly ain't what they used to be.

As we all know, properly done, editing requires almost as much work as writing our own articles or even monographs. And yet we get virtually no credit for it. Edited books are of secondary significance when a promotions committee considers an applicant's publication record. They rate a remarkable zero points (*nul point, null punkte*) in the arithmetical tables now foisted upon us in Scandinavia by ardent administrators who believe they can actually measure "scholarly value." The only credit you'll get for editing a book is 0.75 points for writing its Introduction (compared with similar absurdities, like 3 points for an internationally refereed journal article and just 5 points for a monograph). This princely sum is divided accordingly if you are rash enough to write your Introduction with one or more colleagues.

Logic suggests that, in future, edited books will cease to feature very much on an academic landscape devoted to arithmetical formulae rather than to scholarship. Publishers will probably breathe a sigh of relief, but wonder how they'll now increase their annual turnover. Libraries will take advantage of the trend as they struggle with financial cuts. As an academic, all I can say is: thank God for old age!

Brian Moeran is a social anthropologist by training and has conducted research on advertising, art marketing, ceramics, fashion magazines, olfactory marketing, and the publishing industry—mainly in Japan, but also in cross-cultural comparative perspective. He is founding editor of the online Open Access *Journal of Business Anthropology* (www.cbs.dk/jba), and is partially retired.

NOTE

1. None of my doctoral students, alas, has ever followed my suggestion that they write their theses in the same way.

REFERENCES

Barthes, Roland. 1977. *Image, Music, Text.* London: Fontana.

Becker, Howard S. 1982. *Art Worlds.* Berkeley: University of California Press.

———. 1986. *Writing for Social Scientists.* Chicago: University of Chicago Press.

———. 1998. *Tricks of the Trade: How to Think about Your Research while Doing It.* Chicago: University of Chicago Press.

Benjamin, Walter. 1985. *One Way Street and Other Writings,* with an Introduction by Susan Sontag. London: Verso.

Csikszentmihalyi, Mihaly. 1996. *Creativity: Flow and the Psychology of Discovery and Invention.* New York: HarperCollins.

Geertz, Clifford. 1995. *After the Fact: Two Countries, Four Decades, One Anthropologist.* Cambridge, MA: Harvard University Press.

Kadushin, Charles. 1979. "The Managed Text: Prose and Qualms." *Change* 11, no. 2: 30–5, 64.

Lampel, Joseph, and Alan D. Meyer. 2008. "Field-Configuring Events as Structuring Mechanisms: How Conferences, Ceremonies, and Trade Shows Constitute New Technologies, Industries, and Markets." *Journal of Management Studies* 45, no. 6: 1025–1035.

Moeran, Brian. 2005a. *The Business of Ethnography.* Oxford: Berg.

———. 2005b. "More than Just a Fashion Magazine." *Current Sociology* 54, no. 5: 725–744.

Moeran, Brian, and Jesper Strandgaard Pedersen, eds. 2011. *Negotiating Values in the Creative Industries: Fairs, Festivals and Competitive Events.* Cambridge: Cambridge University Press.

Page, Gillian, Robert Campbell, and Jack Meadows. 1997. *Journal Publishing.* Cambridge: Cambridge University Press.

Powell, Walter W. 1985. *Getting into Print: The Decision-Making Process in Scholarly Publishing.* Chicago: University of Chicago Press.

Thompson, John B. 2005. *Books in the Digital Age.* Cambridge: Polity.

———. 2010. *Merchants of Culture: The Publishing Business in the Twenty-First Century.* Cambridge: Polity.

Van Maanen, John. 1988. *Tales of the Field.* Chicago: University of Chicago Press.

Chapter 5

The Anglicization of Anthropology
Opportunities and Challenges

Máiréad Nic Craith

Is English the primary language of publication for anthropologists today? This is probably the case with most academic disciplines at the beginning of the twenty-first century. Why do academics publish primarily—or even solely—in English? Where does the impetus come from? This chapter considers the drive toward English in the academic world and the implications of that language choice on anthropological publications as well as on the discipline itself. While I do not propose that anthropologists disregard English as their primarily language of publication, my core argument is that that there are good academic (and ethical reasons) for considering other languages when taking up the pen or switching on the computer to express our deliberations.

ENGLISH AND "CULTURAL CAPITAL"

The impetus to publish in English is overwhelming. For many academics, it is their first and, sometimes, their sole language. However, the desire to publish in English is not necessarily driven by a sense of loyalty to some "native language" or "mother tongue." Instead, other factors are usually at play. The global character of English is, without doubt, a major factor. If one wishes to reach a global audience, one must write in a language that the wider public understands. Although we cannot absolutely determine the numbers of speakers of different languages, we can be reasonably specific about the languages that have a global reach. De Swaan (2001: 5) argues for twelve supra-central languages, which, in alphabetical order, are: Arabic, Chinese, English, French, German, Hindi, Japanese, Malay, Portuguese, Russian, Spanish, and Swahili. All of these with the exception of Swahili have more than one hundred million speakers. Ethnologue lists the world's largest languages (in terms of native speakers) in the following order:

Table 5.1. World's Languages (first language speakers).

Rank order	Language	Countries	Millions of first-language speakers
1	Chinese	33	1,197
2	Spanish	31	399
3	English	101	335
4	Hindi	4	260
5	Arabic	60	242
6	Portuguese	12	203
7	Bengali	4	189
8	Russian	16	166
9	Japanese	2	128
10	Lahnda	6	88.7

(*Source:* Ethnologue: http://www.ethnologue.com/statistics/size)

Although the two lists are not identical, English appears on third place in both. However, not all large languages enjoy similar "cultural capital" (Bourdieu 1991) and of the languages cited above, English probably has the greatest prestige in the academic world (Nic Craith 2006). It is the vehicle of global communication. "It is so to speak at the centre of the twelve solar language systems, at the hub of the linguistic galaxy." (de Swaan 2001: 6) Given that the "inner circle of English" is located in the United States and the UK, the linguistic status of English may reflect the political power and material wealth of speakers of English (Crystal 2003). The rise of English appears unstoppable—although some academics are now challenging this perspective (see, for example, Ostler 2010). About a quarter of the world's population is fluent or has considerable competency in English, and the proportion is increasing steadily. No other language can compare. Even Chinese, the name of eight different spoken languages, which are unified by a common writing system, is known to only 1.1 billion people (Crystal 2003: 6). Universities are increasingly switching to English as a language of instruction for postgraduate courses—with a total of 6,407 English-taught masters programs being offered in continental Europe in June 2013 (see Table 5.2). This represents a rise of 38 percent in eighteen months.

Table 5.2. Continental European Postgraduate Courses Taught in English (June 2013).

Country	Number of postgraduate courses taught in English (June 2013)	Percent increase since December 2011
Netherlands	946	16
Germany	733	13
Sweden	708	73
France	494	43
Spain	373	14
Denmark	327	74
Italy	304	60
Switzerland	281	19
Finland	261	52
Belgium	253	18

(*Source:* Grove 2013)

Many Asian countries, such as Hong Kong or China, also offer postgraduate programs in English.

RANKING HOMO SAPIENS

Writing is an occupation that anticipates an audience. Although people sometimes jokingly suggest that they write "for themselves," the reality is that academics publish to engage with their disciplinary peers and clearly the language of writing has a direct impact on the potential (rather than the actual) number of readers. A publication in Irish (Gaelic), for example, is unlikely to reach a huge international audience. This is not any reflection of the academic merits of the Irish-language publication, but a simple recognition of the limited numbers of potential readers with skills in Irish when compared with those with skills in English. Although French, German, and Spanish are international languages, works published in these languages are less likely to attain the same level of internationality as those written in English.

Of course, it is not just any kind of colloquial English that we write in. When publishing, most anthropologists write in an "academic style" using the terminology, concepts, and framework of the discipline. This point has already been made by others. Talal Asad (1986) suggests that when anthropologists "write up 'their people'," they engage with the conventions of the discipline and the academic institution. Stoller (2009: 48) describes the process of writing up fieldwork "using institutionally sanctioned plain style—the bloodless prose of the natural and human sciences." More recently Eileen Kane has complained about being "constrained by the arcane corsetry of our traditional reporting format." She argues that the contrast between what anthropologists do and how they write is "almost comical." She asks "[w]hy then do we report our findings in such a prissy, constipated manner?" (Kane 2010: 183).

There is the added pressure of "world rankings" on the language of academic publications. In October 2013, the *Times Higher Educational Supplement* in the UK published the rankings for the top-ranked universities worldwide. The top ten universities for the year 2015–16 are as follows:

Table 5.3. The World's Top 10 Universities 2015–16.

Ranking	Institution	Country
1	California Institute of Technology	US
2	University of Oxford	UK
3	Stanford University	US
4	University of Cambridge	UK
5	Massachusetts Institute of Technology	US
6	Harvard University	US
7	Princeton University	US
8	Imperial College, London	UK
9	ETH Zurich	Switzerland
10	University of Chicago	US

(*Source:* Reuters)

Not only did the United States and the UK dominate the top 10 universities, they also dominated the top 200 list. Of these, 63 are located in the United States The UK consolidated its position as the number one country after the United States for world-class higher education. Thirty-four of its institutions were in the top 200. With the exception of the Swiss Federal Institute of Technology in Zurich, all of the top 20 are in the English-speaking world. If one examines the social sciences table, one can easily see that this table is composed almost exclusively of English-language academic institutions that are located in the United States, the UK, Canada, and Australia. Overall, the United States has 43 institutions in the top 100 Social Sciences list. Top of the list is Massachusetts Institute of Technology. In fact nine of the top 10 are located in the US. Of the UK universities, the University of Oxford is top of the league for Social Sciences. In fourth place overall, it heads the UK's 17 institutions in the top 100 for Social Sciences.

Fortunately or unfortunately, universities are required to "participate in the game." Not only must they endeavour to appear on the list of top institutions, they are required to aim higher and higher each academic year. The scramble for status is unending and an ever-increasing number of academic institutions wish to participate in rankings that will enable them to achieve credible "academic performance." Ulf Hannerz (2010: 114) cites the example of the rector of his university, who encouraged its academics to conduct more of their writing in English rather than Swedish with the aim of enhancing Stockholm University's place on the list of world-ranked academic institutions. This is a situation we are all familiar with. In the scramble for world rankings, there is impetus on all of us to publish in English—a situation that can be difficult to deal with, and impossible to ignore. Unfortunately, such prestige is difficult to acquire without a major proportion of publications in English. The reasons for this are not difficult to follow.

I recently participated in a panel of international assessors for sociology/anthropology in a country in Eastern Europe. When I was allocated my quota of publications for evaluation, I found myself unable to deal with a considerable proportion of them as they were published in a language with which I am unfamiliar. (I suspect that many of my international colleagues on the panel were in a similar position.) Ultimately, these publications were reliant on a small number of internal evaluators to allocate their scores. It may well be the case that these publications were of a far higher academic quality than any English language ones—but they were not verified internationally and their scores lack the "legitimacy" or "credibility" of the English language works that had been verified by the wider academic community.

The bias toward English in world rankings is an ongoing problem faced by institutions whose employees write in languages other than English. In an effort to counteract this, there has been an effort in Europe to introduce a new system of academic ranking that takes account of linguistic and cultural diversity as opposed to current rankings systems, which favor the English-speaking academic world. The first interim report from U-Multirank criticizes the Thomson Reuter database (WoS) in particular because it is largely focused on English-language publications. "Hence publications from non-English speaking countries, including large countries with a long science tradition, are underrepresented (e.g. in French, German, Chinese, Japanese)" (U-Multirank 2010: 24). Their conclusion has been that since sciences are mostly international in their modes of publication (i.e., they publish in English) and humanities/social sciences tend to deal more with national issues and publish in "native" languages, this entire rankings system operates in favor of sciences.

THE COSMOPOLITAN NATURE OF ANTHROPOLOGY

Anthropologists cannot afford to ignore the flow of the tide toward English when publishing their findings and yet it is a discipline that has frequently engaged with the non-English-speaking world. In their ethnographic forays, anthropologists "have become acquainted with complex multilingual situations, whether in the Amazon rainforest or on the highlands of New Guinea" (Hannerz 2010: 115). In many instances, anthropologists have endeavored to engage with the "natives" in their own language. This derives in part from Malinowski's emphasis on the "native's point of view." A much overquoted comment suggests that "the final goal ... is to grasp the native's point of view, his relation to life, to realise his vision of his world" (Malinowski 1961 [1922]: 25).

Not all anthropologists have necessarily argued for the extensive use of native languages as fieldwork tools and the extent of knowledge required has generated different perspectives. In 1939, Margaret Mead, for example, advocated some knowledge of native languages in certain circumstances of fieldwork, but made a distinction between "using" the native language and "speaking" it. She argued that, in some instances, a very basic knowledge of the native language is sufficient since "the field worker is not in the field to talk but to listen" (Mead 1939: 196)—although I'm not convinced that one can really listen to a language one barely understands!

Others have taken a more proactive approach in relation to the acquisition of "native" languages. Maxwell Owusu (1978) complained vigorously of the arrogance of European anthropologists undertaking fieldwork in Africa with little or no knowledge of local languages. His position was that "no person, not even a de Toqueville studying African cultures, can understand another whose language he does not speak, read and understand, and hence, whose world view he cannot truly share" (Owusu 1978: 327). Whether or not they subscribe to either of these views, most anthropologists have at least considered the significance of using "native languages" for fieldwork. However, less emphasis seems to have been placed on the language in which we write our texts.

It could be argued that this question has become less relevant with the spread of English—that since "everyone speaks English anyway," fieldwork is increasingly being conducted in and through English. Yet, this can hardly be the case. According to the Ethnologue website, there are still 7,105 languages spoken in the world. One might quibble with the exact figure since languages resemble clouds in that it is hard to tell where one begins and the other ends (see Nic Craith 2000). And yet, most languages and clouds are obvious enough (de Swaan 2001: 3). According to Ethnologue, the breakdown of living languages per continent is as follows:

Table 5.4. Distribution of World Languages by Area of Origin.

Area	Living languages	Percentage
Africa	2,138	30.1
Americas	1,064	15.0
Asia	2,301	32.4
Europe	286	4.0
Pacific	1,313	18.5
Total	7,102	100.0

(*Source:* Ethnologue: http://www.ethnologue.com/statistics)

Given the numbers and locations of speakers and the nature of the discipline of anthropology, it is highly likely that the greatest proportion of anthropological fieldwork is still conducted in languages other than English, and anthropologists can still find themselves in situations where knowledge of English is not that useful. Yet, chances are that publications arising from such fieldwork will ultimately be written in English.

Does the language of writing matter that much? Is the process of writing down ideas in English a neutral practice or is it "a crucial aspect of the production of ethnographic knowledge?" (Aguiar et al. 2009: 7). Where anthropologists are monolingual English speakers, the issue does not arise. There is no choice. If they are to publish at all, it will be in English. Moreover, if the fieldwork is conducted in English, then regardless of the linguistic competence of the anthropologist, there is some logic to writing up that fieldwork in English. But I am particularly interested in cases where the fieldwork has not occurred in English and where the anthropologist has a choice of languages in which to write. What are the issues that arise then? This is the context in which I write for the remainder of this chapter.

THE OBJECTIVE ANTHROPOLOGIST

Apart from obvious economic argument as well as the potential engagement with the wider academic community, there may be very good reasons to publish one's academic reflections on fieldwork in English—especially when the fieldwork itself has been conducted in another language. "The reality of fieldwork is a liminal phase for both subjects and objects, in which the distinction between them is dissolved" (Hastrup 1995: 20). Yet this liminality is not always fully acknowledged and anthropologists are expected to distance themselves from the "raw material." "Thus, one was to maintain a polite distance from those studied and to cultivate rapport not friendship, compassion not sympathy, respect not belief, understanding not identification, admiration not love" (Tedlock 2009: 24).

The urge "to keep oneself at a distance" also applies to the process of writing and the use of a different language can enhance the process of "removal." The writing up of fieldwork is not of a personal nature and yet the person of the anthropologist is involved. While anthropologists endeavor to present the experience in a nonpersonal manner it may well be the case that some element of "authorial signature" is unavoidable. Some anthropologists argue for the inevitable authorial presence in the writing up of fieldwork, since anthropologists are human beings who have private as well as public lives. "Whatever they did or said as anthropologists was simply a 'structural/ metaphoric transformation' of what they did and said in quite non-anthropological contexts" (Leach 1984: 3). From Edmund Leach's perspective, there is an inevitability about this, since the only ego that anthropologists know firsthand is their own. "When Malinowski writes about Trobriand Islanders he is writing about himself; when Evans-Pritchard writes about the Nuer he is writing about himself. Any other sort of description turns the characters of ethnographic monographs into clockwork dummies" (Leach 1989: 140–141).

Clifford Geertz (1988: 9) has argued that "the question of signature, the establishment of an authorial presence within a text, has haunted ethnography from very early on," although in many instances that problem has not been openly acknowledged. Instead, it has been lost in questions of epistemology. How does one present the story in an objective manner and "prevent subjective views from coloring objective facts" and is that really possible? Most ethnographies do not deal explicitly with the issue of the "signature dilemma." Instead they attempt to "keep it at bay," giving possibly "overly detailed descriptions of the natural environment, population" and/or "extended theoretical discussions." The issue of authorial presence tends "to be relegated, like other embarrassments, to prefaces, notes, or appendices" (Geertz 1988: 16).

This is an issue that is not simply confined to anthropologists but has relevance for writers in the field of literature as well (see Nic Craith and Kockel 2014). In a recent exploration of mine on language and place, I conducted life-story interviews with a number of migrant authors who wrote memoirs in a language that was not that of their childhood (Nic Craith 2012b). For many authors, the use of a different language was an important element in presenting their childhood experiences in a neutral fashion—in a manner that was not too subjective either for themselves or for the readers. Indeed, it appeared that the act of writing in a different language was an essential tool in creating the necessary distance between the author and his experiences. "Writing about one's earliest memories against the mother tongue or against the tongue in which they occurred involves a process of reassessment and rewriting" (Miletic 2008: 32).

Many authors interviewed suggested that the use of a different language offered freedom from the direct reexperiencing of past memories (Nic Craith 2012b). The Irish-German author Hugo Hamilton said that in his instance, the use of a different language is:

> very important because it removes the events into sort of a fictional place. By calling it a fictional place, I am trying to describe the dramatic distance that is needed in order to tell these family events. Every story is a removal from reality. Otherwise it would have been too close to me. Writing in English became a fictional medium in itself, far away from the language in which the events happened. I was joining the people from outside who had come inside to look around our house and our secrets. When I started reading passages from *Speckled People* in German, after it was translated, I found them initially too overwhelming, emotionally. It put me in this kind of dangerous vulnerable place again where I was exposed to the reality of being back in the kitchen with my mother again. (Hugo Hamilton, interview)

The use of the second language becomes an act of removal from the original since "stories told in the language in which the original events took place are higher in emotional intensity and amount of detail" (Pavlenko 2007: 171). However, this does not imply that somehow the true story becomes a sort of fiction. Instead, its truth-value is possibly enhanced as the writer stands back and looks with "a cool eye" at the scenes he or she wishes to describe. Could one argue that the same benefit applies to anthropologists and writers of a particular genre alike—particularly where there is an issue of truth to be considered? Both need to distance themselves from the original experience and both need to present their material in an objective manner. In those circumstances, the use of a language other than the one of the original fieldwork could have considerable benefits.

Such benefits could also be seen to apply to informants as well. Take, for example, Esperanza, Ruth Behar's *Translated Woman*. Initially, she was very happy that the life-story would be published in English rather than

Spanish. In such circumstances, she would not suffer the embarrassment of neighbors reading and commenting on the book. A volume that is published in a language that is not spoken by the community under observation may "liberate" the informant as much as the anthropologist him- or herself. However, Esperanza subsequently changed her mind when the local priest congratulated her on being the subject of a book in the library. She was no longer afraid of the other women in Mexquitic gossiping about the things she has told the anthropologist (Behar 1993). However, there are also potential inherent dangers in the process of what is effectively the translation of fieldwork from one language to another.

THE DILEMMA OF TRANSLATION

Translation has always played a major role in ethnographic writing (Di-Giacomo 2002; Hymes 2002; Rosman and Rubel 2013) as anthropologists enter the field to "study others" (although increasingly, anthropologists are "coming home"). The exploration of different cultural experiences, and the subsequent production of text, of necessity involves some form of cultural translation. Despite an anthropologist's best intentions, the process can hardly be described as neutral and the issue of objectivity also emerges here. "The notion of the neutral translator as an unseen conduit for pure meaning recalls the image of the objective ethnographer carefully expunging all traces of his or her presence from the text in order to represent 'pure' Otherness" (DiGiacomo 2002: 10). There is always some element of displacement or dislocation in the process. Shreve (2002) describes the process as "kind of brokering in which the translator comprehends in one language and produces in another."

There are also the conditions of power to be acknowledged—not least of which relates to the frequent inequality in the status of the languages involved. This is an issue that Talal Asad had highlighted: "'Cultural translation' must accommodate itself to a different language, not only in the sense of English as opposed to Dinka, or English as opposed to Kabbashi Arabic, but also in the sense of a British, middle class academic genre as opposed to the modes of life of the 'tribal Sudan'." (Asad 1986: 159) Then there is the dilemma of the "un-translatable" as it is not always possible to translate cultural differences and specificities directly from one language to another (see for example Cassin et al. 2014). This issue has long been debated in anthropology and goes back to the notions of cultural determinism and cultural relativity (for example Sapir 1949). Ruth Behar comments on such difficulties in relation to her fieldwork in Mexquitic when she explains a subtle language shift that occurs between Esparanza (the Translated Woman) and her son Julio:

> A subtle linguistic shift takes place in her story when she [Esparanza] finds Julio with his mistress, which is impossible to render in the English translation. In Spanish, however, she ceases to refer to Julio as *usted,* the formal you and now she begins to call him *tú,* the informal you, used to speak to equals, children and women and people of inferior rank. The formal you is always used by rural Mexicans in relationships of respect and deference; that is the way children should address their parents, younger siblings older siblings, wives their husbands (particularly of Esparanza's generation). (Behar 1993: 285)

Some years ago, I conducted some fieldwork in Germany and during that time I engaged with many concepts that were unfamiliar. Although I could understand the words, I did not always empathize with the meaning (Nic Craith 2012b). Sometimes words are translated but that does not necessarily mean that the concept is understood. *Heimat* is an obvious and often-quoted example of a concept that gets lost in English translation. Although it is frequently translated as home or native country, it has many other connotations for Germans. Blickle (2002) writes that *Heimat* is a concept that is shared among German-speaking cultures and that it is a "crucial aspect in German self-perceptions." He suggests that *Heimat* "uses a patriarchal way of seeing the world." (Blickle 2002: 2–3). Suhr proposes that "there are no satisfactory English equivalents for 'Heimat' or 'Fremde'" since both "imply far more than simply 'homeland' or 'a foreign place'." Interestingly, she argues that this is not simply a matter of translation as it also depends on the context. Perhaps the closest I could get to *Heimat* is the Irish word *dúchas,* which can be used to describe something that is local or native or inherited or ancestral (Nic Craith 2012b: 63).

The concept of time is also expressed differently in German and can be quite confusing—at least for those of us from the English-speaking world. In the Anglophone world, one defines the half-hour in terms of the time that has already occurred. 10:30 happens half an hour after the clock strikes ten. In contrast, in the German language it is expressed in terms of time that is yet to come. *Halb zen* (literally half ten) occurs 30 minutes before 10, that is, at 9:30 (Nic Craith 2012b: 68). Expressions of time are of great interest to linguistic anthropologists and Heinrich Böll (1957) famously suggested that the Irish have a fairly relaxed attitude toward the concept of time. Growing up in a bilingual household, I was already aware of a different sense of time between Irish and English-speaking cultural worlds. This is clearly signaled in the way the verb "to be" is managed in both languages. Although there is only one verb "to be" in English, there are two in Irish Gaelic—one that is used for a permanent state of being and another that is reserved for simple activities that have a distinct point of completion (Nic Craith 2012a).

Colors do not translate easily from one language to another. The traditional Irish Gaelic language, for example, has a system of color terms that are quite distinct from those of many other European languages including English. In Irish, for example, there are two terms for red: *dearg* and *rua*. *Dearg* can be used to refer to many shades of red, including bright red, crimson, gold-red, bloody, etc. *Bróga dearga* can refer to tan-colored shoes. *Rua,* on the other hand, is more brownish-red, foxy, brown. It is the adjective used when referring to red hair. However a *capall rua* is a chestnut horse, *leathar rua* is brown leather, *arán rua* is brown bread. *Gorm* is the Irish-Gaelic adjective for blue—but it can also be used correctly to describe green grass or a black or chocolate horse. The color green has become an important marker of Irishness (Wulff 2012) and our varieties of "green" are reflected in our color adjectives in Irish. *Glas* refers to shades such as grey and blue-grey. It is the adjective used for green grass, a grey horse, or a cold, raw morning. On the other hand, if one wants to describe green water, one will use *uaithne* (Ua Duinnín 1948 [1904]). These shades of difference are not easily translated and are a very small indication of matters that can get lost in translation.

Apart from the issue of moving between languages there is the issue of the extent to which language determines the content. Geertz (1988: 18–19) asks "how important is the language in which we write for what we write"? Is it the case that language is "merely an instrument of communication" or is it instead "a vehicle of thought"? Some scholars are clearly of the opinion that language matters—considerably more than we might appreciate. Manguel (2008: 63) argues that stories do not simply emerge in a particular language from our experience. "They are also the product of language itself, and depend on the specific language in which they are told." Space restrictions do not allow for a more nuanced consideration of that issue in this chapter but it suffices to raise the question with reference to the example of the French-American author, Julian Green, who originally began writing about his French childhood in French. However, as the prospect of finding a French publisher for his writing looked doubtful, Green switched to English. Interestingly, when he compared the two beginnings in the two different languages, he judged them to be significantly different.

Green himself writes about this difference—suggesting that on rereading his English "version," it became apparent that he was "now writing another book, a book so different in tone from the French, that a whole aspect of the subject must be deleted." It was as if he "had become another person" by opting to write in English rather than in French. He writes: "There was so little resemblance between what I wrote in English and what I had written in

French that it might almost be doubted that the same person was the author of these two pieces of work" (Green 1985: 182). Green was writing about the same experience in both languages, yet his choice of language had a major impact on the written text (Nic Craith 2012b: 43).

Could such a proposition apply to writing in the field of anthropology? Were I to write about my German fieldwork in German rather than in English, would a different publication emerge? Would I emphasize different concepts or different aspects of my fieldwork and would this be as a conscious or unconscious result of using a different language for writing? Would my writing intentions be colored by the different target language audience? How does our language choice impact our writing? Has the primary use of English for writing enhanced or impoverished the contribution of anthropologists to academia? In our quest to engage with the international community, have we impoverished other languages themselves by failing to develop them to their full academic potential? Have we failed the integrity of our fieldwork by effectively translating it into English?

ANTHROPOLOGY IN OTHER LANGUAGES

In this chapter I am hardly recommending that anthropologists suddenly desist from publishing in English. This is neither feasible nor desirable. Hannerz (2010: 129) has described English as the "only fully functioning academic world language." If he is right, then the argument for maintaining an overwhelming publishing profile in English is powerful. However, I do propose that we give serious consideration to the impact of the overwhelming drive toward publishing primarily in English. "Can this be the discipline whose legitimacy is wrapped up in foreign languages and worlds?" (Behar 1993: 299).

However, this is not to imply that anthropologists might reserve local/national languages for publications on local/national issues while seeking to develop the more general problematic in the world language of English. This division of profile may already be active. A Swedish anthropologist with a strong sense of loyalty to Swedish (for example) may opt to publish regional or national issues in Swedish while developing more international issues in English texts (Hannerz 2010). The real question is whether one can serve "two masters" and publish issues of international relevance in both English and another language. I think anthropologists can and should consider the options. There is also an ethical question to be considered here, that is, should the writings by anthropologists reflect the world in which they live? If the writings we produce as academics signal a monolingual world, what does that say about our representation of a world in which more than seven thousand languages are still spoken on a regular basis?

In association with the Society for the Anthropology of Europe (a subsociety of the American Anthropological Association), Berghahn has launched a series on European Anthropology in Translation. The series presents English-language versions of important publications on European anthropology that were previously published in a different language. The series is not confined to recent books but also welcomes proposals based on older works that have not previously appeared in English. Five volumes have already been published in this series and publications to date profile anthropology originally published in German (Müller 2007), Croatian (Čapo Žmegač 2007), Italian (Grasseni 2009), Portuguese (Ferraz de Matos 2013), and Galician (Medeiros 2013).

In another initiative, *Anthropological Quarterly* has introduced a series of review articles on books written in languages other than English. In the original introduction laying out the basis for the initiative, the editors suggest that the journal aims to emphasize "less widely used languages in which a nascent anthropology is already making important contributions which may be invisible to the larger international community" (Grinker and Herzfeld 2009). While English is the language of mainstream anthropology, they argue that it is important to remember the cosmopolitan nature of anthropology as a discipline that "seeks to recognize and study politically less powerful cultures and languages" (Grinker and Herzfeld 2009).

The initiative was launched with a review of a book about alterity written by Greeks in and about Greece. The review was authored by Hertzfeld himself, who argued that Greece's fascination with anthropology derives in part from its own political marginality, which is in tension with its ideological centrality to the construction of "the West"—that is, the home of the discipline of anthropology (Herzfeld 2009). A subsequent piece featured the contribution of Philippe Descola to the present landscape of French ethnology (Berliner 2010) while Stephan Feuchtwang and Michael Rowlands interviewed Wang Mingming on Chinese Directions in Anthropology (Feuchtwang, Rowlands, and Mingming 2010).

These two initiatives draw attention to ongoing research in anthropology that is conducted in a language other than English—although ultimately they too are "translating" into English. On their own, initiatives such as these will hardly serve to redress the balance in favor of other languages, and there are other ideas that might be considered by major publishers. Could international journals, for example, routinely publish abstracts of articles in languages other than English? Would it be possible to have occasional special issues of journals published in a language other than English? Would it be feasible to regularly reserve one article per journal for a "foreign language" contribution? Some journals already publish articles in more than one language; see, for example, the French language article in a recent edition of *Social Anthropology* (Angé 2011). Book reviewers could easily help by regularly seeking out books for review that are published in a language other than English and publishing reviews that are written in languages other than English.

None of these initiatives in themselves will stem the bias toward publications in English and I am hardly arguing for a reversal of that trend. However, given the nature of the discipline, which seeks to explore human diversity (both in its specificity and its universality), I am arguing that for academic and possibly even ethical reasons, anthropologists should pause and consider the implications of the language in which they publish. Where feasible, it might serve humanity better to occasionally publish our contributions in a language other than English. A garden consisting solely of roses will deprive human beings of the beauty and fragrance of daffodils, carnations, lilies, snowdrops, and even wee daisies…

Máiréad Nic Craith is Professor and Deputy Assistant Principal (Research) at Heriot Watt University, Edinburgh. Author and editor of fifteen volumes, her most recent monograph (*Narratives of Place, Belonging and Language*) explores the role of language in shaping a sense of belonging in society for migrant writers. Along with Ullrich Kockel and Jonas Frykman, she co-edited the *Blackwell Companion to the Anthropology of Europe* (2012). Máiréad has served on numerous research evaluation panels in Australia, Europe, and Canada.

REFERENCES

Aguiar, José Carlos, et al. 2009. "Editorial." *Ethnofoor: Writing Culture* 21, no. 1: 7–8.

Angé, Olivia. 2011. "Yapa. Dons, échanges et complicités dans les Andes méridionales." *Social Anthropology* 19, no. 3: 239–253.

Asad, Talal. 1986. "The Concept of Cultural Translation in British Social Anthropology." In *Writing Culture: The Poetics and Politics of Ethnography,* ed. James Clifford and George Marcus. Berkeley: University of California Press.

Behar, Ruth. 1993. *Translated Woman: Crossing the Border with Esparanza's Story.* Boston: Beacon Press.

Berliner, David. 2010. "Polyglot Perspectives: Levi-Strauss and Beyond, a Presentation of Phillippe Descola, Par-deal Nature et Culture [Beyond Nature and Culture], Paris, Gallimard, 2005." *Anthropological Quarterly* 83, no. 3: 679–689.

Blickle, Peter. 2002. *Heimat: A Critical Theory of the German Idea of Homeland.* New York: Camden House.

Böll, Heinrich. 1957 *Irisches Tagebuch.* Köln Kiepenheuer and Witsch.

Bourdieu, Pierre. 1991. *Language and Symbolic Power.* Cambridge: Polity Press.

Čapo Žmegač, Jasna. 2007. *Strangers Either Way, the Lives of Croatian Refugees in their New Home.* Oxford: Berghahn.

Cassin, Barbara, Emily Apter, Jacques Lezra, and Michael Wood, eds. 2014. *Dictionary of Untranslatables: A Philosophical Lexicon.* Princeton: Princeton University Press.

Crystal, David. 2003 [1997]. *English as a Global Language.* Cambridge: Cambridge University Press.

de Swaan, Abram. 2001. *Words of the World: The Global Language System.* New York: Wiley-Blackwell.

DiGiacomo, Susan M. 2002. "Translation as/and Ethnographic Practice." *Anthropology News* May: 10.

Ferraz de Matos, Patricia. 2013. *The Colours of the Empire: Racialized Representations during Portuguese Colonialism.* Trans. M. Ayton. Oxford: Berghahn.

Feuchtwang, Stephan, Michael Rowlands, and Wang Mingming. 2010. "Polyglot Perspectives: Some Chinese Directions in Anthropology." *Anthropological Quarterly* 83, no. 4: 897–926.

Green, Julian (1985) *Le langage et son double/The Language and its Shadow.* Paris: Editions de la Différence.

Geertz, Clifford. 1988. *Works and Lives: The Anthropologist as Author.* Stanford: Stanford University Press.

Grasseni, Cristina. 2009. *Developing Skill, Developing Vision, Practices of Locality at the Foot of the Alps.* Oxford: Berghahn.

Grinker, Richard, and Michael Herzfeld. 2009. "Introducing Polyglot Perspectives." *Anthropological Quarterly* 82, no. 1: 5–6.

Grove, Jack. 2013. "Euro Rivals Adopt English in Fight for Overseas Students." *Times Higher Education.* www.timeshighereducation.co.uk/news/euro-rivals-adopt-english-in-fight-for-overseas-students/1/2007978.article.

Hannerz, Ulf. 2010. *Anthropology's World: Life in a Twenty-First Century Discipline.* London: Pluto.

Hastrup, Kirsten. 1995. *A Passage to Anthropology: Between Experience and Theory.* London: Routledge.

Herzfeld, Michael. 2009. "Peripeties tis eterotitas: I paraghoyi tis politismikis dhiaforas sti simerini Elladha [Adventures of Alterity: The Production of Cultural Difference in Modern Greece] (review)." *Anthropological Quarterly* 82, no. 1: 311–330.

Hymes, Dell. 2002. "Translations of Oral Narratives." *Anthropology News.* May: 23.

Kane, Eileen. 2010. *Trickster: An Anthropological Memoir.* Toronto: University of Toronto Press.

Leach, Edmund R. 1984. "Glimpses of the Unmentionable in the History of British Social Anthropology." *Annual Review of Anthropology* 13: 1–24.

———. 1989. "Works and Lives: The Anthropologist as Author" (book review). *American Ethnologist* 16, no. 1: 137–141.

Malinowski, Bronislaw. 1961 [1922]. *Argonauts of the Western Pacific.* New York: EP Dutton.

Manguel, Alberto. 2008. *The City of Words.* London: Continuum.

Mead, Margaret. 1939. "Native Languages as Fieldwork Tools," *American Anthropologist* 41, no. 2: 189–205.

Medeiros, António. 2013. *Two Sides of One River: Nationalism and Ethnography in Galicia and Portugal.* Trans. M. Earl. Oxford: Berghahn.

Miletic, Tijana. 2008. *European Literary Immigration into the French Language: Readings of Gary, Kriostof, Kundera and Semprun.* Amsterdam: Rodopi.

Müller, Birgit. 2007. *Disenchantment with Market Economics, East Germans and Western Capitalism.* Oxford: Berghahn.

Nic Craith, Máiréad. 2000. "Contested Identities and the Quest for Legitimacy." *Journal of Multilingual and Multicultural Development* 21, no. 5, 399–413.

———. 2006. *Europe and the Politics of Language: Citizens, Migrants, Outsiders.* Basingstoke: Palgrave.

———. 2012a. "Legacy and Loss: The Great Silence and its Aftermath." In *Atlas of the Great Irish Famine, 1845-1852,* ed. John Crowley, William J. Smyth, and Mike Murphy. Cork: University Press.

———. 2012b. *Narratives of Place, Belonging and Language: An Intercultural Perspective.* Basingstoke: Palgrave.

Nic Craith, Máiréad, and Ullrich Kockel. 2014. "Blurring the Boundaries between Literature and Anthropology: A British Perspective." *Ethnologie française* 44, no. 4: 689–697.

Ostler, Nicholas. 2010. *The Last Lingua Franca: English Until the Return of Babel.* New York: Allen Lane.

Owusu, Maxwell. 1978. "Ethnography of Africa: The Usefulness of the Useless." *American Anthropologist* 80, no. 2: 310–334.

Pavlenko, Aneta (2007) "Autobiographic Narratives as Data in Applied Linguistics," *Applied Linguistics* 28, no. 2: 163–88.

Rosman, Abraham, and Paula G. Rubel, eds. 2003. *Translating Cultures: Perspectives on Translation and Anthropology.* Oxford: Berg.

Sapir, Edward. 1949. *Selected Writings of Edward Sapir in Language, Culture and Personality,* ed. DG Manderbaum. Berkeley: University of California Press.

Shreve, GM. 2002. "Translation, Fidelity and Other Mythical Beasts I Have Sited." *Anthropology News.* October: 7.

Stoller, Paul. 2009. "Re-Writing Culture." *Ethnofoor: Writing Culture* 21, no. 1: 45–59.

Tedlock, Barbara. 2009. "Writing a Storied Life: Nomadism and Double Consciousness in Transcultural Ethnography." *Ethnofoor: Writing Culture* 21, no. 1: 21–58.

Times Higher Education. 2013. "The University World Rankings." http://www.timeshighereducation/news/world-university-rankings-2015-16-results-announced.

Ua Duinnín, Pádraig. 1948. [1904] *Foclóir Gaedhilge agus Béarla.* Dublin: Irish Texts Society.

U-Multirank. 2010. Interim Progress Report Design Phase of the Project "Design and Testing the Feasibility of a Multi-dimensional Global University Ranking." CHERPA-Network. http://www.u-multirank.eu/UMR_IR_0110.pdf.

Wulff, Helena. 2012. "Color and Cultural Identity in Ireland." In *Color and Design*, ed. Marilyn DeLong and Barbara Martinson. London: Berg/Bloomsbury.

II.

Ethnographic Writing

Chapter 6

The Anthropologist as Storyteller

Alma Gottlieb

OF MELTED WATCHES AND MONOPOLIES

At the workshop in Stockholm where I presented an earlier version of this chapter, I found inspiration for my talk in an unexpected place. The day before the workshop, fellow panelist Paul Stoller and I toured the Stockholm Museum of Modern Art. Anticipating a pleasant diversion before the hothouse of our conference, we were amazed to see our prior images of surrealist artist Salvador Dali expand dramatically beyond what we had known of his *oeuvre*. The iconic melted watches and lobster phone of my memory were quickly replaced by all manner of other objects. We saw women's fashions and magazine covers that Dali had designed; we learned that he made commercials and films, wrote parodic newspapers, designed an exhibit for a world expo, and was even a contestant on a US game show; he also used his own body as a canvas in cultivating his famous moustache. Dali's restless imagination impeded him from settling into a single genre; his playful engagement with all these genres surely contributed to his genius.

We anthropologists might learn from Dali's creative spirit. In the academy, until recently we largely left unchallenged the hold that the scholarly article and monograph have long held on our discipline. Of course, when led by creatively thinking editors, scholarly journals can themselves become sites for scholarly innovation (Dominguez 2010). Even so, the academic journal and its book-length counterpart have inherent limitations that even innovative editors acknowledge (Dominguez 2010). Yet notwithstanding the occasional adventurous scholar who tries writing in other genres from time to time, in effect the combined dominance of the scholarly journal and monograph have long constituted a veritable monopoly. Over a century ago in the United States, the famous Sherman Antitrust Act of 1890 effectively restricted the reach of monopolies in business[1]—but we have not passed our own Antitrust Act in the academy. Still, anthropologists have begun to challenge de facto the notion that the scholarly journal article and book-length monograph embody the only legitimate means to share knowledge. In exploring this point, let me begin with a brief autobiography.

In high school, I fancied myself a poet. Writing poetry allowed me to sort through all manner of adolescent angst. A national magazine even published one of my poems, "Worry Stone," that put a name on my teenage anxieties. My best friend also loved to write, and together we founded a literary magazine, *The Purple Dragan,* that (literally) cranked out issues for a good two years, thanks to an office mimeograph machine that my friend's businessman-father allowed us to use.[2] A few years later, speaking to my love of writing, the college I chose to attend boasted the nation's strongest undergraduate curriculum in creative writing, and most academic classes substituted semester- or year-long research and writing projects for tests. The unusual curriculum attracted teachers who encouraged creative approaches to scholarly material.[3] The most enthusiastic scribbled comments I recall receiving from a professor accompanied a Chinese art history class paper I wrote that opened with a dream I'd had about the paper topic—Neolithic-era Chinese bronze vessels—and the meanings my dream had suggested for the designs on the ancient goblets and bowls.

So I found myself in some shock in graduate school, when faculty feedback on my papers looked drastically different. Far from penning anything as creative as a dream-based interpretation of Karl Marx or a poem about Max Weber, my uses of the first person in my class papers remained restricted to such scholarly phrases as "In this paper, I will argue that ..." or "I find this argument problematic insofar as ..." Even so, on the first paper I wrote for a History of Theory seminar, all such phrases received angry-looking red strikethroughs, accompanied by suggested revisions such as "It will be argued that" or "This argument is problematic insofar as ..." In case I missed the logic to the red-penned marks, my professor noted that any use of the first person was inappropriate in academic writing. Period. I remember staying after class to discuss our divergent writing strategies. My instructor remained adamant about this line-in-the-sand-I-could-not-cross. Faced with a clear choice—write in the first person, or remain in graduate school—I retrained myself to hide behind passive constructions and went on to produce hundreds of pages of scholarly writing suitable for obtaining a doctorate as a social scientist.

Further sidelining the human foundations of ethnographic research, my late-1970s doctoral program offered no course in how to conduct ethnographic fieldwork, beyond a technical (albeit helpful) course in field linguistics. My classmates and I heard snippets of more realistic scenarios of what to expect in the field from some of our professors, who peppered their office hours, and sometimes their class lectures, with stories from their fieldwork experiences. Victor Turner and his wife Edie warned me about snakes hiding in thatched roofs in rural central Africa, Roy Wagner injected Melanesian Pidgin into his lectures, and Chris Crocker counteracted his French structuralist persona by joyfully recounting (and sometimes demonstrating) dancing in Bororo villages from his fieldwork in Brazil. Senior graduate students regaled us at parties with their own field adventures and disasters: a West Africanist scared us with his claim that he'd spent months learning how to say Hello (thanks to very complicated greeting patterns), while eating nothing but rice for a year and deploying CIA-style tactics to penetrate closely guarded cultural secrets; a North Africanist alarmed us with his confession that the spoken Arabic he encountered in the streets of Morocco had little relationship to the standard Arabic he'd spent years studying in the United States and Egypt; by contrast, a Central Asianist loved recounting the pleasure he took in playing the traditional horse-racing game of *buzkhashi* in Afghan villages (cf. Azoy 2012). But none of these adventures—or the light they might shed either on the societies these scholars studied or on the fieldwork process itself—made their way into the work we read by our professors, or even our older peers. Our takeaway lesson: write theory, and save the dramatic, scary, or charming stories for parties and the occasional classroom lecture.

While building up my tenure dossier, I made this lesson my mantra and kept to the straight and narrow, producing two scholarly books and enough journal articles to satisfy my tenure committee (Buckley and Gottlieb 1988; Gottlieb 1992). I even turned down an offer from a trade press in New York to publish one of those books, after the chair of my tenure committee warned me to run, not walk, away from that tempting offer. (The lack of the talismanic peer review in the acquisition process would have doomed such a book as Dead on Arrival to my tenure committee.) Still, while writing up my field materials in the language of science for peer-reviewed scholarly journals, memories of my (always intense and often tumultuous) fieldwork tugged at me, beckoning me to revisit the Beng in a more humanistic register than that which I had used in writing about them thus far.

It was not just the poet in me who was dissatisfied with my writing decisions, but also the political activist. I had chosen anthropology as a career that encourages us to boldly rethink social institutions and explore novel solutions, with the goal of increasing equality and decreasing exploitation, from social to ecological. In the rain forests of West Africa, I had found lessons that I thought my fellow citizens in Euro-America might find inspirational. Commitment to community … ingenuity in the face of material deprivation … attention to mind-body connections … respect for elders … devotion to the memory of ancestors … energy to recycle everything until it becomes undeniably unusable … assertion that human activity has a notable impact on seemingly unconnected natural processes … constant awareness of the spiritual side of human life … insistence on treating infants and toddlers as full persons—these were among the many ethical principles and lifestyle commitments I admired in Beng villages. But if I couldn't induce even friends and relatives to read my academic writing about these life lessons, how could I hope to reach a broader audience beyond the small group of scholars already interested in the issues I explored in my professional works?

And so, while publishing the books and articles that had the greatest chances of earning me tenure, I secretly began a different sort of writing. During the fifteen months of my first research stay in Côte d'Ivoire, my fiction writer–husband Philip Graham had frequently suggested—often in the middle of our latest efforts to cope with the challenges of making human connections in such a different cultural world—that we write a book together about our experiences. Later, back in the United States, in spare moments we each jotted down notes about incidents that remained seared in our memories, and Philip patiently reschooled me in aspects of writing narrative that my graduate training had squelched. Mentally revisiting the Beng, I started writing my heart back into the lessons I had to impart—this time, via stories. Slowly, we fashioned a text of alternating first-personal-singular narratives in short, successive sections, so that each of our stories followed the other's while allowing us to explore our individual experiences and reflections. One day I timidly mentioned this co-authored parallel output to a senior colleague—who immediately urged me to divulge nothing of this endeavor to any other colleagues until I had received tenure. And so I concealed the fact that Philip's literary agent had sold our co-authored memoir, now titled *Parallel Worlds,* to a major New York trade publisher, and I received tenure solely on the basis of my scholarly *oeuvre.*

A few years later, that "trade book" proved troublesome when a committee discounted it in evaluating my bid for promotion, precisely because it lacked references and footnotes. The fact that the book had by then won the Victor Turner Prize in Ethnographic Writing may have further doomed it from helping my promotion case—for the members of this committee, clear writing for a broad audience apparently served as a mark against a text.

Only when I demonstrated that the book had been widely taught in graduate-level courses were my colleagues on this interdisciplinary committee convinced that our memoir had scholarly merit; the fact that it had also been taught, in its first two years in print, in over sixty undergraduate-level courses was deemed at best irrelevant, and at worst a further sign of negligible scholarly value.

What is it that makes the academy so nervous about becoming "popular" in the wide arena beyond the immediate charmed circle of fellow scholars?

FROM RETREAT TO REVIVAL

In high school, the urge to "be popular" overcame many of us as otherwise reasonable teenagers. Motivated by the dream of joining whatever friendship circle with which we craved to be associated, we might have studied the walking and speech styles of our most popular classmates, drunk more beer than we liked, pretended interest in the weekend football games, taken after-school and weekend jobs to earn money for the latest fashion trend. At an earlier stage, even we academics yearned to be popular.

But something happened on the way to the academy. Perhaps moved by a range of fears—oversimplification, overgeneralization, distortion, misquotation, vulgarization—many of our colleagues have learned to disdain popularity beyond the invisible but nonetheless real walls of the academy. And sometimes they have good reason to be wary. As Wendy James has pointed out, in writing for a broad audience, authors often "produce Punch and Judy versions of some of the classic texts" (1996: 91). If we don't "dumb down" our texts ourselves, others may do it for us—in the process, wantonly misinterpreting in appalling ways. For example, Dominique Casajus (1996) has documented how the work of Louis Dumont was misappropriated by some ultra-right forces in France as endorsing hierarchy and condemning egalitarianism—an interpretation Dumont roundly rejected. Given the possibility of such troubling misinterpretations, anthropologists may follow the "once burned, twice shy" principle.

Yet scholars in other fields are often less nervous. Philippe Descola (1996) has pointed out that both physicists and historians often seem far less wary than do anthropologists when it comes to spreading understanding of their discipline. Joy Hendry (1996) has further speculated that it may (ironically) be because anthropologists classically paid attention to demographically small, rural, seemingly "exotic" societies that we remain afraid of being mocked as antiquarian—and, thus, have retreated from the public gaze.

It is a twofold retreat. Not only do many among us never even consider writing for a nonspecialized audience; we may even resist the attempt by journalists and other writers to popularize our findings for us, and we often condemn their attempts, once made. Perhaps we are nervous to have the tables turned on us: in effect, to be used as informants. Howard Morphy (1996) suggested that this reaction occurred with Bruce Chatwin's popular book about Australian Aboriginal religion, *Songlines,* which received an icy reception from most of the informed anthropological community—in Morphy's view, unjustifiably.

We may be at least partly responsible, then, for the fact that our opinions don't matter much to journalists when they seek "experts" to comment on all manner of issues confronting modern society.[4] If we are consulted at all, it is usually the archaeologist who fields questions about an early hominid find; very occasionally, an Africanist cultural anthropologist may be questioned (when the political scientists have run out) about the latest crisis in a seemingly "other" country such as Rwanda or Somalia. Rarely are properly anthropological issues that lie at the power-heart of the modern world the occasion for anthropologists to be tapped for comments in the mass media. The "Arab Spring" uprisings, the housing crisis that has produced downward class mobility in some 750,000 formerly middle-class homeowners in the United States, the Occupy movement, the epidemic of eating disorders among teenage girls and young women—all these contemporary issues and many more speak to anthropological expertise, yet (at least in the United States) the scholars quoted in the major newspapers and interviewed on the major television news shows on such issues are rarely, if ever, anthropologists.

While we often shy away from such publicity in mass media contexts, I suggest that even scholars yearn for a certain level of popularity—in our own community. Who among us does not at least occasionally sneak furtive peaks at citation indexes and the bibliographies of colleagues' books and articles, to count up references to their own work? And what is this effort if not a primitive, post-secondary-school rite rooted in a yearning to join that ever-elusive in-crowd? Were we not trying to find a place in the "restricted code" of fellow scholars (Bernstein 1964), we would publish our work anonymously or pseudonymously (Campbell 1996). The problem enters when we lose control of the limited circle of admirers.

Still, all this is starting to change. Since the time that my promotion committee questioned the value of a book intended for a broad audience back in 1997, the discipline of anthropology (along with some others) has begun reassessing its priorities to expand its audience. It may remain impossible to earn tenure at research-oriented campuses on the basis of popular rather than scholarly writing, but writing for a broad readership increasingly garners value even in elite institutions. If it won't win a junior colleague tenure, work aimed at the mythical "general reader" is now frequently valued at least as complementary to scholarly texts. In my own department, far from being concealed by nervous junior colleagues, professional blogs, photography exhibits, dance performances, theatrical productions, and DVDs have all weighed in on the positive column in assessing tenure and promotion cases in recent years.

No longer are most of us content to write ethnographies that are, as Jeremy MacClancy wrote of an earlier generation of scholarship, "boring, and ... virtually unreadable" (1996: 237). No longer is it a badge of honor for many of us when a friend or relative expresses excitement on hearing about our research, only to confess (or at least try to hide) boredom after dipping into any of our actual (scholarly) publications. Fewer among us are content to write scholarly texts that turn off ordinary readers despite the fascination of our topics.

Moreover, fewer academic publishers are willing to publish such works. Anthropology editors at four of the major university-based presses in the United States have told me that their "bottom line" print runs have increased significantly in recent years. In past days, a scholarly author could count a book a success if it sold 500 copies. Nowadays, that number is up to 1,500 or even 2,000, by the major academic publishers' reckoning. To sell more books, these editors now advise authors: "More stories, less theory." For our *homo narrans* species, good writing sells, and that means, in one way or another, good stories.[5]

And many among the generation of new scholars-in-the-making are listening to the editors. Indeed, more graduate students I know from my own and other programs increasingly express a desire for either a nonacademic career, or a career that combines academic research with nonacademic projects. In both cases, their goal is to use their expertise to make a difference in arenas beyond the classroom. For many, key to success in achieving this aim is honing the ability to write for readers beyond fellow scholars.

In fact, the last dissertation-writing workshop I led for advanced doctoral students in cultural anthropology renewed my hope for reviving and expanding interest in the discipline. I had become familiar with the projects and writing styles of that group of students before they left to conduct their year or more of fieldwork in either partly or wholly non-English-speaking spaces of Africa, Latin America, and Europe. From doctoral seminars they had taken with me, I had previously found the English writing style mastered by most of this group of scholars-in-the-making rather turgid. Substituting excess syllables, nested dependent clauses, theory-laden jargon of the moment, and passive constructions for clarity, these young authors had mastered the required fussiness of scholarly writing early in graduate school and seemed confidently headed toward careers in which they would labor to replicate the wordy pretensions of academic-ese that we often feel obliged to read and pretend to love.[6]

But in working through early drafts of these students' dissertations-in-progress, I discovered that every one of the young scholars in my seminar had somehow become remarkably engaging writers of English since returning from their various fieldsites. In our seminar, they found themselves easily writing in the first person (some for the first time), telling stories from their fieldwork, and using dialogue, scene setting, and other classic narrative techniques to engage a reader in their scholarly themes—writing strategies that none of these student-writers would have dared consider before they departed for their far-flung fieldwork locales.

It is true that I had encouraged these recently-back-from-the-field students to approach the challenge of completing a dissertation by writing from the heart (Aronie 1998). As I had designed the workshop, the long-ago words of a graduate school professor had still resonated with me, over a quarter century later. After returning from fifteen months of living in the rain forest of West Africa to conduct my own doctoral research, I had hoped that the respected East Africanist, Ed Winter, might offer me helpful recommendations for how to write my dissertation.

"Alma, I just have one bit of advice," he'd offered. "Don't look at your fieldnotes."

"What?" Surely I'd misunderstood.

"Just write what you remember. Don't look at your notes. You'll remember the good stuff. The important stuff. You can always check your notes later, make sure you got the details right."

"Hmmm," I replied, and the senior scholar returned to whatever he had been doing.

Fat chance I'll take that ridiculous advice, I thought, and proceeded to write a dissertation steeped in the details of my thousands of pages of field notes.

It took me nine years to de-dissertation-ize my thesis enough to publish it as a book (Gottlieb 1992). But by then, I had also begun writing a book of a very different sort—that fieldwork memoir co-authored with my writer-husband that took as a starting point the emotional intensity that characterized our stays with the Beng people of Côte d'Ivoire (Gottlieb and Graham 1994). Over the years, that fieldwork memoir (*Parallel Worlds*) has sold thousands more copies, and has been taught in hundreds more classrooms, than has my revised dissertation (*Under the Kapok Tree*)—and for good reason. Composed dutifully while continually consulting my copious field notes, my rewritten dissertation spoke to disciplinary issues but elided emotional ones.

Yet psychologists tell us that we humans live our lives at least as much in our feelings as we do in our thoughts.[7] For example, when neuroscientist Antonio Damasio studied people who could no longer feel emotions due to brain injuries, he discovered that these individuals had difficulty making decisions about matters ranging from what to eat to where to live, despite being able to articulate rationally the advantages and disadvantages of their options (Damasio 2010).[8] A recent theory of politics posits that a combination of emotion and reason accounts for the political stances we all take as citizens (Marcus, Neuman, and Mackuen 2000). A growing number of cultural anthropologists now suggest that the same reality characterizes the methodological heart of our discipline—our fieldwork.[9] That is, we bring our emotional biographies with us to the field, where they meet up with myriad emotional biographies of those in the communities we are studying. However else we might portray it, the anthropological field encounter can also be described as an emotional cauldron. Increasingly, anthropologists are acknowledging that it does not make intellectual sense to divorce affective considerations from our analyses when they are a key component of the experiences that formed the bedrock of our understanding. Accordingly, anthropologists are concluding that narrative and other writing genres may offer more accurate means to convey the full range of the human experience than do the conventional scholarly journal article and monograph. Echoing the wisdom of this growing interdisciplinary body of research, the best ethnographies, I suggest, engage our hearts and minds in equal doses. In urging me to adopt a dissertation-writing strategy that relied (however unconsciously) on this insight, my late teacher Ed Winter may have had it right.

Keeping his long-ago advice in mind when I designed the first in-class assignment for my dissertation-writing seminar, then, I exhorted my students to jot down notes about the most striking event either that had happened to them, or that they had witnessed or heard about, during their fieldwork. Maybe it was an ethical dilemma (theirs or someone else's)—or a trauma—or a challenge—or even just a conversation. Why did it affect them so strongly? What were their reactions at the time, and how did they perceive the situation now, months later? What did/might it teach them—and others—about the society they had studied? Would they include a discussion of this event or conversation in their dissertations? Why—or why not?

As I listed these writing prompts, I worried that this intellectual crowd would balk at what might have sounded like a Mickey-Mouse assignment devoid of the high theory they had worked hard to master in our demanding doctoral program. To further encourage them, I pointed out that if we ever develop Alzheimer's, it will be such old, haunting memories that remain—that they stick in our minds for a reason.

"Later, you can analyze the reasons for the durability of a particular memory," I assured them. "Later, you can support the big picture with relevant statistics and other details; later, you can add *caveats* and exceptions in footnotes and references galore. For now, just pick the memory that most stands out when you think back about your fieldwork, and write about it. If you write your passion, it will come out with excitement and energy."

I need not have bothered with my words of encouragement. Well before I had reached the end of my prepared short speech, some of the heads before me were already face down, intent on their pages filling with ink; the others were staring at some distant, invisible memories they were wrestling to narrate. A half-hour later, the students all emerged from writing frenzies with prose that told intercultural stories of connection and betrayal.

One of the seminar participants read aloud a disconcerting but gripping scene of an entire community that had run in fear as soon as she had stepped out of the bus in front of the rural village she'd hoped to call home for the next year. In a more cheering narrative, another young scholar recounted how, in the course of conducting "native ethnography" in her hometown in South America, a wary market trader long reluctant to grant an interview had nevertheless shown up unexpectedly at a funeral to express her condolences when the fieldworker's own aunt died. A third student recounted her momentous decision to marry a resident of her fieldsite in the midst of conducting her research, and the ways this new relationship shaped her project. These potential dissertation snippets engaged the human side to fieldwork at the same time that they spoke eloquently—and movingly—to important themes redolent in the students' respective fieldsites; they also embodied broader theoretical issues important to the discipline. So different from the more stilted prose that these young scholars had mastered before they had left the country, these first stabs at dissertation writing were all the more impressive given that several of the students in question were not native English speakers.

Over the years, I have noticed a few such before-and-after writing conversions in returned-from-the-field doctoral students; but I had always chalked the transformations up to idiosyncratic developments in the lives of those young professionals. Now, seeing this group of advanced doctoral students collectively charting parallel intellectual transformations, I wondered what might account for this unexpected development that suddenly appeared systematic, even predictable.

Perhaps doing ethnography changes our "writing brain." For one thing, in many research projects, cultural anthropologists either think continually in a second language, or they commute between two (or more) languages while doing fieldwork. After a good year or more of engaging in such a demanding linguistic dance, something may happen in the brain to provide a new perspective on the structure and possibilities of English (or whatever language in which the anthropologist writes). Feeling more comfortable with a personal approach to writing may be one effect.[10] If this hypothesis were ever demonstrated, we would do well to attend to the pedagogical implications, as teachers and mentors, to help returned-from-the-field students tap into such a newfound relationship to writing. Yet previous generations of mentors routinely endeavored to squelch such impulses in their students. Rather than encouraging early dissertation writers to think through the issues they found most challenging in the field and write about the process of confronting them, the previous inclination of many faculty was to direct students to elide such reflexive discussions and (as I experienced in graduate school) instead aim for a definitive analysis, bypassing any personal odysseys of intellectual discovery along the way.

A related factor that may contribute to the phenomenon I observed in my ABD students concerns the intellectual frameworks that inspire our writing. For a year or more, fieldworking students live far from the graduate school immersion in scholarly literature and conversations that characterized their previous three to five years in a doctoral program. Returning to the academy, many students may feel newly comfortable in pursuing a different relationship to the written word. Again, such an impulse was not regularly promoted in previous generations of anthropological instructors. Yet if it informs the returning-from-fieldwork brain, perhaps our graduate programs should take these changes into account and invite—or even train— students to write their theses differently from the usual model. Incorporating critical personal reflections and the politics of their field experiences into the heart of their analysis, rather than relegating such discussions to a preface or even a mere footnote, might produce dissertations that would at once engage more readers, humanize distant Others, and add transparency to what might otherwise remain opaque field methods.

A third factor that might explain the writing changes I saw in my ABD students concerns more emotional considerations. In some cases, a traumatic incident in the field may have so shaken new fieldworkers that they felt compelled to write about it in some deeply personal way. The usual distanced academic prose just won't capture enough of such events to satisfy either author or reader. In my case, I recall the first professional talk I gave (to the New York Women's Anthropology Conference), after I returned from fifteen months of doctoral research in Côte d'Ivoire: I detailed a public rape I witnessed in "my village," and my anguish at how to react at the time. Although the incident haunted me, I found no way to include any responsible discussion of it in my dissertation. It remained imprisoned as a troubling memory until, a decade later, I discovered the memoirist's style, which allowed me to explore honestly my reactions to the traumatic moment (Gottlieb and Graham 1994: 151ff.). The fact that witnessing or (in other fieldworkers' cases) experiencing sexual violence has produced riveting narratives by female anthropologists evoking their experiences to explore powerful theoretical issues suggests that emotionally engulfing events can be turned into compelling platforms from which to think frankly about the workings and bodily effects of power inequities in ways that more conventional scholarly accounts cannot accomplish (di Leonardo 1997; Winkler 1991, 2002). Other returned fieldworkers may not experience such a single dramatic moment but nevertheless may have felt every aspect of newness so deeply, and attended so deeply to these feelings, that the cumulative result compels them to work through their emotions on the printed page. In either case, encouraging students to pay attention to the emotional core of their fieldwork involvement is likely to produce rich texts that leave an impact, and much to contemplate, well beyond the last page.

I take the writing transformations I observed in my last group of dissertation-writing students as emblematic of important changes occurring in our discipline. The group of young authors I shepherded through their final stage of training may have felt inclined to try new modes of writing because of the liminal moment they straddled, for all the reasons sketched above. Still, unlike those of earlier generations, these advanced doctoral students did not resist such transformations but, rather, embraced them, and they still seem inclined to incorporate their new writing voices in what they are writing for publication. In short, during my first years in the profession, the clamor for alternative writing formats, while increasingly loud, remained marginal, with few among us feeling courageous enough to venture beyond the strict contours of the scholarly article or book. Today, the new generation of scholars seems inclined to write from the heart as much as from the mind.

WRITING AN ENGAGED ANTHROPOLOGY

I see both reasons for and signs of transformation well beyond my dissertation-writing seminar. In recent years, the discipline's flagship professional association in the United States, the American Anthropological Association (AAA), has strongly encouraged anthropologists to share our expertise with a broad public and increase our relevance, and has created a host of new initiatives to offer realistic means for achieving this new goal.[11] At the heart of all these exciting programs to considerably enlarge the audience for anthropology lies a mandate for creating texts to engage readers beyond doctorate-bearing scholars. No matter how compelling our topic, an article of overstuffed and jargon-laden prose further weighed down by endless caveats and footnotes will surely constrict our readership to a small group of professional colleagues. By contrast, an accessible text will easily draw new readers to our research and our insights. And who better than anthropologists to provide the comparative framework linking the global and the local, to humanize both near and distant Others, to explain seemingly inexplicable behavior … in short, to propose creative ways to address the extraordinary challenges of the twenty-first century?

The mandate to communicate our knowledge to a broad public becomes more realistic if we provide training for scholars in the writing skills that can convey the content of our research in an inviting manner. Thankfully, more and more scholars now teach such writing skills. Workshops on writing ethnographic fiction, poetry, and other "alternative" genres that the Society for Humanistic Anthropology sponsors at the annual American Anthropological Association conference are increasingly oversubscribed, as was an intensive, week-long workshop in ethnographic writing held for some years every summer at Lewis and Clark College in Oregon.

Each time I have (co-)taught such workshops (often with Philip Graham), I have been amazed to see the passion—even desperation—that enrollees brought with them. In initial discussions about why participants had joined the workshop, we typically hear stories from anthropologists who describe themselves as refugees from an intellectual space that some said felt like a textual prison. I recall one senior colleague—a department chair—describing in a shaky voice the ethnographic novel she had been working on for a decade but had not yet had the courage to show anyone, until she brought it, with much trepidation, to our workshop. The most junior member of that workshop—a young woman who had just graduated with a B.A. in cultural anthropology and was taking a couple of years off before applying to graduate school—listened to this senior colleague's story with alarm. She wanted to continue writing in a variety of styles (I recall a moving fictionalized ethnographic account of a fishing community she knew well) and suddenly worried that graduate school might silence her writing voice. Still, some graduate programs are less conventional than others; new emphases in public anthropology now characterize increasing numbers of graduate programs.[12] Increasingly easy access to well-written op-ed pieces, letters to the editor, magazine articles, radio pieces, satires, and blogs provides further tools that encourage us to experiment with writing that can draw readers to our work beyond the small circle of colleagues who already share our scholarly interests.

THE CLASSROOM WRIT LARGE

Efforts to engage a broader public in anthropology can include the classroom. In my own life as a teacher, and inspired by growing interest, I introduced a seminar on Ethnographic Writing into my department's curriculum
some years ago. In the workshop, we take as our starting point Geertz's observation—so obvious yet, until he made the case, mostly overlooked—that
scholars are also authors (1988). From that basic assumption, we focus on
the ways in which scholars-as-authors may take unexpected license to cross
the seemingly unbroachable frontiers that divide writing genres. Exploring
a selection of anthropological texts that experiment with writing ethnography to expand the readership of the discipline, students discover a range
of writing genres practiced by early anthropologists from Edward Sapir (a
poet-linguist) and Zora Neale Hurston (an anthropologist-folklorist-novelist)
to contemporary scholars pushing the bounds of academic writing. Com-
plementing our reading of experimental texts by respected scholars, students try their hand at ethnographic styles of their choosing by writing a
set of interpretive texts in three different genres about a society they select
for their focus. Over the years, I have seen undergraduate students decide
to major in anthropology after discovering the world of writing options
available to them; other students—declared anthropology majors who had
already decided to abandon the discipline after they graduated—have found
themselves reinvigorated by the potential of their major and have applied to
graduate schools in anthropology when they realized the field offers more
writing options than they had assumed.

Beyond these excited undergraduate students, every year several graduate students confess that although they would like to take this course, they
are reluctant because they fear it would not help them with their qualifying
exams or, further down the line, that "alternative" writing styles will not
help earn them tenure. Still, each time the course appears on the schedule,
a couple of intrepid graduate students in cultural anthropology enroll. Our
local experience echoes a national trend: courses on ethnographic writing
such as this are sprouting up in top-rated anthropology programs across the
United States and even internationally.[13] As colleagues increasingly create
similar courses, our programs will increasingly train students to take the
craft of writing seriously.

Skeptics might wonder about the merit of such courses. Yet, as I have
suggested, ethnographic writing workshops often (re)excite students about
the writing process, and about anthropology. Beyond this welcome emotional
effect, the texts I have seen students produce are sometimes little short of
spectacular. For example, a play featuring Roma people in Russia written

by an undergraduate student at once thoughtfully highlighted and problematized ethnic stereotypes and "othering" discourses about this historically marginalized group by embedding serious issues in a moving drama
(Parada 2008). Another memorable piece (this one by a doctoral student)
creatively considered the challenges of globalizing forces in the lives of East
African refugees in the United States, and of anthropologists who might
wish to study their situation, by creating a narrative embedded in an online, interactive Google map (Balakian 2011). When students share such innovative pieces in class with one another, their classmates often marvel at
their colleagues' ingenuity and find themselves inspired to produce creative
pieces for their next assignments. In such courses, students learn that if they
hold ambitions to write for readers beyond colleagues with doctorates in
their subfields, the possibilities of alternative genres await.

* * *

The example of Salvador Dali beckons. Beyond award-worthy journal
articles and monographs, anthropologists are staking out new territory by
dipping into other genres, in a dual quest to reinvigorate traditional reader-
ships and find new ones. Some anthropologists venture beyond even these
genres to create their own. Back in the 1960s, not content with the conventional genres, the ever-maverick Gregory Bateson went so far as to invent a
charming genre of writing that he called "metalogues," in which he wrote
partly fictionalized conversations about the most arcane of topics—conversations that he supposedly held with his partly imagined daughter (whose
real-life model grew up to become anthropologist Mary Catherine Bateson)
(G. Bateson 1972). While few anthropologists have followed Bateson's lead in
crafting such a creative format, plenty try their hands at writing ethnographically informed poetry and short stories. In fact, the Society for Humanistic
Anthropology now offers annual awards in these two genres, with winning
pieces published in its peer-reviewed journal, *Anthropology and Humanism*.[14]
Beyond these conventional literary genres for adults, the world of writing
offers a plethora of genres that we normally exclude from our scholarly pur-
view, though we may engage them daily outside our academic lives. Dieting
books—advice columns—repair manuals—greeting cards—package warning
labels—shopping lists—bookstore receipts ... the kinds of texts that literate people now encounter daily abound. As participants in what we might
term a veritable riot of literacy, we scholars are intimately acquainted with
a dazzling array of texts of every shape, size, and sort. Limiting ourselves
to a single genre—the scholarly article (or its book-length equivalent)—dramatically reduces our options for how we can convey our knowledge, and
to whom.[15]

Acknowledging the small but growing corpus of alternative writings, I invite you, as reader, to find your own jig to dance with genre. Perhaps even the shyest among us might be encouraged to disseminate our knowledge and our analytic acumen more broadly if we classify the world beyond the academy as the classroom writ large. With that model, a much larger cohort of students awaits.

ACKNOWLEDGMENTS

Small portions of this chapter appeared in different forms as: "Ways of Writing Anthropology," talk presented at the Stockholm Roundtable on "The Anthropologist as Writer: Training, Practice, Genres"; "Dancing a Jig with Genre" in *Anthropology News*; and "The Perils of Popularizing Anthropology" in *Anthropology Today*.

I thank Helena Wulff for the gracious invitation to participate in the Stockholm Roundtable and to expand my talk for this collection. For comments on this and all my writing efforts, I am forever grateful to my partner in life and work, Philip Graham.

Alma Gottlieb is past president of the Society for Humanistic Anthropology, with interests in religion, children, gender, and migration/diaspora (especially in Côte d'Ivoire and the Cape Verdean diaspora). Her work has been supported by the Guggenheim Foundation, Social Science Research Council, National Endowment for the Humanities, and other agencies. Most recently she has edited *The Restless Anthropologist* and authored, with Philip Graham, *Braided Worlds* (2012) (a sequel to their Victor Turner Award–winning memoir, *Parallel Worlds*). Gottlieb teaches at the University of Illinois at Urbana-Champaign and has also held appointments at Princeton University, Brown University, École des Hautes Études, Catholic University of Leuven, and elsewhere.

NOTES

1. The United States law has its analogue in most other modern nations; for some overviews and discussions, see Hylton and Deng (2007), C. James (2001), and Joelson (2006).
2. Unlike me, this friend, Miriam Sagan, became a professional poet (see, e.g., Sagan 2004, 2007, 2008).

3. Perhaps not coincidentally, another contributor to this volume, Kirin Narayan, also attended this very small but distinctive college as an undergraduate student.

4. This journalistic invisibility is especially relevant in the United States; it is less so in several other nations in which public anthropology boasts a more robust and valued profile; on Latin America, see Chelekis (2015), Ribeiro (2012), Uquillas and Larreamendy (2006); on Europe, see Afonso (2006), Barth, cited in Borofsky (2001), Eriksen (2006, n.d.), Hastrup et al. (2011), Howell (2010), Rogers (2001); on India, see Mahapatra (2006).

5. The notion that storytelling is central to our survival and nature has been proposed by thoughtful observers of the human condition in diverse times and places. For a selection of such work, see, for example, Coles (1989), Eckstein and Throgmorton (2003), Fisher (1985, 1987), Gabriel (2000), Gottschall (2012), Niles (1999), Sandercock (2003), and Scolari (2009).

6. For some provocative critiques of the insults to the language wrought by scholarly writing in English and pleas for more reader-friendly writing, see, for example, Germano (2013), Leonard (2014), Limerick (1993), Nida (1992), Ruben (2012), and of course the Bible of all English style guides, Strunk and White (2011); for a playful parody of academic writing, see University of Chicago (n.d.).

7. For a small sampling of this growing literature, see, for example, LeDoux (1998), Salovey and Mayer (1990), and Solomon (2003).

8. For additional research on the role of emotion in decision making, see Isen (1993), Markic (2009), and Sanfey, Rilling, Aronson, Nystrom, and Cohen (2003).

9. For some examples, see Ahmed (2004), Boellstorff and Lindquist (2005), Dickson-Swift et al. (2007), Dutton (2007), Hovland (2007), Hubbard et al. (2001), Hunt (1989), Irwin (2007), Kleinman and Copp (1993), Kulick and Willson (1995), Monchamp (2007), Mossière (2007), Pertierra (2007), Rosaldo (1984), and Shrestha (2007); also cf. Wulff (2007).

10. Research by psychologists on the "bilingual brain" now demonstrates other distinctive cognitive profiles that suggest that this hypothesis bears pursuing (e.g., Bialystok et al. 2004; Craik et al. 2010; Kousaie and Phillips 2010).

11. Although based in the United States, the AAA increasingly (and intentionally) attracts members from around the world, in an effort to internationalize the organization that was vigorously promoted by Virginia Dominguez during her term as president (2009–11). A Committee on Practicing, Applied and Public Interest Anthropology now also addresses "the increasing number of anthropologists in and outside the academy doing practicing, applied and public interest work" (American Anthropological Association 2015a), and a Committee on Public Policy encourages anthropologists to participate in public policy debates (American Anthropological Association 2015b). Furthermore, in the organization's flagship journal (*American Anthropologist*), a new section of Public Anthropology Reviews further supports this increasing commitment to engage public issues by printing reviews of "anthropological work principally aimed at

non-academic audiences, including websites, blogs, white papers, journalistic articles, briefing reports, online videos, and multimedia presentations" (American Anthropological Association 2010).

12. At the time of this writing, the list includes the University of Pennsylvania, the University of Oregon, Wayne State University, and the University of South Florida, among others. To increase the likelihood that members of the faculty in such programs receive tenure, the AAA has developed guidelines for tenure and promotion committees to use in judging efforts beyond scholarly writing (American Anthropological Association 2011).

13. Such courses are now taught at the University of Chicago, the University of Michigan, and the University of Wisconsin, among other premier doctoral departments. In Belgium, a short course in ethnographic writing that Philip Graham and I co-taught at the Catholic University of Leuven in 2002 attracted an excited cohort of international graduate students. The demand for such courses appears to be spreading across Europe.

14. In recent years, cultural anthropologist Renato Rosaldo has won the widely respected American Book Award for his poetry (Rosaldo 2007). Other anthropologists have written up their ethnography in the form of plays (e.g., Allen and Garner 1997; Saldaña 2005), memoirs (e.g., Behar 1993; Briggs 1970; Campbell 2001; Cesara 1982; Dumont 1978; Orlove 2002; Stoller and Olkes 1987; Tedlock 1992), literary novels (e.g., Narayan 1994; Stoller 1999), mysteries (Berger 1997; Nanda and Young 2009; Price and Price 1995), biographies (Crapanzano 1980; Shostak 1981), and "factional ethnography" (Sillitoe and Sillitoe 2009).

15. In recent years, a few experimental works by anthropologists and other social scientists have begun to draw creatively from other genres to convey ethnographic information in lively formats. Examples include a graphic exposition of the discipline (Galman 2007), an imagined Socratic dialogue among European and African historical figures (Nzegwu 2006), an extended photo essay (Behar 2007), a political cookbook (Fair 2008), imagined childcare guides *à la* Dr. Spock (DeLoache and Gottlieb 2000, Gottlieb and DeLoache 2016), and an ethnographic "flip book," children's book–style (Taylor 1998).

REFERENCES

Afonso, Ana Isabel. 2006. "Practicing Anthropology in Portugal." *NAPA Bulletin* 25, no. 1: 156–175. doi: 10.1525/napa.2006.25.1.156.

Ahmed, Sara. 2004. *The Cultural Politics of Emotion.* New York: Routledge.

Allen, Catherine J., and Nathan C. Garner. 1997. *Condor Qatay: Anthropology in Performance.* Prospect Heights, IL: Waveland Press.

American Anthropological Association. 2010. "Public Anthropology Reviews Debut in American Anthropologist." 3 March. AAA Blog. http://blog.americananthro.org/2010/03/03/public-anthropology-reviews-debut-in-american-anthropologist/.

———. 2011. "Guidelines for Evaluating Scholarship in the Realm of Practicing, Applied, and Public Interest Anthropology for Academic Promotion and Tenure. AAA Statement Produced by the Committee on Practicing, Applied and Public Interest Anthropology, Adopted by the AAA Executive Board, May 28, 2011." http://s3.amazonaws.com/rdcms-aaa/files/production/public/FileDownloads/pdfs/cmtes/copapia/upload/Final-T-P-Document-2011.pdf.

———. 2015a. "Committee on Practicing, Applied and Public Interest Anthropology." http://www.americananthro.org/ParticipateAndAdvocate/CommitteeDetail.aspx?ItemNumber=2224 /.

———. 2015b. "Committee on Public Policy." http://www.americananthro.org/ParticipateAndAdvocate/CommitteeDetail.aspx?ItemNumber=2226

Aronie, Nancy S. 1998. *Writing from the Heart: Tapping the Power of Your Inner Voice.* New York: Hyperion.

Azoy, Whitney. 2012. *Buzkashi: Game and Power in Afghanistan.* 3rd ed. Long Grove: Waveland Press.

Balakian, Sophia. 2011. "Mapping a Lost Friend: Technology and Tracing a Transnational Life." Paper presented at the 110th Annual Meeting of the American Anthropological Association, 16–20 November, Montréal. https://www.google.com/maps/d/viewer?ie=UTF&msa=0&mid=zKCba1oFPteg.kJvHABRwjL44.

Bateson, Gregory. 1972. "Metalogues." In *Steps to an Ecology of Mind: Collected Essays in Anthropology, Psychiatry, Evolution, and Epistemology.* Chicago: University of Chicago Press.

Behar, Ruth. 1993. *Translated Woman: Crossing the Border with Esperanza's Story.* Boston: Beacon Press.

———. 2007. *An Island Called Home: Returning to Jewish Cuba.* New Brunswick, NJ: Rutgers University Press.

Berger, Arthur Asa. 1997. *Postmortem for a Postmodernist.* Walnut Creek: AltaMira Press.

Bernstein, Basil. 1964. "Elaborated and Restricted Codes: Their Social Origins and Some Consequences." *American Anthropologist* 66, no. 6 Part 2: 55–69. doi: 10.1525/aa.1964.66.suppl_3.02a00030.

Bialystok, Ellen, Fergus IM Craik, Raymond Klein, and Mythili Viswanathan. 2004. "Bilingualism, Aging, and Cognitive Control: Evidence from the Simon Task." *Psychology and Aging* 19, no. 2: 290–303. doi: 10.1037/0882-7974.19.2.290.

Boellstorff, Tom, and Johan Lindquist. 2004. "Bodies of Emotion: Rethinking Culture and Emotion through Southeast Asia." *Ethnos* 69, no. 4: 437–444. doi: 10.1080/0014184042000302290.

Borofsky, Robert. 2001. "Envisioning a More Public Anthropology: An Interview with Fredrik Barth." Center for a Public Anthropology RSS. 18 April. http://www.publicanthropology.org/interview-with-fredrik-barth/.

Briggs, Jean L. 1970. *Never in Anger: Portrait of an Eskimo Family.* Cambridge: Harvard University Press.

Buckley, Thomas, and Alma Gottlieb, eds. 1988. *Blood Magic: The Anthropology of Menstruation.* Berkeley: University of California Press.

Campbell, Alan. 1996. "Tricky Tropes: Styles of the Popular and the Pompous." In *Popularizing Anthropology,* ed. Jeremy MacClancy and Chris McDonaugh. London: Routledge.

Campbell, Howard. 2001. *Mexican Memoir: A Personal Account of Anthropology and Radical Politics in Oaxaca.* Westport, CT.: Bergin & Garvey.

Casajus, Dominique. 1996. "Claude Lévi-Strauss and Louis Dumont: Media Portraits." In *Popularizing Anthropology,* ed. Jeremy MacClancy and Chris McDonaugh. London: Routledge.

Cesara, Manda. 1982. *Reflections of a Woman Anthropologist: No Hiding Place.* London: Academic Press.

Chelekis, Jessica. 2015. "Brazilian Anthropology—A National Discipline." Indiana University, Deptartment of Anthropology. http://www.indiana.edu/~wanthro/theory_pages/Brazilian.htm.

Coles, Robert. 1989. *The Call of Stories: Teaching and the Moral Imagination.* Boston: Houghton Mifflin.

Craik, FIM, E. Bialystok, and M. Freedman. 2010. "Delaying the Onset of Alzheimer Disease: Bilingualism as a Form of Cognitive Reserve." *Neurology* 75, no. 19: 1726–1729. doi: 10.1212/WNL.0b013e3181fc2a1c.

Crapanzano, Vincent. 1980. *Tuhami, Portrait of a Moroccan.* Chicago: University of Chicago Press.

Damasio, Antonio R. 2010. *Self Comes to Mind: Constructing the Conscious Brain.* New York: Pantheon Books.

DeLoache, Judy S., and Alma Gottlieb, eds. 2000. *A World of Babies: Imagined Childcare Guides for Seven Societies.* Cambridge: Cambridge University Press.

Descola, Philippe. 1996. "A *Bricoleur*'s Workshop: Writing *Les Lances Du Crépuscule.*" In *Popularizing Anthropology,* ed. Jeremy MacClancy and Chris McDonaugh. London: Routledge.

Dickson-Swift, Virginia, Erica L. James, Sandra Kippen, and Pranlee Liamputtong. 2007. "Doing Sensitive Research: What Challenges Do Qualitative Researchers Face?" *Qualitative Research* 7, no. 3: 327–353. doi: 10.1177/1468794107078515.

di Leonardo, Micaela. 1997. "White Lies, Black Myths: Rape, Race, and the Black 'Underclass.'" In *The Gender/Sexuality Reader: Culture, History, Political Economy,* ed. Roger N. Lancaster and Micaela Di Leonardo. New York: Routledge.

Dominguez, Virginia R. 2010. "Wiggle Room and Writing." *Iowa Journal of Cultural Studies* 12: 118–126.

Dumont, Jean-Paul. 1978. *The Headman and I: Ambiguity and Ambivalence in the Fieldworking Experience.* Austin: University of Texas Press.

Dutton, Edward C. 2007. "Eye-glazing and the Anthropology of Religion: The Positive and Negative Aspects of Experiencing and Not Understanding an Emotional Phenomenon in Religious Studies Research." *Anthropology Matters Journal* 9, no. 1: 1–15. http://www.anthropologymatters.com/index.php/anth_matters/article/view/58/112.

Eckstein, Barbara J., and James A. Throgmorton, eds. 2003. *Story and Sustainability: Planning, Practice, and Possibility for American Cities.* Cambridge, MA: MIT Press.

Eriksen, Thomas Hylland. 2006. *Engaging Anthropology: The Case for a Public Presence*. Oxford: Berg.

——. n.d. "Engaging with the World: Eriksen's Site." http://hyllanderiksen.net.

Fair, C. Christine. 2008. *Cuisines of the Axis of Evil and Other Irritating States: A Dinner Party Approach to International Relations*. Guilford: Globe Pequot Press.

Fisher, Walter R. 1985. "The Narrative Paradigm: In the Beginning." *Journal of Communication* 35, no. 4: 74–89. doi: 10.1111/j.1460-2466.1985.tb02974.x.

——. 1987. *Human Communication as Narration: Toward a Philosophy of Reason, Value, and Action*. Columbia, SC: University of South Carolina Press.

Gabriel, Yiannis. 2000. *Storytelling in Organizations: Facts, Fictions, and Fantasies*. Oxford: Oxford University Press.

Galman, Sally Campbell. 2007. *Shane, the Lone Ethnographer: A Beginner's Guide to Ethnography*. Lanham, MD: AltaMira Press.

Geertz, Clifford. 1988. *Works and Lives: The Anthropologist as Author*. Stanford, CA: Stanford University Press.

Germano, William. 2013. "Do We Dare Write for Readers?" *The Chronicle Review*. The Chronicle of Higher Education. 22 April 2013. http://chronicle.com/article/Do-We-Dare-Write-for-Readers-/138581.

Gottlieb, Alma. 1992. *Under the Kapok Tree: Identity and Difference in Beng Thought*. Bloomington: Indiana University Press.

——. 1995. "Of Cowries and Crying: A Beng Guide to Managing Colic." *Anthropology & Humanism* 20, no. 1: 20–28. doi: 10.1525/ahu.1995.20.1.20.

——. 1997. "Guest Editorial: The Perils of Popularizing Anthropology." *Anthropology Today* 13, no. 1: 1–2.

——. 2004. *The Afterlife Is Where We Come From: The Culture of Infancy in West Africa*. Chicago: University of Chicago Press.

——, ed. 2012. *The Restless Anthropologist: New Fieldsites, New Visions*. Chicago: University of Chicago Press.

Gottlieb, Alma, and Judy S. DeLoache, eds. 2016. *A World of Babies: Imagined Childcare Guides for Eight Societies*. Fully revised second edition. Cambridge: Cambridge University Press. In press.

Gottlieb, Alma, and Philip Graham. 2012. *Braided Worlds*. Chicago: University of Chicago Press.

Gottlieb, Alma, and Philip Graham. 1994 [1993]. *Parallel Worlds: An Anthropologist and a Writer Encounter Africa*. Chicago: University of Chicago Press.

Gottschall, Jonathan. 2012. *The Storytelling Animal: How Stories Make Us Human*. Boston: Houghton Mifflin Harcourt.

Hastrup, Kirsten, et al. 2011. *Social and Cultural Anthropological Research in Norway: An Evaluation*. Oslo: Research Council of Norway.

Hendry, Joy. 1996. "The Chrysanthemum Continues to Flower: Ruth Benedict and Some Perils of Popular Anthropology." In *Popularizing Anthropology*, ed. Jeremy MacClancy and Chris McDonaugh. London: Routledge.

Hovland, Ingie. 2007. "Fielding Emotions: Introduction." *Anthropology Matters Journal* 9, no. 1: 1–6. http://www.anthropologymatters.com/index.php/anth_matters/article/view/51/99.

Howell, Signe. 2010. "Norwegian Academic Anthropologists in Public Spaces." *Current Anthropology* 51, no. 2: 269–277. doi: 10.1086/652907.

Hubbard, Gill, Kathryn Backett-Milburn, and Debbie Kemmer. 2001. "Working with Emotion: Issues for the Researcher in Fieldwork and Teamwork." *International Journal of Social Research Methodology* 4, no. 2: 119–137. doi: 10.1080/13645570116992.

Hunt, Jennifer C. 1989. *Psychoanalytic Aspects of Fieldwork.* Newbury Park: Sage Publications.

Hylton, Keith, and Fei Deng. 2007. "Antitrust around the World: An Empirical Analysis of the Scope of Competition Laws and Their Effects." *Antitrust Law Journal.* Boston University School of Law Working Paper No. 06-47. http://papers.ssrn.com/sol3/papers.cfm?abstract_id=950964.

Irwin, Rachel. 2007. "Culture Shock: Negotiating Feelings in the Field." *Anthropology Matters Journal* 9, no. 1:1-11. http://www.anthropologymatters.com/index.php/anth_matters/article/view/64/124.

Isen, Alice M. 1993. "Positive Affect and Decision Making." In *Handbook of Emotions,* ed. Michael Lewis and Jeannette M. Haviland. New York: Guilford Press.

James, Charles A. 2001. "International Antitrust in the 21st Century: Cooperation and Convergence." Speech, Address by Assistant Attorney General Antitrust Division US Department of Justice before the OECD Global Forum on Competition, 17 October. OECD Global Forum on Competition, Paris.

James, Wendy. 1996. "Typecasting: Anthropology's *Dramatis Personae.*" In *Popularizing Anthropology,* ed. Jeremy MacClancy and Chris McDonaugh. London: Routledge.

Joelson, Mark R. 2006. *An International Antitrust Primer: A Guide to the Operation of United States, European Union and Other Key Competition Laws in the Global Economy.* Alphen Aan Den Rijn: Kluwer Law International.

Kleinman, Sherryl, and Martha A. Copp. 1993. *Emotions and Fieldwork.* Newbury Park, CA: Sage Publications.

Kousaie, Shanna, and Natalie A. Phillips. 2010. "Age-related Differences in Interlingual Priming: A Behavioural and Electrophysiological Investigation." *Aging, Neuropsychology, and Cognition* 18, no. 1: 22–55. doi: 10.1080/13825585.2010.510555.

Kulick, Don, and Margaret Willson, eds. 1995. *Taboo: Sex, Identity, and Erotic Subjectivity in Anthropological Fieldwork.* London: Routledge.

LeDoux, Joseph E. 1996. *The Emotional Brain: The Mysterious Underpinnings of Emotional Life.* New York: Simon & Schuster.

Leonard, David. 2014. "In Defense of Public Writing." 12 November. *Chronicle Vitae.* Chronicle of Higher Education. https://chroniclevitae.com/news/797-in-defense-of-public-writing.

Limerick, Patricia N. 1993. "Dancing with Professors: The Trouble with Academic Prose." *New York Times,* 31 October. Book Review section.

MacClancy, Jeremy. 1996. "Fieldwork Styles: Bohannan, Barley, and Gardner." In *Popularizing Anthropology,* ed. Jeremy MacClancy and Chris McDonaugh. London: Routledge.

————. 1996. "Fieldwork Styles: Bohannan, Barley, and Gardner." In *Popularizing Anthropology*, ed. Jeremy MacClancy and Chris McDonaugh. London: Routledge.

Mahapatra, LK. 2006. "Anthropology in Policy and Practice in India." *National Association for the Practice of Anthropology Bulletin* 25, no. 1: 52–69. doi: 10.1525/napa.2006.25.1.052.

Marcus, George E., W. Russell Neuman, and Michael MacKuen. 2000. *Affective Intelligence and Political Judgment*. Chicago: University of Chicago Press.

Monchamp, Anne. 2007. "Encountering Emotions in the Field: An X Marks the Spot." *Anthropology Matters Journal* 9, no. 1: 1-7. http://www.anthropologymatters.com/index.php/anth_matters/article/view/57/110.

Morphy, Howard. 1996. "Proximity and Distance: Representations of Aboriginal Society in the Writings of Bill Harney and Bruce Chatwin." In *Popularizing Anthropology*, ed. Jeremy MacClancy and Chris McDonaugh. London: Routledge.

Mossière, Géraldine. 2007. "Sharing in Ritual Effervescence: Emotions and Empathy in Fieldwork." *Anthropology Matters Journal* 9, no. 1: 1–14. http://www.anthropologymatters.com/index.php/anth_matters/article/view/59/114.

Nanda, Serena, and Joan Young. Gregg. 2009. *The Gift of a Bride: A Tale of Anthropology, Matrimony, and Murder*. Lanham, MD: AltaMira Press.

Narayan, Kirin. 1994. *Love, Stars, and All That*. New York: Pocket Books.

Nida, Eugene A. 1992. "Sociolinguistic Implications of Academic Writing." *Language in Society* 21, no. 3: 477–485. doi: 10.1017/S0047404500015530.

Niles, John D. 1999. *Homo Narrans: The Poetics and Anthropology of Oral Literature*. Philadelphia: University of Pennsylvania Press.

Nzegwu, Nkiru. 2006. "The Conclave: A Dialogic Search for Equality." In *Family Matters: Feminist Concepts in African Philosophy of Culture*. Albany: State University of New York Press.

Orlove, Benjamin S. 2002. *Lines in the Water: Nature and Culture at Lake Titicaca*. Berkeley: University of California Press.

Parada, Anais. 2008. "Playing Carmen: A One-Act Play in Three Scenes." Play written for ANTH 414 (Ethnographic Writing), University of Illinois at Urbana-Champaign. Unpublished manuscript.

Pertierra, Anna C. 2007. "Anthropology that Warms Your Heart: On Being a Bride in the Field." *Anthropology Matters Journal* 9, no. 1: 1–14. http://www.anthropologymatters.com/index.php/anth_matters/article/view/55/106.

Price, Richard, and Sally Price. 1995. *Enigma Variations*. Cambridge, MA: Harvard University Press.

Markic, Olga. 2009. "Rationality and Emotions in Decision Making." *Interdisciplinary Description of Complex Systems* 7, no. 2: 54–64.

Ribeiro, Gustavo. 2012. "From Local to Global Ethnographic Scenarios." In *The Restless Anthropologist: New Fieldsites, New Visions*, ed. Alma Gottlieb. Chicago: University of Chicago Press.

Rogers, Susan C. 2001. "Anthropology in France." *Annual Review of Anthropology* 30: 481–504.

Rosaldo, Renato. 1984. "Grief and a Headhunter's Rage: On the Cultural Force of Emotions." In *Text, Play, and Story: The Construction and Reconstruction of Self and Society*, ed. Edward M. Bruner. Washington, DC: American Ethnological Society.

———. 2007. *Prayer to Spider Woman: Rezo a La Mujer Araña*. Saltillo, Coahuila: Gobierno del Estado de Coahuila, Instituto Coahuilense de Cultura, 2003.

Ruben, Adam. 2012. "Life and Career. How to Write Like a Scientist." 23 March. American Association for the Advancement of Science.

Sagan, Miriam. 2004. *Rag Trade: Poems*. Albuquerque: La Alameda Press.

———. 2007. *Gossip*. El Rito, NM: Tres Chicas Books.

———. 2008. *Map of the Lost*. Albuquerque: University of New Mexico Press.

Saldaña, Johnny. 2005. *Ethnodrama: An Anthology of Reality Theatre*. Walnut Creek, CA: AltaMira Press.

Salovey, Peter, and John Mayer. 1990. "Emotional Intelligence." *Imagination, Cognition, and Personality* 9: 185–211. http://www.unh.edu/emotional_intelligence/EI Assets/EmotionalIntelligenceProper/EI1990%20Emotional%20Intelligence.pdf.

Sandercock, Leonie. 2003. "Out of the Closet: The Importance of Stories and Storytelling in Planning Practice." *Planning Theory & Practice* 4, no. 1: 11–28. doi: 10.1080/1464935032000057209.

Sanfey, AG, James K. Rilling, Jessica A. Aronson, Leigh E. Nystrom, and Jonathan D. Cohen. 2003. "The Neural Basis of Economic Decision-Making in the Ultimatum Game." *Science* 300, no. 5626: 1755–1758. doi: 10.1126/science.1082976.

Scolari, Carlos A. 2009. "Transmedia Storytelling: Implicit Consumers, Narrative Worlds, and Branding in Contemporary Media Production." *International Journal of Communication* 3: 586–606. http://ijoc.org/index.php/ijoc.

Shostak, Marjorie. 1981. *Nisa, the Life and Words of a !Kung Woman*. Cambridge, MA: Harvard University Press.

Shrestha, Celayne H. 2007. "Emotional Apprenticeships: Reflection on the Role of Academic Practice in the Construction of 'The Field.'" *Anthropology Matters Journal* 9, no. 1: 1–11. http://www.anthropologymatters.com/index.php/anth_matters/article/view/53/101.

Sillitoe, Paul, and Jackie Sillitoe. 2009. *Grass-clearing Man: A Factional Ethnography of Life in the New Guinea Highlands*. Long Grove, IL: Waveland Press.

Solomon, Robert C. 2003. *What Is an Emotion? Classic and Contemporary Readings*. 2nd ed. New York: Oxford University Press.

Stoller, Paul. 1999. *Jaguar: A Story of Africans in America*. Chicago: University of Chicago Press.

Stoller, Paul, and Cheryl Olkes. 1987. *In Sorcery's Shadow: A Memoir of Apprenticeship among the Songhay of Niger*. Chicago: University of Chicago Press.

Strunk, William, and EB White. 2011. *The Elements of Style*. Kindle ed.

Taylor, Julie M. 1998. *Paper Tangos*. Durham: Duke University Press.

Tedlock, Barbara. 1992 *The Beautiful and the Dangerous: Dialogues with the Zuni Indians*. New York: Penguin Books.

University of Chicago Writing Program. n.d.. "Write Your Own Academic Sentence." http://writing-program.uchicago.edu/toys/randomsentence/write-sentence.htm.

Uquillas, Jorge E., and Pilar Larreamendy. 2006. "Applied Anthropology in Ecuador: Development Practice and Discourse." *NAPA Bulletin* 25, no. 1: 14–34. doi: 10.1525/napa.2006.25.1.014.

Winkler, Cathy. 1991. "Rape as Social Murder." *Anthropology Today* 7, no. 3: 12–14. http://www.stopviolence.com/winkler/social-murder.htm.

——. 2002. *One Night: Realities of Rape.* Walnut Creek, CA: AltaMira Press.

Wulff, Helena, ed. 2007. *The Emotions: A Cultural Reader.* London: Berg/Blooomsbury.

Chapter 7

Writing for the Future

Paul Stoller

In June 1984, I traveled to the Republic of Niger to sit with my mentor of things Songhay, the late Adamu Jenitongo. By then I had been learning from him for more than sixteen years. Among the Songhay people of western Niger, Adamu Jenitongo was considered a powerful sorcerer who had spent much of his life healing the sick of physical and emotional disorders. During our long time together, he patiently taught me about medicinal plants, ritual incantations, spirit possession, divination, and the rites of sorcery. By 1984, I had amassed a wealth of "data" about sorcery and had begun to write an academic book about Songhay sorcerous practices. Most of my information, of course, had come from long sessions with Adamu Jenitongo, who considered me to be one of his apprentices. Like any properly trained anthropologist, I "wrote up" the field data and by May 1984, I had completed an early version of what was to become my first book, *In Sorcery's Shadow*. Like any young anthropologist and writer, I was a bit anxious about what I had written. In that early version, I had tried to refine anthropological thinking about sorcery. Even so, I wondered if I had included in the manuscript erroneous information—an improperly transcribed incantation, a poorly translated interview, or a blatant misinterpretation. I also worried whether the rather dry text—a theoretical introduction, a no- nonsense presentation of data, long passages of arcane analysis, and a modest conclusion—had faithfully represented the nuanced reality of the Songhay world of sorcery, the complex world of my mentor.

In short, I needed to get my mentor's response to my work. Accordingly, I printed a copy of my manuscript and took it with me to Tillaberi, Niger, Adamu Jenitongo's home. I arrived in Niger on a very hot June afternoon, made my way through immigration and customs, and hired a taxi, a sturdy Peugeot 504 with a cracked windshield. We slowly made our way through the Niamey's dusty streets, typically clogged with cars, trucks, carts, camels, donkeys, and pedestrians. Exiting the city limits, we headed north into the bush. City clutter soon thinned out as did the vegetation, buttes giving way to dunes, trees giving way to clay plains dotted with rocks and scrub. We arrived in Tillaberi just before sunset, the smoke of cooking fires mixing with dust to form a bank of clouds above a maze of mud brick houses. We exited the main road and made our way across sandy tracks to the edge of town. We lumbered up a sandy dune and finally arrived at a millet stalk fence, perhaps a meter in height, that marked the "wall" of Adamu Jenitongo's compound. Beyond the fence stood four two-room mud brick houses and a conical grass structure, the "spirit hut," where Adamu Jenitongo slept, kept his power objects, and consulted with clients. As always, the family received me warmly. After a long absence I felt happy to see them, especially my mentor, who at this point was well over 100 years old. He seemed frail, but motioned for me to come into his hut.

"You'll stay here with me, Paulu," he said. "In the black of night, we'll have important things to talk about."

Throughout our long master-apprentice relationship, we always talked in the "black of the night"—to avoid eavesdroppers, people wanting access to precious words or recipes. I explained to Adamu Jenitongo my project for that summer of fieldwork.

"You want to read me your book?"

"I need to know what you think."

"This is what we'll do." he said. "I'll talk and when I'm done, you'll talk."

We quickly established a working pattern. I made sure to complete my evening visits by 11:00 P.M., after which I'd return to Adamu Jenitongo's hut. He'd talk about the spirits and plants, and then ask me to begin reading my manuscript. Each night I'd translate five to ten pages of the work. Each night, Adamu Jenitongo would listen silently. Even when I asked for his reaction, he'd avoid responding.

"Let's wait until you're finished."

Although it took almost three months to complete the task, my teacher remained silent—not a word of criticism, no corrections of factual errors, and no encouragement. On the night before my departure, I finally finished.

"Baba," I said, using the term "father" to connote my respect for Adamu Jenitongo, "I have spent so much time reading but you've said nothing." In fear that my text had failed to represent the realities of the Songhay world of sorcery, I finally marshaled the courage to ask: "What do you think?"

As I had expected, Adamu Jenitongo was unimpressed with the work. He then said something that would change my life as anthropologist and writer. "You must produce something that will be remembered, something that describes me and you, something that my grandchildren and your grandchildren will use to remember the past, something they will use to learn about the world."

DISCIPLINARY EXPECTATIONS

For scholars, it is a profound challenge to write a text that our grandchildren will use to remember the past and learn about the future. In the academy there has always been a tension between institutional expectation—what we are expected to do to advance on our scholarly path—and creative desire— what we want to produce to fulfill our deep existential obligations. Given the power of academic institutions, most of us, and here I certainly include myself, tend to do what is expected: to produce academic texts that are markers of intellectual distinction. These texts, usually written with the "dead hand of competence" in a bloodless plain style, may well raise eyebrows and make important contributions to knowledge. Like the text I read to Adamu Jenitongo in 1984, they are usually documents that seek "the truth of statements," a truth formed in the logical precision of discourse. No matter the sophistication of the argument these texts usually do not endure. In relatively short periods of time, they are stored away—to make room for newer works that reflect the next moment. Once in storage, these texts remain closed to the world.

But there is another path that Adamu Jenitongo revealed to me more than thirty years ago. In the dim lantern light of the spirit hut, he suggested that I write a text that sought the "truth of being," a truth that is, in part, evoked through narrative and image. As my teacher well knew, works that feature good stories have a much better chance of remaining open to the world. In a powerful way, Adamu Jenitongo challenged me to take an institutional risk and attempt to create a work that would pass the test of time, a work that might produce knowledge that would somehow make life a little sweeter.

In this chapter I suggest how anthropologists might write texts that seek the "truth of being," representations that reflect a measure of mastery. For the Songhay of Niger, mastery is reached when the specialist—a custodian of knowledge—is finally ready to take on the greatest obligation: to pass on what he or she has learned to the next generation. Stories are told, lessons are learned and the work moves on to a future in which the specialist's thoughts, images, and texts remain open to the world (see Stoller 1989, 2004, 2008; Stoller and Olkes 1987).[1]

THE CONSTRAINTS OF THE PAST

The forces that led me to "write up" an academic text about my experiences in the Songhay world of sorcery have long been set in place. Our Enlightenment ancestors laid the foundation for social science in the eighteenth century. Although thinkers like Leibniz, Hume, Locke, Montesquieu, and Rousseau took a variety of paths in their search for Truth, they agreed that the Platonic penchant for reasoned reflection would (1) guide human beings toward truthful insight and (2) provide the wherewithal for a utopian society freed from the constraints of religious and emotional irrationality. They linked their search to the dispassionate gaze of empirical science, which, in time, became what Michel Foucault termed the modern episteme. If thinkers followed the way of the modern episteme, or so it was argued, they might bring a degree of shape and order to ongoing natural and social chaos. Such knowledge, it was said, might tame the beast of nature and provide a reasoned rationale for social orders, which, in turn would bring us closer to a utopian society (see Foucault 1982, 1994; see also Stoller 1998). In this vein, Jean-Jacques Rousseau, who was arguably the first person to think about anthropological method, suggested that scholars travel to far-off places in order to encounter pristine, egalitarian societies that had not yet fallen from grace, societies in which people had not yet forgotten how to live well in the world. Knowledge acquired during these encounters would create sharp contrasts that would reveal the hidden dimensions of the human condition. Spirited cultural critiques that would articulate such lost knowledge would, in turn, bring those home societies a step closer to a utopian social order. (Rousseau 2004 [1755]; Diamond 1981).[2]

Using this strong philosophical foundation, scholars began to build social science's complex edifice. In rooms on the lower floors scholars would use rationally contoured empirical methods to gather information, employ various theoretical lenses to assess the data, and suggest modest insights about the central elements of the human condition. When social scientists had gathered more and more data, which provided more refined insights, they would gradually move up the edifice's stairwell, eventually reaching the high floors of theoretical reflection. Here they would evaluate what they and others had produced and would use meta-theory to isolate human universals, the key to a deep comprehension of the human condition.

In those lofty, higher rooms of social science's edifice, a space far removed from the interminable swirl of ground-level realities, elders set the standards for research and academic writing. They suggested that research should have a contemporary conceptual focus—whatever that might be—and should feature sound empirical methods. When scholars published the research results, the elders decided, the reports and essays were to be done in a plain style—a bloodless prose—that presented the data and analysis in a dispassionate discourse that would demonstrate disciplinary mastery. If a text were to be published, it would have to be logically sound and follow a distinct form: introduction, review of the relevant literature, presentation of results, and a conclusion that, like the introduction, would pinpoint the work's theoretical contribution. This stylistic and structural framework has long set the standard for (social) scientific texts—research proposals, dissertations, scholarly essays, monographs, and, lest we forget, ethnographies.

When I began to "write up" the results of my ethnographic research on Songhay religion, the framework for my early drafts had long been established. Graduate school was a process of academic socialization. Most of us who had just returned from the field wanted to write about our extraordinary experiences, but our dissertation advisors, all representatives of disciplinary institutions, said no. They pushed us to write more standard texts, full of third-person reference, passionless prose, a healthy dose of jargon, and judicious interpretation, all of which led to a modest addition to the literature. We knew that if we incorporated those structures into our writing, the pathway toward a doctoral degree would remain open. If we became junior scholars, this formula would ensure that the pathway toward tenure would also remain open. We needed to publish essays in the "best" journals, which required that we follow the aforementioned set of institutionally prescribed rules—the same set of rules that framed the evaluation of highly competitive grant applications and book manuscripts at the "best" academic publishing houses. In short, I wrote the kind of text that the anthropological elders expected me to write. I, too, wanted to work my way up to the higher floors of the social science edifice.

Despite this bedrock of institutional constraint, Adamu Jenitongo's challenge compelled me to rethink my project. The earlier versions of *In Sorcery's Shadow* had never "worked" for me. They seemed far removed from what I had experienced. Quite frankly, my work had disappointed my teacher. Because of my love and respect for this man, I realized that I had to rewrite the work entirely and attempt to create a text that would be about me and him, a text that our grandchildren might use to learn about their past and imagine their future.

In response to Adamu Jenitongo's response, I wrote a memoir of my early fieldwork in Niger. Instead of long passages of dispassionate theoretical digression, followed by the voiceless presentation of "informant" data, followed by academic arguments of potential disciplinary significance, I attempted to produce a description of place (the villages of Mehanna and Wanzerbe), fused with the sensitive portrayal of character and laced with the nuanced representation of idiosyncratic dialogue—all to craft narratives that recounted faithfully the ethnographic world in which Songhay sorcery was practiced. These would be narratives that honored the practice and wisdom of Adamu Jenitongo.

To cover my bases, I submitted *In Sorcery's Shadow* to six trade and six academic publishers, all of whom rejected it. The trade publishers said the book was "too academic." The academic publishers said the book was "not academic enough." Seizing upon an experimental moment in ethnographic representation (see Rabinow 1977; Crapanzano 1981, 1985; Marcus and Fischer 1985; Clifford and Marcus 1986), David Brent of the University of Chicago Press took the substantial risk of publishing an unconventional work.[3] As the Songhay people like to say, *andurnya kala suuru,* "life is patience." From what I hear and see, *In Sorcery's Shadow* is still widely read and debated, and this after twenty-five years after its publication. Sometimes I wonder why that has been the case. Maybe *In Sorcery's Shadow* has withstood the test of time because it is a straightforward narrative about two very different men—one old, one young—whose paths cross in a remote place. It is a book in which the narratives are laced with examples of fear, courage, love, jealousy, fidelity, betrayal, and curiosity—emotional elements that readers themselves have experienced in their lives. Perhaps the emotional contours of the book continue to connect with many readers, creating linkages that transcend space, place, gender, age and culture—themes that sometimes trigger debates about the existential nature of the human condition. In the end, ongoing conversations about these philosophical themes bring us closer to a truth of being. They also show us the existential rewards of writing for the future.

WRITING FOR THE FUTURE

Scholars often think that there are formulae for constructing a text that will transcend the moment of its publication. I once presented a paper about sorcery and cancer that blended scholarship and personal experience. It was a text in which I attempted to discuss themes of life and death, courage and fear. At the end of the presentation, the audience, esteemed anthropologists all, seemed to be in a state of shock. No one knew how to respond. Finally an internationally prominent anthropologist spoke up.

"You know," he said, "you've given a powerful presentation. You had us on the edge of our seats." He paused for effect and looked at his colleagues. "How do you do that?" he asked.

"What do you mean?" I asked.

"Is there a formula or a system that you follow?"

Truth be told, I didn't have direct answer for him. "I don't know."

He pressed on. "Surely, you do. How do you do it?"

"There is no one way to construct a text like this," I said to an audience looking for ways to transform data into memorable text. "I can only speak for myself. I live with my materials—my data, if you will—and eventually the material, which, of course, differs from context to context and study to study, shows me the way."

Judging from the reaction, the audience thought I had given an inappropriate mystical response. Indeed my response was not unlike those given by fiction writers who talk about "living" with their characters, which, in time, speak to them, often quite critically, about the state of their characterization. In the end, our disconnect arose from two distinct orientations to writing. The audience approached writing from the truth of statements epistemology in which logical cohesion and the economy of language are front and center on Wittgenstein's straight highway, which marks the shortest and fastest journey from origin to destination. My approach to writing had more in common with the truth of being epistemology in which you wander into boundless spaces, to quote Nietzsche, where "logic curls about itself and bites its own tail" on sinuous less traveled roads that mark more distant and longer journeys from origin to destination. (See Nietzsche 1956 [1876]: 93; Wittgenstein 1953).

Even if such writing cannot be reduced to formulae, there are elements along the path that help you find your way. Along the sinuous path that seeks a truth of being, writers are compelled to think metaphorically. For me, ethnographic writing is a tapestry. In a fine West African blanket, the weaver employs minute thread patterns to produce an aesthetically balanced textile. In this way these masters "weave the world." In memoir and ethnography, the weave of cultural threads and personal motifs can also create a distinct world. Yet the memoir is often too narrowly stitched to the personal, while the ethnography is more often than not overburdened with impersonal detail. In weaving a textual world, the ethnographer, no matter the genre he or she employs, attempts to strike an aesthetic balance, transforming turgid academic prose into sensuously evocative writing that connects her or him to an audience of readers. One way to reach this felicitous destination is through the textual incorporation of place, dialogue, and character.

Any reader of James Agee's classic ethnographic text, *Now Let Us Praise Famous Men,* has experienced his masterful evocation of space and place. In this book, Agee's sensuously poetic prose evokes the sights, sounds, smells, and tastes of poverty in Alabama during the 1930s. The palpably descriptive passages of cabins and fields give the reader the texture of poverty in rural America, creating an experiential link—between writer and reader—in the text. You get the same sensuously evocative mastery of place in Michael Jackson's work of ethnographic fiction, *Barawa and the Ways Birds Fly in the Sky.* Spaces and spaces are filled with meaning, which means their evocation can be a powerful way to write for the future.

Dialogue is devilishly difficult to construct, and yet a faithfully idiosyncratic representation of how people converse can also create connections between readers, writers, and the characters featured in an ethnography or memoir. Are the dialogical representations in books like Marjorie Shostak's, *Nisa* (1981) or Kevin Dwyer's *Moroccan Dialogues* (1982) mere exercises in representational experimentation or do they provide a window into a person's character? Clearly, carefully crafted dialogue that faithfully portrays a person's particular way of speaking can attract a reader to a character, making him or her memorable. Is their talk choppy and scattered? Do they struggle over words? Do they speak quite fast or slow? Do they ramble or do they speak sparingly?

Dialogue, then, is one thread in the weave of character. Who are the people we attempt to represent? What physical, linguistic, or emotional traits distinguish the individuals in the text? Do they walk with a limp? Do they have particularly erect postures? Do they look you in the eye or avoid the gaze of others? Ruth Behar's careful construction of character in *Translated Woman* (1993) is the source of that book's widespread and longstanding appeal.

It is possible for ethnographers to combine representations of place, dialogue, and character to create works that give the readers a real sense of locally lived life—the trials and tribulations of people as they struggle to find a measure of well-being in an increasingly complex and unforgiving world. These are the texts that speak directly to the human condition. These are works that our grandchildren, to return to the prophetic insights of Adamu Jenitongo, might use to make sense of their past and chart their future.

If anthropologists attempt to write for the future and follow the sinuous paths that lead to a truth of being, they are also compelled to think about their scholarly obligations. There are, of course, disciplinary obligations. Having been socialized into the discipline, most anthropologists want to make significant contributions to anthropological thought. We spend much of our time thinking about how we might refine anthropological thinking about culture and social life. These are contributions of the moment. What about our contribution to the next generation?

Unlike Songhay specialists, much of our thinking and writing is lodged in the reward-rich here and now. As previously mentioned, Songhay bards, weavers, and healers, by contrast, usually have a different orientation. When they are young, they learn the nuts and bolts of specialization. They are like junior scholars following entrenched disciplinary paths that lead to institutional recognition and advancement. If the young specialists have talent, they increase their know-how and eventually become seasoned poets, weavers, and healers—all becoming masters who are first and foremost masters of specialized knowledge and practice. In the Songhay world, masters continue to practice what they have learned during a long and difficult apprenticeship. And yet, the Songhay master's greatest obligation, to reiterate, is not simply to effectively put into practice what he or she has learned, but to pass his or her knowledge on to the next generation. Stories are told and retold and in this way the knowledge lives on, marking a path toward the future—a gift to our grandchildren. Is such an obligation not worthy of our anthropological attention?

ACKNOWLEDGEMENTS

A special thanks to Helena Wulff for inviting me to participate in the conference, The Anthropologist as Writer, held at Stockholm University. Some of the ideas in this chapter were developed when I taught a workshop on ethnographic at the Writing Culture Summer Institute held at Lewis and Clark College. I thank Joann Mulcahy for inviting me to participate. I also had the opportunity to develop my ideas on writing for the future at Academic Writing Conference held at Emory University and during School of Humanities lecture I gave at Rhodes University in South Africa. Feedback from these varied audiences has been invaluable. Funds for ethnographic research in Niger as well as for time to write ethnography and memoir have been generously provided by West Chester University, The American Philosophical Society, The Wenner-Gren Foundation for Anthropological Research, the National Endowment for the Humanities, and the John Simon Guggenheim Memorial Foundation.

Paul Stoller is Professor of Anthropology at West Chester University and has been conducting anthropological research for more than thirty years in West Africa (Niger) and among African immigrants in New York City. This body of research has resulted in the publication of twelve books, which include ethnographies, memoirs, a biography, and collections of academic essays. His most recent work, published in October 2014, is *Yaya's Story: The Quest for Well-Being in the World.* In April 2013 the King of Sweden, Carl XVI Gustav, awarded him the 2013 Anders Retzius Gold Medal for his significant scientific contributions to anthropology. In 2015, the American Anthropology presented him the Anthropology in Media Award.

NOTES

1. These works provide the broad context for my early ethnographic work on Songhay religion as well as illustrating how my field experiences prompted the development of my anthropological and existential thinking.
2. Space precludes a more thorough account of Enlightenment thought and its impact on processes in academic institutions.
3. The list of works that shaped anthropology's experimental moment is long and I've omitted many important titles. The key, though, is that these early works, especially the meta-ethnographic contributions, made it more acceptable for publishers to put forward unconventional ethnographies and memoirs.

REFERENCES

Agee, James. 1939. *Now Let Us Praise Famous Men.* New York: Houghton Mifflin.
Behar, Ruth. 1993. *Translated Woman: Crossing the Border with Esperanza's Story.* Boston: Beacon Press.
Clifford, James, and George E. Marcus, eds. 1986. *Writing Culture: The Poetics and Politics of Ethnography.* Berkeley: University of California Press.
Crapanzano, Vincent. 1981. *Tuhami: Portrait of a Moroccan.* Chicago: University of Chicago Press.
———. 1985. *Waiting: The Whites of South Africa.* New York: Random House.
Diamond, Stanley. 1981. *In Search of the Primitive.* New Brunswick, NJ: Transaction Books.
Dwyer, Kevin 1982. *Moroccan Dialogues.* Baltimore: The Johns Hopkins University Press.
Foucault, Michel. 1982. *The Archaeology of Knowledge.* New York: Vintage.
———. 1994. *The Order of Things.* New York: Vintage.
Jackson, Michael D. 1968. *Barawa and the Way Birds Fly in the Sky.* Washington, DC: The Smithsonian Institution.
Marcus, George E., and Michael MJ Fischer 1985. *Anthropology as Cultural Critique.* Chicago: University of Chicago Press.

Nietzsche, Frederick 1956 [1876]. *The Birth of Tragedy Out of the Spirit of Music.* Trans. Francis Groffling. Garden City, NJ: Doubleday, Anchor Books.

Rabinow, Paul 1977. *Reflections on Fieldwork in Morocco.* Berkeley: University of California Press.

Rousseau, Jean-Jacques. 2010 [1755]. *A Discourse on the Origin of Inequality Among Men.* Trans. Helena Rosenblatt. New York: St. Martin's Press.

Shostak, Marjorie 1981. *Nisa: The Life and Words of a Kung Woman.* Cambridge, MA: Harvard University Press.

Stoller, Paul. 1998. "Rationality." In *Critical Terms for Religious Studies,* ed. Marc C. Taylor. Chicago: University of Chicago Press.

———. 1989. *Fusion of the Worlds: An Ethnography of Possession among the Songhay of Niger.* Chicago: University of Chicago Press.

———. 2004. *Stranger in the Village of the Sick: A Memoir of Cancer Sorcery and Healing.* Boston: Beacon Press.

———. 2008. *The Power of the Between: An Anthropological Odyssey.* Chicago: University of Chicago Press.

Stoller, Paul, and Cheryl Olkes 1987. *In Sorcery's Shadow: A Memoir of Apprenticeship Among the Songhay of Niger.* Chicago: University of Chicago Press.

Wittgenstein, Ludwig 1953. *Philosophical Investigations.* Trans. GEM Amscombe. London: Blackwell.

Chapter 8

Life-Writing

Anthropological Knowledge, Boundary-Making, and the Experiential

Narmala Halstead

INTRODUCTION

In this chapter, I consider different trajectories that constitute forms of life-writing and the entanglement of these forms with anthropological knowledge. I consider that this entanglement is an ongoing engagement with processual spaces vis-à-vis both anthropological discipline-specific approaches and "everyday life experiences." These spaces illustrate the anthropological as deeply bounded in particular forms of knowledge conventions. It is also being constantly "written in" as extensions of data and translations of our world-views, practices, and trajectories. I consider in this entanglement a space for the popular as a form of knowledge, which, however, is often rendered invisible or explicitly written out. In this regard, anthropological knowledge achieves privileged status through a visibility marked by distance from the popular.

The concern with authentic anthropological knowledge construction echoes within anthropology in varying ways. Within the discipline itself, how knowledge is produced as authentic has been subjected to extended critiques as part of debates about ethnography in terms of a production of texts seen to be marked by unreflexive viewpoints and inadequate recognition of participants "co-authorship," for instance (see Clifford and Marcus 1986).[1] The discipline has at different times foregrounded written-up knowledge through models that shift, for instance, from bounded, cohesive units, to unstable (unbounded) forms of organization (see Radcliffe-Brown 1952; Leach 2002). Through critiques, anthropologists reexamine, extend, and write outside of particular models (Halstead, Hirsch, and Okely 2008; see also Hirsch 2001: 137; Stocking 1985, 1991).

The boundaries between the popular and the privileged anthropological knowledge approach emerge in talk about what is real and not real: forms of distance from the popular have often been reflected on in the positioning and status of media anthropology, for instance, although this has been much contested. In a related manner, anthropological knowledge is held distinct from journalism and fiction as other notable forms of the popular. These distinctions and others have been mistranslated to position anthropology as an exotic discipline, leading to intense reflections against this misreading and also to calls for wider engagement (see, for instance, Eriksen 2006). In these calls, anthropology is being made central to contemporary debates: this centrality relies on its privileged forms of knowledge construction. In this chapter, I consider what is less visible within this boundary: I explore a role for the popular that attaches to processual spaces of anthropological knowledge construction as an understanding of anthropology in practice. I consider the popular as life-writing, ways of being in the world represented by forms of knowledge construction that are easily understood by lay publics. I consider this space as part of life-writing, an anthropological co-presence that can draw in other experiences to redefine the boundaries of knowledge-making, where anthropology is also part of "being in the world." I draw on a few related works, a research project on five anthropology departments in the UK, research and teaching, and my life experiences as anthropologist, author, and journalist to reflect on these forms of boundary-making and drawing in of the popular. I point to various examples of being drawn in and written out as combined spaces of life-writing vis-à-vis the anthropological. I consider that processual engagement contributes to anthropological knowledge and extends in a way that argues against popularization as always being a problem affecting epistemological boundaries. I reflect on how this might be recategorized as spaces of life-writing and particular trajectories of joined experience in constructing knowledge. This also relates to an anthropology of landscape as a cultural process with different "sites" for interpretation and making meanings (see Hirsch 1995: 22).

CO-PRESENCE

I place emphasis on the idea of "life-writing" as embedded experiences that might be easily represented in popular forms, but are drawn in and distilled to add to and be a part of the anthropological. To elaborate, I point to the ways anthropology has attracted people from other professions: I consider that rather than a career change, this could be read as a progression for some along a particular trajectory that inevitably discloses the co-presence of the anthropological. In my case, I first defined myself as a writer before becoming an anthropologist. My conversion to anthropology followed an experiential path, based on my writing as well as engaging with people as discussed further below. A perusal of staff profiles in some anthropology departments will also indicate current examples of such trajectories. Examples include Glen Bowman at University of Kent: the first line of his staff page reads: "I came to anthropology out of a literature background, but one which had always focused on the social context of representation and symbolization."[2]

Anthropology "ancestors" who became anthropologists as a shift from their original training or vocation include Edmund Leach and Franz Boas. Leach, who originally studied mathematics and then trained as an engineer, noted, in an interview with Adam Kuper (1986: 376), the varied influences that led him to a "life-long discipleship." He noted that the "family tradition" of going overseas was followed when he joined with a trading company. His travels led him to China, where he was "fascinated by the whole cultural system, which was so very different from anything that I had encountered in Europe, but I had no plans as yet to become an anthropologist." Leach jokingly noted an attempt to study the Yamis as part of an after-party activity. While discussing his "pre-anthropological" stage, Leach recalled that at a British embassy party in Peking a "very drunk American" and former missionary, Kilton Stewart, invited anyone interested to join him to "Bottle the Bugger" (Kuper 1986: 375–376). Leach followed up on this invitation and found himself on an island named Botel Tobago. He noted: "The inhabitants, the Yami, were 'real primitives,' in the classical ethnographic sense, the sort of people whom 'real' anthropologists are expected to study! We were not real anthropologists, but we did our best" (Kuper 1986: 376).[3] As I immersed myself in my ethnographic research, I would sometimes hear, spoken and unspoken, and in a more serious manner, the distinctions that Leach had jokingly thrown into the mix of being among the Yami on this island near Taiwan.

EPISTEMIC BOUNDARIES

The distinctions are about protecting epistemic boundaries; however, I consider that there exists an overprotection that has failed to consider the transferability of life experiences that might contribute to the core or the ways anthropological knowledge is itself constructed through an idea of practice, and, thus, also, both anthropological research and its knowledge conventions become applicable to wider settings.[4] Further, we might consider that these conventions are supported by processual spaces of life-writing that draw in and draw upon the popular as a privileging of the specific disciplinary boundaries. This is a separate issue from ensuring disciplinary integrity in a context where interdisciplinarity, increasingly, is espoused as a form of desired research collaboration to diffuse knowledge without attention to an epistemic base, as Marilyn Strathern noted in her 2004 Huxley Memorial Lecture "A Community of Critics." Strathern (2006)[5] notes the problem of tolerance that pedagogically allows the flourishing of many viewpoints to the detriment of arguing from any one viewpoint.[6] She goes on to discuss the construction of expertness and distinctions vis-à-vis interdisciplinarity and multidisciplinarity and the management of research in the knowledge economy. The debates raise questions about whether researchers are experts within one discipline contributing to others or whether in collapsing disciplinary boundaries they lose claim to being experts. Strathern notes: "By contrast with multi-disciplinary transfers, which align different voices and provide simultaneous translation, there is with interdisciplinarity, a promise of a pidgin, an epistemic transfer, affecting the very knowledge base in which one works" (2006).

This problem of interdisciplinarity supports the need for anthropological knowledge to follow and be known to be produced through rigid knowledge approaches. The ways these boundaries are drawn allow for anthropological knowledge to be sought across disciplines. The issue highlights the need to protect boundaries and suggests the ready displacement of the popular. The related issue of knowledge approaches jostling for attention also attaches itself to the co-presence of anthropology and the popular, and renders invisible the subjective processes located outside of these disciplinary boundaries.

The visibility of anthropological knowledge approaches in relation to technology and media comes under similar scrutiny as a problem of perceived unstable disciplinary boundaries. In 2001, I conducted a C-SAP[7] research project jointly with Edward Simpson on five anthropology departments in the UK. The project was to explore the relationships between ICT and anthropology. We interviewed a number of anthropologists across the departments: while the data brought out practical issues on changes and new use of technology, underlying this material were debates about what constituted real anthropology and how these boundaries had to be protected in relation to media and technology. Our project report reflected on these issues and discussed the privileged spaces of anthropological knowledge where there was some concern about how anthropologists' visibility through these technologies, by studying or using them, might affect the integrity of anthropological knowledge construction and its epistemic base. In a sense, an engagement with the popular, through technologies or fiction-writing, immediately engaged the boundary.

PROCESSUAL SPACES AND LIFE HISTORIES

I had other opportunities to reflect on these boundaries through my research and teaching. I taught for one year at Brunel University after completing my Ph.D. I subsequently joined Cardiff University. I taught at Cardiff University between 2001 and 2005.[8] I taught large groups of masters and undergraduate students. I engaged with various knowledge debates as I developed my research and teaching at Cardiff University: I considered interdisciplinarity and the *credibility* of particular forms of knowledge and delved into texts about "the ethnographic turn" in media, made famous by David Morley and other audience studies researchers. I taught in interdisciplinary settings: many international postgraduate students had worked as established journalists. Some of these students became very interested in acquiring ethnographic skills to conduct research.[9] Those students who had been professionals wanted to go beyond *usual writing practices;* those without experience became motivated to produce ethnographic research after *seeing* the ready connections to everyday settings.

The "turn to ethnography" (people writing) did not just materialize in this smooth manner, however; internally, ethnography could not be described simply as seamless as many debates have illuminated. I was also making distinctions between different kinds of writing and forms of knowledge construction. Further, at different times I was illustrating how these boundaries could be intertwined in understanding research. I converted various forms of writing by drawing on discussions with students, their experiences and mine as teaching and learning resources. A number of the M.A. students came to their studies from diverse professional backgrounds with significant experiences. I came to understand at an early stage that their experiences as life-histories could be utilized in the teaching and learning processes. My teaching and my encounters with students and visiting speakers also provided spaces to consider particular examples of how knowledge construction might be privileged and the ways others from different disciplines might be drawn into a specific approach, in this instance, ethnography. The cooptation of ethnography by different disciplines[10] has also led to other debates about what could be defined *as proper ethnography as distinct from that which apparently is just ethnography* (see Moores 2006).

Although I came to understand the processual spaces that drew in and were made valuable through life experiences that might include other forms of knowledge construction, I also had to compartmentalize different modes of writing: by definition, the categories of novelist, journalist, and anthropologist had their own territorial boundaries as I was to explore in a research paper presented at Fudan University, China (following Strathern 2006). The paper, "Modes of Knowing: The Instant-Expert Frame, Popular Representations and Reflexivity" (Halstead 2005) explored the different claims to knowledge and expertness. The paper reflected upon the importance of boundaries in different kinds of writing and knowledge construction.

But I also considered how one set of experiences and writing skills could become points of access and translation into another setting and drew on work with professionals who had drawn on their life histories and skills in relearning in order to become postgraduate students. While this work has led to pedagogical exploration of the use of life-histories and experiences in teaching and learning, I consider it here to return to the distinctions between "real" and "proper" in how we might use a particular set of experiences as forms of "life-writing" and where these spaces become discipline-specific, that is to say, through the processual, we become an expert in a particular field grounded through specific knowledge conventions. To return to Strathern's point, expertness as interdisciplinary is faced with the problem of an unstable epistemic base. The other issue, however, is that while we are paying close attention to knowledge conventions within disciplinary boundaries and being grounded epistemologically, other influences and knowledge spaces might be enriching to particular modes of knowledge production and writing. This process of *drawing in* occurs simultaneously alongside the closing or renewal of boundaries as I learned through self-critiques of my own work and the superseding of anthropological writing over fiction.

I became immersed in anthropological knowledge debates during doctoral fieldwork. As my research developed, I was simultaneously considering fieldwork encounters, not dissimilar to the experiences and written-up accounts of many anthropologists among others exploring relations with research participants (see, for instance, Narayan 1993); in exploring these fieldwork encounters, my *writing* drew definitively on particular epistemological conventions. The idea of anthropologist-writer meant different things in two distinctive areas of knowledge construction. The first notes boundaries in approaches to the written word that establish particular approaches to fiction and academic writing; the second brings out an ongoing consciousness embedded in moments of recognition and reflection, similar to the way "ethnographic moments" are significant in anthropological knowledge construction (see Strathern 1999; see also Halstead 2008). As indicated, opportunities emerged in various ways to reflect on the interfaces of these different genres of writing that were inevitably embedded in larger issues about knowledge construction.

TRAJECTORIES

Toward the end of 1994, I completed a novel. It was the second of my main novels.[11] This added to plays, poems, and short stories I had also written. The significance of this moment was that I immediately commenced my Ph.D. studies. I did not have time to write any more novels. I did not have time to read them. I drew a distinction with much commitment. Simultaneously as I embarked on doctoral fieldwork, I had to "unlearn" confident approaches to writing, honed through work as a writer and later as journalist. At the same time, I refined existing "people skills" to walk into strangers' homes in my designated fieldsites, at various times without a local guide, to reach out, to "listen" to what they understood about my research and follow these and other pathways to obtain the data for the intensive writing that I was to carry out for the doctoral thesis. The processes of unlearning, discovery, writing, and rewriting were also a continuation in "life-writing." While there were established boundaries between different kinds of writing and, thus, knowledge construction, accompanying the different approaches was an understanding of writing that commences and continues as unwritten, implicitly part of the written text. The "background" was one of expectations, plans, and what it meant to be a writer as a life-view, that is to say, seeing through lens guided by imagination and marked by reflection and reflexivity.

My consideration of the different settings that influenced my work emerges through varied pathways, in conversations, through research and, generally, an ongoing engagement with knowledge and its different forms. As a journalist, I had worked for a state-controlled media under censorship conditions. Despite editorial policy constraints, a space for dissent flourished that was much more open than the off-stage production of hidden transcripts so well theorized by James Scott (1990).[12] A notion of transience (people were passing through in various non-physical ways[13]) was part of this ordered *and* disordered landscape.[14] As a writer, I too was passing through and did not remain in the job. Some years later I published a novel—it was fiction and did not name a country or any contemporary historical figures (Shewcharan 1994). Researchers and reviewers (see, for instance, Muneshwar 2009) have examined this work in efforts to uncover or make connections to real-life accounts. At a writing conference in Twickenham,[15] several participants were interested in this book although I did not speak about it. My talk was on "work in progress."

WRITING AND LIFE-WRITING

I had given some thought to what I might discuss in terms of fiction at this conference; after commencing ethnographic fieldwork in the mid 1990s, my fiction, it seemed, had changed direction. In fact, I was not really writing much fiction as the space to do so had become, it seemed, futuristic: my growing interest in my research, which would become combined with anthropological knowledge debates, came to dominate my attention well past my Ph.D viva. I considered two pieces of fiction to discuss at this conference. I had published a short story (Shewcharan 2000), which had been commissioned in 1999; the request had come while I awaited my viva. I had written it quickly as a character, Bhola Ram, materialized and took over the story through a "diatribe." Connections hovered to my academic research. A somewhat accidental protagonist, Bhola Ram, started by complaining about his wife and her "strange" desire to migrate: it seemed she wanted to do so because everyone down the street was doing it. He was unstoppable. His monologue encompassed multiple connections on corruption, migration, and everyday living all the time while it remained centered on his wife, an unassailable figure who grew more "omnipresent" in his very efforts to evade her machinations.

I had conducted fieldwork in urban and rural areas in Guyana over a sustained period. At an earlier stage, I had worked as a journalist: subsequently, I had written my first novel (Shewcharan 1994). I never met anyone like Bhola Ram: he could have been a composite, or existed in his own right. He was "pure invention," but his story resonated with the life experiences of others. He came alive as a Creolese speaker, an experimental writing mode for me; later on, I thought of "declaring" his additional language skills so that he could "tell" his story to wider audience. But mainly because this was a short story, and already published, it did not seem to be what I should talk about. At an early stage in the field, I had half begun a novel then left it aside. One of the characters was a male anthropologist who wandered around seemingly unaware of how the locals saw him; as the fictional account developed, he was compassionate and more local than was credited by his appearance; by their gentle and affectionate mockery, his interlocutors knew this too. It sounded familiar and delving into texts and critiques, he could have some synergies with various historical figures. I saw it developing away from these critiques, partly into a comical series of errors and where locals had central voices and told "stories." Its unfinished state put it down as a work in progress. I stopped working on it to continue my research, which also brought out critical examining of my positionality within the field and encounters with participants (Halstead 2001).

My "life-writing" had become centered on my positioning and research as an anthropologist. This was a different mode of representation, studying the "imponderabilia of everyday life" through long-term research in named fieldsites. *The writing* became guided by debates and the fieldwork, garnering a central space that placed limits on the textual bids for "novels in progress." At the time, I thought at some stage I would continue this particular work and at the Twickenham conference read a number of pages from it. It seemed like some kind of continuation.

An anthropology professor was present at another Brunel conference that was being held in the next room and spoke with me during the break. Which conference was I *really* attending? An unspoken question. He was slightly bemused. New questions arose for me as well: Was I collapsing a boundary or returning elsewhere…? What was my *position?* The position of my writing? No one had said anything to me. I was already immersed in various anthropological knowledge debates, which were bringing out distinctions between different kinds of writing: I was making different choices in this processual journey.

For some earlier women anthropologists such as Laura Bohannan, disguised as Eleanor Smith-Bowen, in *Return to Laughter,* such distinctions were deemed absolutely necessary (see Clifford 1986: 13). Judith Okely (personal communication), discussing the experiences of Bohannan, noted that Bohannan "believed correctly that her experience had to be under a pseudonym as it would not be given academic credibility." The emphasis on protecting disciplinary boundaries here comes out in a way that seems to inevitably exclude fiction-writing and related forms of knowledge production.

Critiques about representation and scrutiny of what was unwritten *and* written have also called into question the nature of ethnography as fiction (see Clifford 1986). However, anthropological knowledge construction approaches at the same time answer these critiques and return to/protect the issue of what is privileged: attentiveness to reflexivity and grounded data in constructing the anthropological text have answered some of these critiques. Further, collapsing of the boundary between ethnography and fiction becomes more about knowledge debates that serve to re-embed epistemological integrity than about disciplinary erosion into the popular. However, the necessary anthropological boundary-making can also sweep away the separate issue of the role of the popular in the processual spaces of anthropological knowledge production.

REENGAGING THE POPULAR–JOINED SPACES

In contemporary times, I note that in the work of Amitav Ghosh, there is a reversal of this space. María Elena Martos Hueso considers that Ghosh's aim is to reengage anthropological compartmentalization as a given through his work as researcher and novelist (2007: 55). As Padmini Mongia (2005: 78) notes, he also traverses genres of writing in his book, *In an Antique Land,* which is about an Indian slave, Bomma, and Ghosh, the student anthropologist some eight hundred years after the incident. The book incorporates his anthropological research, but also appears as travel-writing. Mongia's point that the work pushes a rethinking of "traditional disciplinary forms from a post-colonial perspective" as messing with the limits in each genre suggests the subjective process that draws on the production of knowledge through experience as well as disciplinary knowledge conventions. María Elena Martos Hueso (2007: 55) notes the positionality of Ghosh as an "anthropologist from the inside" vis-à-vis knowledge debates about self/other and reflexive anthropology. James Clifford's discussion of Ghosh's work also signals the connectedness between the two domains without the same publicness of rigidly reasserting epistemic boundaries as he writes about Ghosh's locatedness in the West and his subsequent reflections of this presenced positionality. This connectedness also comes out in Ghosh's work: he discusses an ethnographic moment in the field where he is unable to answer his interlocutor's question about his own circumcision and subsequently explores this issue in relation to a childhood memory (as cited in Mongia 2005: 88). This space that seems to be so effortlessly produced, where fiction co-resides or is an extension of the anthropologist's activities, is one that also occupies newly privileged visibility. However, it takes on the processual spaces of what it means to be anthropological and the connections to life-writing.

CONCLUSION

In this account, I have considered forms of life-writing to show the anthropological co-presence as experiential, ways of being in the world. I drew on various debates, teaching, research, as well as personal accounts to reflect on this issue. This is inevitably an engagement with knowledge construction and disciplinary boundaries that simultaneously argues for experiences outside of these boundaries that provide epistemic value. In considering how life-writing contributes to this joined space, I also identified the invisibility of sets of subjective experiences that are unaccounted for or have to be separated in order to maintain particular boundaries. Relatedly, popular forms of knowledge construction are rigidly separated from anthropological knowledge approaches—in particular, the chapter pointed to fiction and journalism and also, through the C-SAP research project, indicated some of the debates in relation to media and technology as forms of the popular. However, by identifying the processual spaces of anthropological knowledge construction, the chapter also brought out a role for the popular that contributes to rather than detracts from anthropological knowledge approaches.

I considered how the distinctions discussed while indicating different kinds of knowledge production also formed a joined space to provide examples of the subjective experiences and trajectories that can be embedded within the anthropological. The chapter has, thus, considered an overlooked role of the experiential in relation to the popular and as invisible subjectivity to bring out understandings of anthropology in relation to processual engagement and, thus, embedded in the contemporary.

Narmala Halstead is an anthropologist with regional expertise on Guyana, and on migrants/Caribbean diaspora in New York. She has also conducted research on migrants in London and in Wales, UK. Her research contributes to contemporary debates on state, violence, and cosmopolitan identities in relation to extensive migration. She explores knowledge debates as a related strand of her work on research participants who see themselves as reflexive "citizens of the world." Narmala is a Reader in Anthropology at the University of East London, UK. She previously held a university lectureship at Cardiff University and also taught at Brunel University.

NOTES

1. As discussed in a previous publication (Halstead 2008), anthropological knowledge approaches are continually reexamined through "crisis modes." These modes engage debates, which undo, remake, and reposition particular forms of writing anthropological accounts: these forms remain within or reformulate disciplinary boundaries.
2. http://www.kent.ac.uk/sac/staff-profiles/profiles/social-anthropology/academic-staff/bowman-glenn.html.
3. Kuper also points to the "mythical charter" that was developed in relation to Bronislaw Malinowski's work (1983: 10).

4. These are now part of wider debates and knowledge exchanges (see Eriksen 2006). Conferences in 2012 by the Royal Anthropological Institute, the American Anthropological Institute, and the American Ethnologist Society all engaged with these themes of anthropology and wider engagement. See also the theme for the 2015 Royal Anthropological Institute conference.

5. This lecture was subsequently published in the Journal of Royal Anthropological Institute (Strathern 2006).

6. Strathern notes: "In order to have argued you needed to have detached yourself—divided yourself off—from competing viewpoints you might otherwise have (in a different life) occupied" (2006: 192).

7. Centre for Sociology, Anthropology and Politics.

8. I obtained a permanent lectureship with Cardiff University in 2003.

9. The then Head of School, Terry Threadgold, would later note my passion for what she saw to be new ethnography as "contagious," adding that "a number of students managed to carry out remarkable and innovative projects" (personal communication).

10. Marcus Schlecker and Eric Hirsch (2001) explore this adoption of ethnography in media and cultural studies as well as science and technology studies to consider perceived limits of ethnography and how these relate to Euro-American knowledge conventions.

11. I have also written two other novels.

12. In effect, this space co-existed with a controlled arena. Some of the journalists participated in high-level state breakfasts or briefings: the more outlandish requests and the ways in which these occurred trickled down as breaches of secrets with little commentary, leaving the actual "disclosure" of these requests to speak for themselves. The talk and knowledge as a particular forms of insider secrets supported an official atmosphere of ordered writing and the fiction that censorship was routine.

13. For anthropological understandings of this notion of distance as being "away" while being involved, see also Clifford Geertz's reference to the Balinese on their initial distance when he turned up to do fieldwork in their village (1972: 2).

14. See Barbara Bender's (2001) point about landscape being about movement.

15. I was teaching at Brunel after finishing my Ph.D. in 2000 when I met by chance a lecturer in the Department of English at Brunel, Paula Burnett, who was organizing a writers' conference at the Twickenham Campus. On learning of my writing and published novelist status (Shewcharan 1994), she invited me to be a speaker at this conference.

REFERENCES

Bender, Barbara. 2001. "Introduction." In *Contested Landscapes: Movement, Exile and Place*, ed. Barbara Bender and Margot Winer. Oxford: Berg.

Clifford, James. 1986. "Introduction: Partial Truths." In *Writing Culture: The Poetics and Politics of Ethnography,* ed. James Clifford and George Marcus. Berkeley: University of California Press.

———. 1997. *Routes: Travel and Translation in the Late Twentieth Century.* Cambridge, MA: Harvard University Press.

Clifford, James, and George Marcus, eds. 1986. *Writing Culture: The Poetics and Politics of Ethnography.* Berkeley: University of California Press.

Eriksen, Thomas Hylland. 2006. *Engaging Anthropology: The Case for a Public Presence.* Oxford: Berg.

Geertz, Clifford. 1972. "Deep Play: Notes on the Balinese Cockfight." *Daedalus* 101: 1–37.

Halstead, Narmala. 2001. "Ethnographic Encounters: Positionings within and outside the Insider Frame." *Social Anthropology* 9: 307–221.

———. 2005. "Modes of Knowing: The Instant-Expert Frame, Popular Representations and Reflexivity." Paper presented at Fudan University.

———. 2008. "Experiencing the Ethnographic Present: Knowing through Crisis." In *Knowing How to Know: Fieldwork and the Ethnographic Present,* ed. Narmala Halstead, Eric Hirsch, and Judith Okely. Oxford: Berghahn.

———. 2012 "Undoing Resistance: East Indians beyond the Culture Bound." *South Asian Diaspora* 10, no. 2: 123–135.

Halstead, Narmala, Eric Hirsch, and Judith Okely, eds. 2008. *Knowing How to Know: Fieldwork and the Ethnographic Present.* Oxford: Berghahn.

Hirsch, Eric. 1995. "Introduction: Landscape: Between Place and Space." In *The Anthropology of Landscape: Perspectives on Space and Place,* ed. Eric Hirsch and Michael O'Hanlon. Oxford: Clarendon Press.

———. 2001. "When Was Modernity in Melanesia?" *Social Anthropology* 9, no. 2: 131–146.

Hueso, María Elena Martos. 2007. "The Subaltern Ethnographer: Blurring the Boundaries through Amitav Ghosh's Writing." *Miscelánea: A Journal of English and American Studies* 36: 55–66.

Kuper, Adam. 1984. *Anthropology and Anthropologists.* London: Routledge and Kegan Paul plc.

———. 1986. "An Interview with Edmund Leach." *Current Anthropology* 27, no. 4: 375–382.

Leach, Edmund. 2002 [1954]. *Political Systems of Highland Burma: A Study of the Kachin Social Structure.* Oxford: Berg.

Orwell, George. 1949. *Nineteen Eighty-Four.* London: Penguin Books.

Mongia, Padmini. 2005. "Medieval Travel in Postcolonial Times: Amitav Ghosh's *In an Antique Land.*" In *Amitav Ghosh: A Critical Companion,* ed. Tabish Khair. Delhi: Permanent Black.

Moores, Shaun. 1996. *Interpreting Audiences: The Ethnography of Media Consumption.* London: Sage Publications.

Muneshwar, Tanita Amanda. 2009. "(Her)stories Written: The Construction of Identity through Politics, Culture and Education in the Novels of Contemporary Indo-Guyanese Women." M.A. thesis, York University.

Narayan, Kirin. 1993. "How Native is a 'Native' Anthropologist?" *American Anthropologist* 95, no. 3: 671–686.

Radcliffe-Brown, Alfred. 1952. *Structure and Function in Primitive Society*. Glencoe, IL: The Free Press

Schlecker, Marcus, and Eric Hirsch. 2001. "Incomplete Knowledge: Ethnography and the Crisis of Context in Studies of Media, Science and Technology." *History of Human Sciences* 14, no. 1: 69–87.

Scott, James C. 1990. Domination and the arts of resistance: hidden transcripts. New Haven: Yale University Press.

Shewcharan, Narmala. 1994. *Tomorrow is Another Day*. Leeds: Peepal Tree Books.

——. 2000. "Janjhat: Bhola Ram and the Going Away Plan." In *Jahaji Bhai*, ed. Frank Birbalsingh. Toronto: Tsar.

Stocking, George W. Jr. 1985 [1983]. "History of Anthropology: Whence/Whither." In *Observers Observed: Essays on Ethnographic Fieldwork*, ed. George W. Stocking. Madison: University of Wisconsin Press.

——. 1991. "Maclay, Kubary, Malinowski: Archetypes from the Dreamtime of Anthropology." In *Colonial Situations: Essays on the Contextualization of Ethnographic Knowledge*, ed. George W. Stocking Jr. Madison: University of Wisconsin Press.

Strathern, Marilyn. 1999. *Property, Substance and Effect: Anthropological Essays on Persons and Things*. London: Athlone Press.

——. 2006. "A Community of Critics? Thoughts on New Knowledge." *Journal of the Royal Anthropological Institute* 12, no. 1: 191–209.

Chapter 9

Chekhov as Ethnographic Muse

Kirin Narayan

Anton Chekhov walked into a book I was writing about fifty pages into the first draft. He wasn't yet leaning on the cane that so often appears in photographs of him from the years that his energy was diminished by tuberculosis, and he didn't yet peer through a pince-nez. He came striding into my manuscript with energetic purpose: a tall bearded young man with dark hair combed back from his forehead.

I had been drafting chapters, trying to work out how ethnographers might acquire tools for vivid storytelling used by writers of creative nonfiction and also how writers of creative nonfiction might gain from ethnographic methods and perspectives. Arriving at the second chapter, "Place," I found myself in the doldrums that so often accompany the start of writing projects. Fidgeting, restless, I broke away from the computer screen to rummage again through files assembled in the course of teaching ethnographic writing classes and workshops. I came up with a few pages that my friend and colleague Frank Salomon had dropped off in my campus mailbox some months earlier. These were from a translation of Anton Chekhov's nonfiction 1895 book, *Ostrov Sakhalin,* about the tsarist penal colony on the island of Sakhalin off Russia's Pacific coast.

Chekhov is celebrated mostly for his short stories and his plays. Almost six hundred stories of varied length, and four major plays—translated, read, performed, adapted, updated—have secured his bright luster in world literature. Yet his one nonfiction book is less well known. Even across time and translation, I was struck by the energetic immediacy of Chekhov's accounts of Sakhalin Island. Assuring myself that this was not procrastination, I set off to the library in quest of the entire work. As I tried to understand why and how Chekhov had turned to nonfiction, and what a writer of his brilliance might offer ethnography, Chekhov began moving through every chapter in my unfolding book.

Other anthropologists have been drawn to the galvanizing energy of celebrated writers of world literature for their own books, whether Jane Austen (Handler and Segal 1990), EM Forster (Rapport 1994), or even William Shakespeare (Hastrup 2004). Scores more anthropologists have written about the ethnographic insights opened by creative writers, especially those associated with their fieldsites (i.e., Archetti 1994; Cohen 2013; Dennis and Aycock 1998; Herzfeld 1997; Wulff 2015). In this essay I share a few highlights about Chekhov's ethnographically informed work. First, I draw on letters reconstructing his own vision for his journey to Sakhalin. Second, I present his accounts of research and the process of writing his book. Third, I reflect on the book's strange form and consider the ways that Chekhov's use of juxtaposition and imagined alternatives open possibilities for ethnographic technique. I end by returning to how Chekhov gave me new ways to think about ethnographic process and also a cord of continuity for structuring my own book on writing. If I start with a writer turning himself into an anthropologist of sorts, then, I conclude with reflections on the anthropologist as writer who may find herself in unexpected apprenticeship to other great writers.

PREPARING THE RESEARCH

The island of Sakhalin lies in the Pacific, just north of Japan and off the eastern coast of the Russian mainland. Since 1947, this has been under Russian administration and a major source of petroleum and gas. In the nineteenth century and again in the early twentieth century, the proximity to two regional powers meant that control of parts of the island or the whole island shifted at various junctures between Japan and Russia. Russia claimed the northern part in 1857, three years before Chekhov's birth, and the southern part was ceded to Russia by Japan in 1875. The tsarist government began actively colonizing the entire island, shipping in large numbers of convicts for both labor and settlement.

Chekhov became interested in Sakhalin in the fall of 1889, when he happened to read the lecture notes on criminal law that his younger brother Mikhail was reviewing for a civil service exam. At this time, Chekhov was on the cusp of thirty, already a trained doctor and a celebrated writer whose earnings helped support his parents and siblings. Widely adored for his charm, talent, and playful humor, he had just won half of the prestigious Pushkin prize for his third collection of stories. So in the spring of 1890, when he announced that he would travel that summer to Sakhalin—the farthest spot from Moscow in the entire multiethnic Russian empire—Chekhov mystified his family, friends, and fans. He then puzzled them even further by shutting himself away to read every book, article, and government report he could find about the Sakhalin penal colony. Writing his friend and patron, the newspaper editor Alexei Suvorin from Moscow that February, Chekhov reported: "The work I am engaged in now is varied but very tedious. I must turn myself into a geologist and then a meteorologist and then an ethnographer, and since I'm not experienced at any of this I get bored. I'll go on doing my research about Sakhalin until March, until I run out of money, and then I'll settle down to write some stories" (A. Chekhov 2004a: 200). With the self-mocking playfulness that glints in many of his letters, Chekhov went on to warn his friend, "My work on Sakhalin will make me look like such a learned son of a bitch that you will simply have to throw up your hands" (A. Chekhov 2004a: 201).

Born in 1860 in the provincial, multiethnic port town of Taganrog (that lies off the Sea of Asov to the northwest of the Black Sea), Chekhov was the grandson of freed serfs on both his mother's and his father's sides. His father, a shopkeeper, was forced to declare bankruptcy and left for Moscow when Chekhov was just sixteen. The rest of the family reassembled in Moscow, where they lived in poverty, but Chekhov was left behind in Taganrog to finish high school. He was able to win a scholarship to medical school in Moscow and joined his parents and siblings. For extra income, Chekhov turned his hand to any kind of paid writing available in magazines and newspapers: short funny sketches, stories, accounts of legal proceedings, reviews, literary gossip, and even the text to accompany cartoons. He wrote under various pseudonyms—particularly "Antosha Chekhonte"—and turned out to possess such a distinctive and abundant talent that even after graduating in 1884, and beginning to practice medicine, he continued writing stories. Eventually, his life as a writer sidelined his medical practice.

Chekhov's younger brother Mikhail's memoir (translated in 2010 as *Anton Chekhov: A Brother's Memoir*), indirectly suggests their mother Evgenia's influence on Chekhov's reasons for writing about Sakhalin. Describing their childhood in the provincial western town of Taganrog, Mikhail recalls how the family watched public executions through the windows, "with our Mother, Evgenia Yakovlevna, sighing deeply and crossing herself. She believed that even criminals were worthy of compassion and that they were oppressed by the powerful, and she instilled in us this attitude" (M. Chekhov 2010: 19). Their mother, Mikhail remembered, also went each year "to the all-night vigil at the jail's chapel to talk to the convicts about what they needed and listen to their stories of why they were in jail" (M. Chekhov 2010: 19).

I looked through the assorted letters of Chekhov now available in English translation in various selections and editions culled from the over five thousand pieces of correspondence that his adoring sister Masha assembled after he died. I wasn't able to locate any evidence of Chekhov himself making a link between traveling to Sakhalin and his mother's actions. Yet perhaps some echo of his mother's compassion, indignation, and determination to listen to prisoners' stories guided his interest. Writing again to Suvorin, Chekhov sharply responded to his friend's suggestion that no one was interested in Sakhalin. Rather, Chekhov emphasized that everyone in Russian society was culpable for allowing such suffering:

> From the books I've read and am now reading, it is evident that we have let *millions* of people rot in jails, we have let them rot to no purpose, unthinkingly and barbarously. We have driven people through the cold in chains, across tens of thousands of versts, we have infected them with syphilis, debauched them, bred criminals and blamed it all on red-nosed prison wardens. Now all educated Europe knows all of us, not the wardens are to blame, but it's still none of our business; it's of no interest to us (Karlinsky 1975: 159–160).

In addition to such outrage, Chekhov also explained his interest through an obligation to medicine. As he wrote his friend: "I want to write at least one or two hundred pages to pay off some of my debt to medicine, towards which, as you know, I've behaved like a pig" (Karlinsky 1975: 158–159).

What was this debt? Chekhov had been intending to write a dissertation ever since he received his medical degree in 1884, as this would enable him to lecture at Moscow University. Chekhov first prepared himself for research through extensive reading, with his younger sister Masha and her friends helping out to assemble a long list of works on Sakhalin. "I spend all day, every day sitting, reading, and copying out excerpts," he wrote a fellow writer, "There is nothing either in my head or on paper except Sakhalin." He then went on to playfully invent a medical diagnosis for his obsession: "Derangement of the mind. *Mania Sachalinosa*" (A. Chekhov 2004a: 199).

Chekhov was not simply reading but also critically evaluating what he read in light of when this text was written as well as the author's degree of engagement, and motive for writing at all. As he wrote his brother Alexander, "The facts and figures are clearly important in themselves, but…I shall need to know the historical context in which they have been set out. The articles were written either by people who had never been to Sakhalin and had no conception of what it was really like, or by interested parties who had invested capital in Sakhalin business and wanted to protect their innocence" (A. Chekhov 2004a: 202).

In April 1890, Chekhov set off on an uncomfortable journey along rutted, barely passable roads across Siberia and toward Sakhalin. Between May and June, he sent Suvorin's newspaper *New Times* nine articles about his travels that are reprinted as "From Siberia" at the beginning of Brian Reeve's translation, *Sakhalin Island* (A. Chekhov 2007: 3–37). He also sent many lively letters to friends and family, describing encounters and adventures en route. With a playful allusion to his ultimate destination, he signed off a letter to his family as, "Your Homo Sachaliensis" (A. Chekhov 2004a: 232). Yet after he sailed across the Tatar Strait to the island in Sakhalin, Chekhov was almost entirely out of contact by mail.

RESEARCH AND WRITING UP

Soon after his arrival on the island on 11 July 1890, while still adjusting to the smell of burning forest, clouds of mosquitoes, and the clank of shackles in the main northwest settlement, Chekhov arranged for ten thousand cards to be printed up at the police department's printing shop that he intended to use for a makeshift census. As he later confessed, these cards were more a pretext for him to interact with people and gain an impression of their lives than to generate exhaustive figures (A. Chekhov 2007: 65). The bureaucratic quality of filling out cards did not disturb the prison administration, who even offered him assistants. Chekhov then began traveling around the island, from settlement to settlement, interacting with as many people as he could. While stacking up cards, he also recorded the living conditions of prisoners doing forced labor, settled exiles, free people who had followed family members to this desolate colony, officials, and to a lesser extent, Sakhalin's indigenous peoples. (He was not, however, allowed to speak with political exiles.)

Each card carried twelve categories. Starting with the settlement's name and house number, it then moved on to the status of the person, listing four subcategories (a straightforward "convict" could with time become a "settled-exile" and then "peasant-in-exile;" and a "free" person could join the settlement by choice). Then came spaces for the person's name, age, religion, place of birth, year of arrival in Sakhalin, chief occupation, literacy, married status, and whether or not they received any support from the state. Gender seems to have been added as an afterthought, with women's cards marked with a lengthwise stroke of a red pencil.

Perhaps Chekhov's own background as a poor provincial boy who had come to interact with the Moscow elite, along with his experience as a doctor who treated many sorts of people, helped him interact with people of many social strata. A prison official later marveled: "Chekhov chatted at length with the convicts in the prisons. He possessed the knack of being able to win them over, and they related to him with an unusual degree of trust" (Reeve 1993 22). That Chekhov's mother had once listened to such stories perhaps also contributed to his finding rapport in these interactions.

Midway through his research, as he sailed from the north to the south of the island, Chekhov was again able to communicate with Suvorin. "I saw everything, so the problem now is not *what* I saw, but *how* I saw it," he wrote his friend. He went on: "I don't know what I'll end up with, but I've gotten a good deal accomplished. I have enough for three dissertations. I got up every day at five in the morning, went to bed late, and spent all my days worrying about how much I had yet to do. Now that I'm done with the penal colony, I have the feeling I've seen it all, but missed the elephant" (Karlinsky 1975: 171). Here Chekhov seems to be drawing a distinction between what was readily apparent and how this should be interpreted. He also offers a glimpse of how hard he worked and the vastness of the undertaking. In mentioning too what he might have missed, hidden in plain sight, he is perhaps also alluding to the sinister structures of power surrounding all the observable details of the northern penal colony.

Through Sakhalin's brief summer season, Chekhov amazingly managed to fill out close to all ten thousand cards, to visit government archives, and to take copious notes. He left Sakhalin on 13 October 1890, and sailed by way of Hong Kong, Ceylon, and Odessa to arrive back in Moscow by rail in early December. Yet on his return, finding the time to write the book amid other obligations was a challenge. The summer after his return, Chekhov reported to Suvorin, "I'm working on my Sakhalin book and, in between times, so as not to starve my family to death, I caress my muse and write short stories" (McVay 1994: 109). Through the next few years, he continued to work on the book even as he wrote short stories and a novella, moved his parents and siblings to the countryside outside Moscow, organized famine relief, worked as a doctor to battle a cholera epidemic, and helped out with a local census.

As someone more accustomed to inventing characters and situations, Chekhov also chafed at being bound to facts, complaining to Suvorin about how he was "forced for the sake of a single mangy line or other to rummage among papers for a full hour" (Coope 1997: 72). After writing a first draft, he started all over again in 1893. He instructed Suvorin:

> Forget what I've shown you, for it is all false. I kept writing and kept feeling I was on the wrong track, until I finally discovered where the false note was. It was in my trying to teach something to someone with my *Sakhalin* and at the

same time trying to conceal something and to hold myself back. But as soon as I started to admit what an oddball I felt like while I was on Sakhalin and what swine live there things became easy and my work surged ahead, even though it is ending up a bit on the humorous side (Karlinsky 1975 271).

Rather than instruct from a distance—teaching "something to someone"—Chekhov allowed his own presence, feelings, and opinions to guide the text. In doing this, he also made readers fellow-witnesses to the horror and the absurdities of all he encountered.

While Chekhov contributed an early chapter about people who tried to escape the island to an edited collection (*Help for the Starving*, intended to raise funds for famine relief) it was only in 1893 and 1894 that he began actively publishing a sequence of chapters in the scholarly journal *Russian Thought*. As Chekhov wrote, his chapters had to be first inspected by the Central Prison Department before publication was approved (Reeve 1993: 26). He walked a fine line of risking censorship as he documented the dreadful living conditions, the smug and callous bureaucracy, and the range of punishments forced on prisoners—hard labor, fetters, being chained to wheelbarrows, brutal floggings, executions. He outlined the further injustices that emerged in this setting where children could not receive a decent education, young girls and women were forced into prostitution, food rations were dismal, medical supplies were minimal, and a brisk profit could be made by pretending to help others escape and instead turning them in for bounty. Censors only began objecting with later chapters (later to form 20 and 21 in the book) in which Chekhov discussed more general issues, such as the bored soldiers, unreliable and exploitative overseers, the prevalence of petty crime and prostitution, local forms of punishment, and a searing account of the flogging he witnessed. Despite not having received approval for those chapters, Chekhov decided to risk publishing an entire volume composed of all he had published so far, the chapters that hadn't been cleared, and a new chapter about disease and medical facilities on the island. As he wrote Suvorin, "Well, we're releasing Sakhalin without waiting for permission. It will be a thick book with endless footnotes, anecdotes and statistics. Who knows? We may get away with it. And if we don't, so be it, we all die in the end" (Karlinsky 1975: 271).

ETHNOGAPHIC ASPECTS OF SAKHALIN ISLAND

As Chekhov warned, *Ostrov Sakhalin* did turn out to be a very thick book, dense with footnotes, anecdotes, and statistics. The censors did not end up blocking the work and its publication brought some limited reforms to the conditions on Sakhalin. Chekhov also looked into the possibility of submitting the book to Moscow University as his dissertation in medicine. Though it was not accepted as a dissertation, writing the book appears to have given Chekhov the sense of having discharged the "debt to medicine" that he had alluded to when preparing for departure. As he wrote Suvorin when the chapters were being serialized, "Medicine can no longer accuse me of unfaithfulness: I've paid my debt to scholarship and to what older writers called 'pedantry.' And I'm glad that this rough convict's smock shall take its place in my literary wardrobe..." (McVay 1994: 143).

Translated into English, *Ostrov Sakhalin* carries such names as *The Island: A Journey to Sakhalin* (A. Chekhov 1967), *A Journey to Sakhalin* (A. Chekhov 1993), and simply *Sakhalin Island* (A. Chekhov 2007). Sections of the book are also extracted in Piero Brunello and Lena Lenček's sparkling short manual, *How to Write Like Chekhov* (A. Chekhov 2008). As a capacious book with twenty-three chapters, this is a frankly daunting read and I suspect confounds most readers who attempt to read it right through (each time I try, in different translations and type faces, I instead skip around, dipping in and flipping ahead). Partly, I think this is because Chekhov himself jumps around abruptly, rarely preparing readers for his transitions between general descriptions, statistics, other people's stories, and vividly observed scenes. The book's structure can seem chaotic. It takes some study with a map to figure out the movement of the first fourteen chapters from the Russian mainland to Sakhalin and then between various settlements: from the northwest to the northeast, and then, after a trip south by steamer, from the southwest to southeast through areas that had been recently occupied by Japan. The sequence of the next nine chapters, organized around themes, is even less clear.

In the final chapter, after enumerating illnesses and commonly reported causes of death on Sakhalin, Chekhov moves from being an observer to being a doctor treating outpatients at an infirmary while an overseer with a revolver and a few other men and women mill around, giving him and the patients no privacy. Trying to lance a boil on a small boy's neck, he notes that he was handed a blunt scalpel, was given antiseptic only after a delay, and that there was "no wash-basin, no balls of cotton-wool, no probes, no decent scissors and not even water in sufficient quantity" (A. Chekhov 1993 358). The absence of supplies and functioning equipment, he shows, absolutely does not match the government records on expenditures. Continuing with this damning portrayal of official versions, the book's final paragraph cites, without comment, laws insisting that labor is not permitted if it harms either convicts' health or the well-being of their breastfeeding infants.

There's no doubt that scenes and sections of *Sakhalin Island* display Chekhov's virtuosity as a writer, yet these are usually welded without break to other sections of a different weight, voice, and seeming purpose. The Chekhov of short stories and novellas who follows characters and their transformations with a subtle, spare tone becomes instead a Chekhov whose commitment to being thorough and scholarly results in an overpacked, even chaotic collage. As the literary critic Janet Malcolm writes in her wonderful book *Reading Chekhov:*

> In the book on Sakhalin, Chekhov wrote from file cards and scholarly books and reports. His customary artist's fearlessness gave way to a kind of humility, almost a servility, before the ideal of objectivity and the protocols of scientific methodology. Like a convict chained to a wheel-barrow (one of the punishments at Sakhalin), he drags along the burden of his demographic, geographic, agricultural, ethnographic, zoological, and botanical facts. He cannot omit anything; his narrative line is constantly being derailed by his data. (Malcolm 2001: 126)

Malcolm goes on to assert that "in rendering the sufferings on this island of the damned, Chekhov could not achieve in three hundred pages what he achieve in a four-page passage at the end of his story 'The Murder' (1895) about Sakhalin convicts in fetters loading coal onto a steamer on a stormy night" (Malcolm 2001: 127). Rereading "The Murder," one sees the skill with which a fiction writer can metamorphose knowledge gained from accessing "the native's point of view" to speak from within that very subjective experience (Narayan 1999).

Other critics have also tried to make sense of this shambling text. In an article titled "Chekhov as Ethnographer," the Slavic Studies scholar Cathy Popkin argues that Chekhov was stymied by the chaos on Sakhalin, and that this "epistemological crisis leads to severe representational distress" (1992: 45); rounding up a wealth of documentation on how other scholars and writers have variously discussed this book, she describes *Sakhalin Island* as "truly one of the strangest documents in any genre" (1992: 48). Responding to Popkin, the environmental historian and historian of medicine Conevery Bolton Valencius (2007) locates the book's form amid writings in the field of medical geography during Chekhov's time, arguing that Chekhov reveals a callous lack of fit, deleterious to health, between the Sakhalin environment and the forms of life that had been imposed on the place. Another Slavic Studies scholar, Juras Ryfa (1999) devotes an entire book to the question of genre in the book, arguing that Chekhov interweaves travel, scientific and literary discourses. Most recently, the writer Akhil Sharma (2015) has insisted that this is a brilliant piece of investigative journalism, and that critics are confused about form because of the "lies" that Chekhov told (for example, claiming that this was for a dissertation, or that he was just doing a survey).

I can only convey the vivid force of Chekhov's descriptions by repro-ducing short sections. To acknowledge different translations, I first quote a scene from the translation by Luba and Michael Terpak, *The Island: A Journey to Sakhalin* (1967). This is a scene that Chekhov had recorded in a letter to a lawyer and writer friend soon after his return (2004a: 261–262). For the book he worked his description into a discussion of religion and of schools. This scene takes place in the course of an improvised funeral for a woman whose husband had returned to the mainland. A clerk named Kelbokiani who had been lodging in the dead woman's quarters was present and dis-traught about his default responsibility for her young children. The children had also been brought to the graveside by another woman.

> The newly dug grave was one quarter filled with water. The convicts, puffing and panting, their faces perspiring, loudly discussed something which had nothing to do with the funeral. Finally they carried up the coffin to the edge of the grave. The coffin was made of boards hastily nailed together and unpainted.
>
> "Well?" said one.
>
> They quickly dropped the coffin, which plopped into the water. Clods of clay knocked against the lid, the coffin shuddered, water splashed, and the convicts working with their shovels continued their own discussions. Kelbokiani looked at us perplexedly, stretching out his hands and complaining helplessly.
>
> "What shall I do with the children? I'm saddled with them! I went to the war-den and begged him to give me a woman, but he won't give me one!"
>
> The woman was leading the little boy, Aleshka, three or four years old, by the hand, and he stood there, gazing down at the grave. He wore a woman's blouse with long sleeves many sizes to large for him, and faded blue trousers. His knees were covered with bright-blue patches.
>
> "Aleshka, where is your mother?" asked my companion.
>
> "They b-b-buried her!" said Aleshka as he laughed and then he waved his hand toward the grave (A. Chekhov 1967: 295).

Chekhov shows the hastily improvised quality of rituals in the flux of convict lives; the casual attitude toward death; the pervasive poverty shaping the unadorned coffins and patched clothing alike; the precarious condition of women who can be abandoned, can die, can be supplied by requests to wardens; and the vulnerability of young children. The momentary glimpse of uncomprehending little Aleshka in his ragtag clothes dramatizes children's bleak prospects with an immediacy that numbers and generalities cannot reproduce.

Just as Aleshka laughs as he waves toward the grave, Chekhov again and again uses juxtapositions to jolting effect. The horror that Chekhov sees and hears is often contrasted to what seems out of place. In *Sakhalin Island* (2007) translated by Brian Reeve, for example, Chekhov describes the well-fed cat in a chaotic, filthy prison barrack (2007: 86), the cheerful singing of a mentally ill convict amid the numbing monotony of clanking fetters, thudding waves, and humming telegraph lines (2007: 129), the District Governor who confides that he couldn't sleep for a month after a convict who wasn't actually guilty survived a hanging, and had to be hung a second time (2007: 297).

Such juxtapositions extend toward imagined parallel realities. I am particularly interested in Chekhov's leap beyond describing immediacies to conjuring up what is not there. In opening out the "imaginative horizons" (Crapanzano 2004) beyond what he perceives, conjuring alternatives, Chekhov intensifies the sense of convict experience in the present. For example, here is how he describes a village square in one of the settlements:

> When walking across the square, one's imagination visualizes the hubbub of a jolly fair being held there, the resounding voices of the Uskovo Gypsies as they trade horses, the reek of tar, manure and smoked fish, the lowing of cows, and the shrill sounds of an accordion blending in with drunken songs: but the peaceful picture dissolves into thin air when you suddenly hear the sounds you have come to detest, the clank of chains and the hollow footfall of prisoners and guards crossing the square to the prison (A. Chekhov 2007: 151–152).

By making present the absent sounds and smells that readers of his time might have associated with settlements on the mainland, Chekhov enhances the bleakness of clanking chains as convicts are marched back into the prison by the guards.

Chekhov also enhances what he sees by juxtaposing how the same scene might flash into other imaginations. For example, after entering a graveyard filled with identical crosses, he thinks of where else these lost lives might be recalled:

> ...these people, lying under little crosses, people who committed murders, escaped, clanked along in shackles, nobody has any need to remember. Only somewhere, perhaps in the Russian steppes, by a bonfire or in a wood, an elderly wagon-driver will, out of boredom, tell a tale about how so-and-so in his village went off on an orgy of violent highway robbery; the listener will glance at

the darkness and shudder, while a night-bird shrieks—and that is all the funeral feast he will get (A. Chekhov 2007: 270).

Here, the faraway imagined scene of a story being told to fill the time, horrifying a listener, adds an extra dimension of poignancy to the silent rows of crosses.

Chekhov also heightens descriptions of what is present with imagined disruptions: "It is always quiet in Dooay. The ear soon grows accustomed to the slow, measured jangling of fetters, the thunder of the breakers on the sea and the humming telegraph wires, and because of these sounds the impression of dead silence grows still stronger. Severity and rigorousness lie not merely on the striped posts. If someone should unexpectedly burst into loud laughter in the street, it would sound harsh and unnatural" (2007: 129). Notice how sound itself is in flux here: the "quiet" morphs into the steadiness of constituent sounds, and then the very severity of silence is further emphasized by the contrast of imagined joyous laughter. This passage goes on, playing with further variations on sound. Not only would laughter be incongruous, but song would too. Chekhov observes that "life here has taken a form which can be communicated only through hopeless and implacably cruel sounds," noting how, though a cold wind seems to sing in key, the singing of a convict sounds out of place (2007: 129).

CONCLUSIONS

When I began my book on ethnographic writing, I had already been thinking of how techniques used by writers of fiction (Narayan 1999) and creative nonfiction (Narayan 2007) might be adapted to ethnography. Meeting Chekhov's practice of ethnography in *Sakhalin Island,* my book was rerouted. Chekhov came to occupy so much of the book that the title, *Alive in the Writing* eventually demanded a subtitle, *Crafting Ethnography in the Company of Chekhov.*

I had thought at first that I might work sections from *Sakhalin Island* into an early chapter titled "Place." For this chapter, as with others, I intended to reproduce short extracts from ethnographies I'd found inspiring, supplementing each extract with a prompt for writing. But in the course of learning about Chekhov's travels to Sakhalin I was increasingly intrigued by Chekhov himself. Who was this person? I felt the presence of a quick, alert sensibility in Chekhov's words and I was drawn to knowing more about him as a person. Simultaneously, I could see that when ethnography enters the hands of writers without stakes in anthropology, the loosening of disciplinary conventions opens out new possibilities in form. I hoped that close reading might help me better comprehend even a small segment of such expanded possibilities.

By the time I needed to draft my next chapter on "Person," I wasn't ready to leave Chekhov behind. I continued bringing home more books from the library: not just further editions of *Sakhalin Island,* but stories in different translations and selections, different collections of letters. I also found Chekhov's notebooks, novellas, and plays, and began venturing toward edited volumes and biographies with "Chekhov" in the title. I was especially drawn to the ways that his contemporaries conjured his presence in reminiscences published after he died of complications from tuberculosis in 1904, when he was just forty-four. I ended up drawing selections from their evocations of his physical being and presence to explore as prompts in my chapter on "Person." Having started on this track, I continued to comb through writings by and about Chekhov as I conceptualized succeeding chapters. For "Voice," I integrated accounts of his spoken and written voice, and his advice to other writers. For "Self," I reflected on Chekhov's self-professed "autobiographobia" and what parts of himself he revealed in different genres. For a chapter on tips for the writing process, I drew on letters describing his struggles with writing about Sakhalin Island.

For a chapter that I wrote last, but that eventually became the first, "Story and Theory," I reflected on the ethnographic aspects of Chekhov's life and wider body of writing, and the ways in which his insights on asking questions to organize insights might speak to ethnography. I noticed how, in Chekhov's wider body of writings and especially the short stories, he displays an ethnographer's ability to move between social locations, making the strange familiar, the familiar strange. I was struck by his capable handling of multiple professional identities: his life as a doctor and a writer in many genres became an inspiration and affirmation for my own need to write in multiple voices and ways. I savored how, in letters and in his notebooks, Chekhov could be so wittily articulate about problems of representation and the very process of writing. Again and again, I perceived how even as Chekhov was partly caught within the prejudices and conventions of his era, he was also changing his mind, growing, refining his craft, and reaching beyond his time to ours.

Even though my book is now published, I continue to learn through revisiting Chekhov. For this essay, I found fresh materials like Chekhov's brother's memoir, and also new ways to think about the force of juxtaposition—not just with what is incongruously and often ironically present but also what might be imagined. Imagination is a peculiar term to juxtapose with ethnography, for as ethnographers we are mostly trained to note the solid contours of what we empirically perceive: in short what is there. Much of our imaginative work comes later, in organizing materials and crafting arguments that connect to larger conversations. Yet the lively imaginative force that Chekhov brings to his fiction and plays adds an unexpected power to his appropriation of ethnography. Conjuring imaginative alternatives, Chekhov deepens the contingency and intensity of what is given. The imaginative horizons opening out around empirical immediacies remind readers not just of what is missing, but also how life in a seemingly set-apart prison settlement is intimately connected with other places, people, and practices of the present and future.

A year after *Sakhalin Island* appeared in print, Chekhov published a novella titled *My Life: A Provincial's Story.* The narrator Misail Poloznev is from a well-off family in a provincial town, but has idealistically resolved to live only off his own labor. At one point, he is invited to dinner by the pretty daughter of a local railway magnate. She assures him that it's dull to be rich and live off others, and then she presses him to tell her more about the housepainters he works with: "What are they like? Funny?" Misail reports, "I began telling about housepainters but was abashed, being unaccustomed, and spoke like an ethnographer, gravely and ploddingly" (A. Chekhov 2004b: 476).

It is precisely so that we can avoid being grave and plodding ethnographers that we might sometimes refresh our perspectives by looking not only to ethnographies written by anthropologists, but also the ethnographic work of brilliant literary figures like Anton Chekhov.

Kirin Narayan is Professor of Anthropology at the Australian National University. She is the author of *Alive in the Writing: Crafting Ethnography in the Company of Chekhov* (2012), *My Family and Other Saints* (2007), *Mondays on the Dark Night of the Moon: Himalayan Foothill Folktales* (1997), *Love, Stars and All That* (1994), and *Storytellers, Saints and Scoundrels: Folk Narrative in Hindu Religious Teaching* (1989). Her next book, *Everyday Creativity,* will appear in 2016.

REFERENCES

Archetti, Eduardo, ed. 1994. *Exploring the Written: Anthropology and the Multiplicity of Writing.* Oslo: Scandinavian University Press.

Chekhov, Anton Pavlovich. 1967. *The Island: A Journey to Sakhalin.* Trans. Luba and Michael Terpak. New York: Washington Square Press.

——. 1987. *Notebook of Anton Chekhov.* Trans. SS Koteliansky and Leonard Woolf. New York: Ecco Press: Distributed by WW Norton.

——. 1993. *A Journey to Sakhalin.* Trans. Brian Reeve. Cambridge: Ian Faulkner.

———. 2004a. *Anton Chekhov: A Life in Letters.* Trans. and ed. Rosamund Bartlett. London: Penguin.

———. 2004b. *The Complete Short Novels.* Trans. Richard Pevear and Larissa Volokhonsky. New York: Everyman's Library.

———. 2007. *Sakhalin Island.* Trans. Brian Reeve. Oxford: Oneworld Classics.

———. 2008. *How to Write Like Chekhov: Advice and Inspiration, Straight from His Own Letters and Work,* Trans. Lena Lenček, ed. and intr. Piero Brunello and Lena Lenček. Cambridge, MA: Da Capo Lifelong.

Chekhov, Mikhail. 2010. *Anton Chekhov: A Brother's Memoir.* Trans. Eugene Alpers. New York: Palgrave Macmillan.

Clifford, James. 1988. On Ethnographic Surrealism. In *The Predicament of Culture: Twentieth Century Ethnography, Literature, and Art.* Cambridge: Harvard University Press.

Cohen, Marilyn. 2013. *Novel Approaches to Anthropology: Contributions to Literary Anthropology.* Lanham: Lexington Books.

Coope, John. 1997. *Doctor Chekhov: A Study in Literature and Medicine.* Chale: Cross.

Crapanzano, Vincent. 2004. *Imaginative Horizons: An Essay in Literary Philosophical Anthropology.* Chicago and London: University of Chicago Press.

Dennis, Phillip A., and Wendell Aycock, eds. 1998. *Literature and Anthropology.* Lubbock: Texas Tech University Press.

Handler, Richard, and Daniel Segal. 1990 *Jane Austen and the Fiction of Culture.* Arizona: University of Arizona Press.

Hastrup, Kristin. 2004. *Action: Anthropology in the Company of Shakespeare.* Copenhagen: Museum Tusculanum Press.

Herzfeld, Michael. 1997. *Portrait of a Greek Imagination: An Ethnographic Biography of Andreas Nenedakis.* Chicago: University of Chicago Press.

Karlinsky, Simon. 1975. *Anton Chekhov's Life and Thought: Selected Letters and Commentary.* Trans. Michael Henry Heim in collaboration with Simon Karlinsky. Berkeley: University of California Press.

Malcolm, Janet. 2001. *Reading Chekhov: A Critical Journey.* New York: Random House.

McVay, Gordon, trans. and ed. 1994. *Chekhov: A Life in Letters.* London: Folio Society.

Narayan, Kirin. 1999. "Ethnography and Fiction: Mapping a Border." *Anthropology and Humanism* 24: 1–14.

———. 2007. "Tools to Shape Texts: What Creative Nonfiction can Offer Ethnography." *Anthropology and Humanism* 32, no. 2: 130–144.

———. 2012. *Alive in the Writing: Crafting Ethnography in the Company of Chekhov.* Chicago: University of Chicago Press.

Popkin, Cathy. 1992. "Chekhov as Ethnographer: Epistemological Crisis on Sakhalin Island." *Slavic Review* 51, no. 1: 36–51.

Rapport, Nigel 1994. *The Prose and the Passion: Anthropology, Literature and the Work of E.M. Forster.* Manchester: Manchester University Press.

Reeve, Brian. 1993. "Introduction." In *A Journey to Sakhalin,* by Anton Chekhov. Trans. Brian Reeve. Cambridge: Ian Faulkner.

Ryfa, Juras T. 1999. *The Problem of Genre and the Quest for Justice in Chekhov's The Island of Sakhalin.* Studies in Slavic Languages and Literature. Vol. 13. Lewiston, New York: The Edwin Mellen Press.

Sharma, Akhil. 2015. "Chekhov's Beautiful Nonfiction." *The New Yorker.* 2 February. http://www.newyorker.com/books/page-turner/chekhovs-beautiful-nonfiction.

Valencius, Conevery Bolton. 2007. "Chekhov's Sakhalin Island as Medical Geography." In *Chekhov the Immigrant: Translating a Cultural Icon,* ed. Michael C. Finke and Julie W. De Sherbinin. Bloomington: Slavica.

Wulff, Helena. 2015. "Anthropologist in the Irish Literary World: Reflexivity through Studying Sideways." In *Anthropology Now and Next: Essays in Honor of Ulf Hannerz,* ed. Thomas Hylland Eriksen, Christina Garsten, and Shalini Randeria. New York: Berghahn.

III.

Reaching Out
Popular Writing and Journalism

Chapter 10

On Some Nice Benefits and One Big Challenge of the Second File

Anette Nyqvist

This chapter deals with a couple of concerns that I suspect many readers already know about and have experience of but that I here wish to emphasize: on the positive side—the multiple benefits of parallel writing; on how working on different kinds of texts based on the same material not only keeps the writing process going in a steadier flow but how such cross-writing may, in fact, sharpen and better the different kinds of texts worked on simultaneously. I am here to remind you about how parallel writing can allow texts to feed into each other, maintain the flow, prevent writer's block, and keep the writer from getting bored with the text. But, and on a more negative note, I am also here to remind you of the main challenge of parallel writing: getting it all out there. For those of us who wish to write for a larger readership than the occasional cockroach in the desk drawer, getting published is a real concern and huge challenge. Getting the academic texts out there, and not only in print but in A-journal's ink (or whatever is used nowadays to fixate these tiny black symbols onto more or less white paper), is hard enough and to get the other nonacademic, parallel written texts published by newspapers, magazines, commercial publishing houses is no slighter task. So here it is— the story of one of my failures of getting that other text past the marketing people at a commercial publishing house.

The dissertation was, of course, the prioritized First file (Nyqvist 2008). After the mandatory courses, fieldwork, seemingly endless transcriptions, and organization of files of notes and documents; after (at last) deciding upon one of many possible outlines and disposition alternatives for the (still imaginary) Ph.D. thesis, I created a new file, named it "Dissertation," and set up subfiles for each chapter inside that First file on the desktop of the computer. I then created yet another new file and placed it along side the first. I named the Second file "Boken."[1] The texts I produced for the First file were all to be in English, and my very first attempt to produce text in the particular format, style, phrasing, and formality of the academic genre. All the texts for the Second file were in Swedish, in the—after more than fifteen years of earning a living writing for newspapers and magazines and nonfiction books—genre of journalistic writing that was so familiar and comfortable (Nyqvist 2003, 1999, 1997, 1995). The first and formal mission, the very reason for being at the university, was to write a dissertation in Social Anthropology. I opted to do so in English for a couple of reasons—making a larger readership possible, although still improbable (very few people read dissertations and even fewer read dissertations in Swedish), and as a personal challenge of trying to learn how to write academically and, thus, setting this specific text apart from all the others I had been writing up until then. Producing academic text *is* different from producing journalistic text and I wanted to make that very clear, not least for myself (Hannerz 2004a, 2004b).

I can think of two very successful and quite recent examples of Ph.D. students in the Department of Social Anthropology at Stockholm University who were able to write their dissertations in Swedish *and* get them published as is at commercial publishing houses (Ambjörnsson 2004; Nordin 2007). Ambjörnsson's thesis became a veritable bestseller and Nordin's is, to my knowledge, the only dissertation that has been turned into a play. I could not imagine myself embarking on such brave endeavors. Instead I aimed to keep my two texts very separate so as not to confuse myself with mixing styles and purposes. But—whatever is written and in what genre, any writer, I assume, *will* want to be read. What is the point of producing text read by no one? I do not know anything else than that the purpose of writing something is that someone reads it. Writing is a way of communicating and if there is no one in the other end, well then there is not much point to it. The mere joy of being able to express oneself is simply not enough. So, from the very beginning I decided to embark on a second, simultaneous task: besides writing the dissertation I would write another book as an investigative journalist and for a broader, Swedish, audience, presenting facts and hoping to stir debate on an important contemporary societal issue.

Being accepted into the Ph.D. program and asked to chose a topic and a field, I decided rather quickly what I wanted to focus on, what I wanted to think about and immerse myself in for the following four or five years...the Swedish national pension system. Friends and family had a hard time understanding why I chose such a boring topic, of all the things an anthropologist could investigate and of all the places one could locate an anthropological fieldwork I stayed at home and began to think about pensions (Hannerz 2010: 59–86). Honestly, I, too, had spurs of doubt and second thoughts over the years and found myself, especially November through February, wishing I were writing about something that had to be studied in a warmer and sunnier part of the world. I soon realized it could very well still be national pension systems since, when you think about it, these technocratic constructions are intriguing and interesting systems of distribution of not only money, but of social issues, of values and ideas.

A national pension system covers enormously large issues in both scale and scope; from individual through national and global levels—and back again. It touches upon everything from birth, through life, up until death. It involves issues of welfare, security, risk, and responsibility; it is both private and public and it deals with things social, economic, and political. Trying to figure out what a rather radically altered, new national pension system does to people, how it might affect their way of thinking and acting. Attempting to understand what expectations those who created the new system had of both the system and of society and the citizens, and investigating how individual citizens, in turn, reacted to the makeover of their national pension system. The main novelties of the remade pension system are that the new one is contribution-based with fixed payments and pensions pending as opposed to the previous one, from 1960, which was benefit-based, with payments pending and pensions being fixed. In the new system each citizen's pension is calculated from an entire life of employment and pension ages are "flexible," i.e., one "chooses" to retire anytime after sixty-one years of age and depending on when and if one can afford to. Also, there is the new and compulsory funded part where each individual must place part of her/his future pension capital in funds on the financial market. The new national pension scheme is constructed to be a self-regulating system where nothing more than what is paid into it is paid out. It is revised every year and if the intricate equations do not add up the entire pension system is "automatically balanced" and pension payments "adjusted," i.e., lowered, so that the system adds up. Bottom line: with the new 1990s design the politically difficult decision of raising pension ages and/or lowering pension payments is transferred to seemingly apolitical mathematical formulas, to effects of the global financial market, and to each individual citizen. How a national pension system is constructed, introduced, and received can say something about an ongoing shift in responsibility from state to citizen and new forms of governance in a contemporary welfare state (Nyqvist 2008). Good stuff to study for those of us interested in issues of power, in politics, in economy and finance and wanting to work within the subdiscipline of the anthropology of policy. Equally good stuff to investigate as a journalist and write a nonfiction, current affairs, and state of the nation kind of a book about.

While conducting fieldwork I interviewed all of the politicians and experts who constructed the new pension system and wrote the law; I also "worked" for one year within the pension system administration, or rather participated in groups that worked with public information at the two government bureaucracies in charge of the administration of the system; and for an entire summer I traveled all over Sweden interviewing "ordinary" Swedes about their views on, reactions to, feelings about, and experiences with the new pension system. After a year and a half I had a collection of surprisingly candid taped interviews with well-known and leading politicians (I soon noted that they said things on the record to me as a researcher that they would never have said to me had I sat in front of them as a journalist); I had revealing interviews with technocrats, economists, lawyers, and bureaucrats; I had been granted access to all kinds of meetings on all levels within the pension system bureaucracy and had detailed notes from innumerous meetings behind closed doors. I had piles of documents, protocols, drafts, and memos produced during a year within the national pension administration and I had my collection of voices from Swedes all over the country. All good stuff for a Ph.D. student to work with and begin to write up into a dissertation—all great stuff for an investigative journalist to write a story about contemporary politics and new expectations placed on citizens. Former and current roles connected with one study and two books. I set out to write the two texts simultaneously aiming to have the critical nonfiction book in print at the same time as the finished thesis; planning to have a dissertation dinner and release party in one. I failed, not with my parallel writing endeavor, but with the simultaneous publishing project.

The benefits of the parallel writing lie in the differences between the two texts and how these differences feed into each other, how sparks may jump from one file to the other, how ideas, words, and phrasings not suitable for texts in the First file might be perfect for those in the Second and vice versa. Some of the differences in the different types of texts are, of course, in language and tone, but also in structure and outline, and, not least, in purpose. In the academically written text one primarily presents facts and findings. The academic article is constructed so that arguments are presented and advanced so that certain points are put up for display and proven. And the backbone of the academic text is theory and analysis expressed and compiled in paragraphs that account for and explain all previous research that in some way or another bares relevance for one's own. Here the proper use of foot- or end notes and the appropriate reference system is of utmost importance. At the core of the journalistic reportage, on the other hand, is the story. Here it is all about capturing the reader's interest immediately and retaining it all through the story that one wants to tell. Journalistic text too needs to have all the facts straight, as in not only right but also double checked and verified. But, whether it is breaking news or investigative reportage, the journalistic text first and foremost tells a story, while the academic text proves a point. The reverse is, of course, to a certain extent also true: an academic text definitely needs a story but the argumentation must come before the storytelling, and, conversely, a good journalistic text certainly also needs evidence, arguments, and facts but without a good story the text crumbles and all the important arguments and revealing facts remain unrevealed.

No matter how much most of us actually enjoy writing–putting words together, building sentences, and constructing texts–it does, at times, get really, really, really boring. One grows tired of the subject, gets sick of the material, questions aims and purposes. Gets totally stuck. The darn words will not come, the thought looks awkward when spelled out, the sentences do not connect, and the paragraphs do not match. The writing is off and sour. You struggle with the simplest words and nothing, absolutely nothing, is good enough. You sit there with a bad idea spelled out in lousy writing. You have opened the faucets but only grey trinkets of still water come dripping out. There is no flow and none in sight. And everything else but writing suddenly seems urgent. Not only reading emails but actually answering them too. You tell yourself you have to check a not-really-that-important fact only to suddenly find yourself surfing way off shore. You realize you must actually have that book before you can finish the sentence and you need that particular page reference right now in order to complete the paragraph. Well, you have to visit the library. You come back with a pile of interesting volumes that you found where the book you looked for should have been had it not been misplaced. You now need a fourth cup of coffee, the kind you have to take a short walk to get. A talkative colleague walks by your room and quite to your own surprise you ask how the research is going. And then you are hungry although it is only 10:25.

All of the procrastination above can be avoided with a Second file. You sense the lack of focus coming, you feel the thoughts begin to drift, the text becomes heavy, and that overly critical voice starts to question every single word and sentence. Save it and close it. Forget about the texts in the First file for now. Open up the Second file and fire away. In different style, in other words, more tempo, more passion, more fun. Forget the references, never mind the notes. Use any word in the world *not* ending with -ization. Engage in the story; let the informants be individuals, play with them and the words

and the text. Have fun, let it flow. Your hands and thoughts have been bur-
dened and tied by decades of other people's scholarly thinking, systems of
referencing and passive, formal, cold, and impersonal sentences—and now
they are free. Free to play, poke, and persuade. Add meat to the story and
juice to the telling. Add color and flavor to the text. Feel free to sprinkle
verbal MSG[2] as a flavor enhancer to the texts in the Second file. Instead
of procrastinating promenades of mind and body you find yourself having
written 535 words and it just keeps coming. The writer's block was just a
bump, the boredom never settled, you have kept your fingertips working and
you have now found fresh air under your thoughts. It is not entirely improbable that some of the newer, lighter thoughts may fit well into the texts in
the First file. While the text gained speed, the words kept flowing, and your
mind opened up for new ideas. You got a nice little stream going and some
of it sprinkled off and found soil in the academic texts. Hmm…cutting that
entire paragraph out and pasting it there instead makes the entire argument
clearer. And having just read through that particular interview once again
looking for a quote I realize this informant's insights should be included in
the third chapter of the thesis. Save all texts in the Second file and close it
down. Open up the First file and enjoy the solemn seriousness of academic
writing, feel the security of your choice of system of reference and the com-
fort, inspiration, and excitement of basing an argument on decades of other
people's scholarly thinking. So I find that parallel writing and alternating between different kinds of texts feeds the various writing processes and keeps
the text production going in a steadier pace. I also find that working through
the same empirical material with different lenses on—or perhaps looking at
it with one eye first, then the other—opens up for alternative readings and
interpretations and paves way for new insights and ideas. Writing two texts
does not necessarily take twice the time, but with parallel writing you might
not get as much procrastination done.

Other differences, than language and style, that may feed both texts and
keep the writing process going are the variations in structure and outline.
The text in the Second file, the journalistic story, needs a hook and a story. It
begins with a hook: a clear and steady, interesting yet intriguing beginning;
a few well-phrased sentences to entice the reader, to lure her to continue,
to make the reader want to know more, to tease him to read on. That is
the hook. Then comes the story. Well told and with a graspable amount of
clearly defined characters, a thickly described environment and one big,
fat red story line running smoothly throughout the beginning, middle, and
end. Reaching the end of the story the reader has learned of a particular
problem through the experiences of others given voice through your writing. The reader swallowed the shiny hook, could not stop reading, followed

the story line until the end where all the minor threads are bound together in a nice knot so that the reader feels both satisfied and enriched from the gulp. The basic outlines of the texts in the First file are rather reversed. Instead of luring the reader into reading out of curiosity and desire to know, the academic text clearly states from the very first paragraph what can be expected, in fact what the entire text is all about: the aim of this text is this, the theoretic framework is that, the methods used in the study are such and such, the results and finding are this and that. I thus suggest that this and such may very well be so and so and I shall now show how I came to reach such a conclusion. The difference in structure and outline of texts can, much like the language and style of different texts, fruitfully feed into each other and spark the joy and flow of writing. The stiff and rigid structure of the academic text can often feel like a firm and secure construction to hold on to and to mold the text upon, especially at the stages when the material is overwhelming, thoughts are blurred and out of focus. Other times that very same structure feels like a cast iron cage, an ill-fitting piece of clothing in an itchy material and with uncomfortable seams in strange places. Save and close down the First file, open up the Second file and see the metal bars melt and the fabric loosen.

Before I go on to what I see as the one and only real challenge of parallel writing, that is if the writer intends to have the two texts read, I would like to mention an issue that can be of benefit to the processes of writing but that can also be a real and hindering challenge as academic scholars embark on what I here have described as joyful and creative writing driven by lust and the pure satisfaction of telling a good story about something really important to a great number of people. I want to clarify some things about simplification.

Yes, the texts in the Second file need to go through a simplification process. I have many times sensed the anxiety that scholars of all ranks seem to feel as they talk about writing other kinds of texts, perhaps an editorial or a response in a debate. Not to mention the high anxiety when they read the printed interview they said yes to, or the feature story based on their research, or the news article about their findings. Journalistic texts are forever and categorically doomed to simplehood. They are all simplified beyond recognition, entirely black and white, totally taken out of context and embarrassingly incorrect. And, yes, journalistic texts are often stripped off any kind of nuance and state things incorrectly due to limited time and space. And do so, at that, in big, fat, bold letters with the poor misunderstood scholar's name and picture forever attached to it. Frightful for sure. But such black and white and simple texts are often enough exactly what the journalist is expected to produce. He or she has done nothing wrong at all, just his or her job. The scholar interviewed or cited or referred to, however, should perhaps have not only asked to see the text before publication (that goes without saying) but also made the effort to better it, to rephrase, to come with suggestions of corrections. Or, even better, the scholar should from the beginning have fed the stressed-out journalist with already prepared simplifications, one-liners, and simple facts phrased by the scholar her/himself to ensure that the reporter did not have to interpret anything, just quote correctly. My point is that the scholar should understand that such are the working terms and conditions of journalists and if one agrees to participate in their arena it will be on their terms and one should be more or less prepared to do so. But my other point with this note on simplification, and in fact with this chapter, is that scholars could and should, I think, participate in the journalist's arena with their own texts, produced under different conditions than the journalist's but somewhat altered to fit to be printed on pages in that arena. Simplification does not necessarily and automatically mean that the research is blown to pieces, that the conclusions are out of whack, that the scholar is made into a fool and a simpleton. It simply means that the texts in the Second file need to focus on *one* point of argument, forward *one* empirical example to illustrate that, have a catchy beginning, have a good story, probably have no references within parentheses and preferably not one single word ending with -ization. The text needs to be simpler but it does not mean it becomes simple. The challenge is to write about a complex, intertwined, complicated, and multifaceted subject in a straightforward manner with perhaps shorter sentences, fewer syllables, and less but more precise words. Simplification does not mean it is all diminished to blunt black and white, nor that it is all a paler shade of grey, but rather that it comes alive with some well-selected prime colors to prove a point.

Now, to the one and only true challenge of having created a Second file of texts of a different kind, aimed for another readership—getting them out there, the texts that is. So—I had my First file, called "The Dissertation," containing the six subfiles, one for each chapter of the thesis-in-progress, each chapter getting more and more finalized with each reading and subsequent rewriting, until one day each part seemed ready to be linked to the other and the chapters were connected in order so that the thesis could take its shape as a whole as one document progressing in a series of versions within the comfortable setting of the First file. And—I had my Second file, called "Boken," it too containing six subfiles, one for each chapter of the investigative journalism critical nonfiction book, with an entirely different outline from the thesis, in a different language literally and in a very different style of writing. As the chapters of the thesis slowly took shape and I began to feel comfortable about the hook and story I had formulated within the Second file I wrote to seven Swedish publishing houses in an attempt to interest them in the book. This was a year and a half before my thesis was to be finished and ample time for the texts in the Second file to be both written and printed. Three publishers never answered, two replied with the standard letter of "Thank you but no thank you," and two editors let me know they were interested: one wanted more text samples and an outline of the book I had in mind, the other one thought it better to meet in person to discuss the project further. Ah, the bliss and joy of callbacks, of being on short lists, of stirring someone's interest. Inspired by the lack of total rejection I finished the most urgent texts of the First file and devoted myself to the texts of the Second. I wrote and sent the required texts to publishing house A and went to meet with editor at publishing house B. The meeting went well. Two editors present, smart and smiling, firm handshakes, nice, bright office, good coffee, large table, both well prepared, professionally excited about my proposition and outline, asking engaged questions about numbers of chapters, content, seemingly impressed by previous work as well as current, claiming to really want to publish a book on the new pension system, saying they had already thought about it, letting me know how well it would fit in with next year's production, asking me how fast I could get it done, liking the idea of simultaneous publication of the thesis and the book, setting up a meeting in two months, promising to have gained clearance "in the house" by then, could I promise to have, say, three chapters ready then? Sure! Great! Of course! Thank you! Me getting to it. Hammering away, getting into the flow of working on the chapters in the Second file, all along at times closing it down to rest in the comfortable structural cage of the chapters in the First file. Almost two months go by and the editor at publishing house A sends an email saying: "Sorry. I like the idea. I know what you want to do and I think it would have been good… But the people at marketing do not. Thanks but no thanks. And good luck." Oh, well. Does not matter. Meeting with publishing house B coming up, three chapters soon finished, idea and outline specified and clarified. *And* thesis in First file coming along nicely too.

Again, the two editors, the good coffee, the large table but smiles slightly smaller, at least that is how I remember them. Me presenting the promised texts, waiting for their part of the deal. Instead: excuses and pardons and: "You know we *had* this. It has been a smooth ride throughout the house—other editors, senior editors, planners… You know it was on the list for next year's Fall publications. And then, just last week we heard from the people at the marketing department. They say they will never be able to sell it. Marketing said No. We are so sorry, we can't do this. We were not able to get it past Marketing. But, hey, good luck!"

I walked home. Cursed Marketing. Stared at the Second file, browsed though the texts, liked them. Looked at the calendar. Closed down the Second file and devoted myself to finishing the texts in the First file. Thinking on the day of defending the dissertation, how nice it would have been to have the finished texts from the Second file there in print too. Thinking about the Third file and how the parallel texts of it kept the writing process going and the words flowing after I closed down the Second file for good. The Third file contains a series of unfinished lines of thought, descriptions of characters and places and parts of a plot with far too many loose ends still. The Third file is the embryo of a thriller, a detective novel based on the same empirical material as the thesis—Sweden's remade national pension system. The story is plotted around a psychopath cum technocrat, a dark white-collar worker, a purely evil pension system bureaucrat who cunningly kills off the majority of his own cohort so that he can afford to retire early and live well during his last 18.6 years of life. The reader does not, of course, know, until way into the story and after gory and detailed descriptions, who or what so brutally, yet ingeniously and with great variation and creativity, kills every single Swedish citizen born in 1961. I wonder if the texts in the Third file will ever get past marketing. I am, however, sure that if they do the profit that such a horror story of greed and gore in safe and secure welfare state of Sweden will generate could very well pay for the publishing of the book in the Second file.

Anette Nyqvist is an Associate Professor in Social Anthropology at Stockholm University and a researcher at Stockholm Center for Organizational Research (Score). Nyqvist's research is focused on issues of power at the nexus of statecraft and market-making. Her ongoing research is on the financial and political strategies of institutional investors and her earlier work was on the financialization and individualization of social security systems. In a new and recent academic endeavor Nyqvist reconnects with her previous occupation as a journalist and author as she studies the role of travel literature as a literary genre that mediates the world.

NOTES

1. "The Book" in Swedish.
2. MSG, monosodium glutamate, is a food additive commonly used in the food industry to enhance flavors.

REFERENCES

Ambjörnsson, Fanny. 2004. *I en Klass för Sig: Genus, Klass och Sexualitet bland Gymnasie-tjejer.* Stockholm: Ordfront.

Hannerz, Ulf. 2004a. *Foreign News: Exploring the World of Foreign Correspondents.* Chicago: University of Chicago Press.

———. 2004b. *Antropologi/Journalistik: Om Sätt att Beskriva Världen.* Lund: Studentlitteratur.

———. 2010. *Anthropology's World: Life in a Twenty-First–Century Discipline.* London: Pluto Press.

Nordin, Lissa. 2007. *Man ska ju Vara Två: Män och Kärlekslängtan i Norrländsk Glesbygd.* Stockholm: Natur & Kultur.

Nyqvist, Anette. 1995. *Mexikansk Matresa.* Stockholm: Alfabeta förlag.

———. 1997. *Vovven och Jag i Mexiko.* Stockholm: Alfabeta förlag.

———. 1999. *Tequila – Staden, Kulturen, Drycken.* Stockholm: Svenska förlaget.

———. 2003. *Rottrådar: Handbok för Historielösa.* Stockholm: Walström & Widstrand.

———. 2008. *Opening the Orange Envelope: Reform and Responsibility in the Remaking of the Swedish National Pension System.* Stockholm Studies in Social Anthropology, 64. Stockholm University.

Chapter 11

The Writer as Anthropologist

Oscar Hemer

The most intriguing literary portrait of an ethnographer that I know of is to be found in one of Jorge Luis Borges's late collections of poetry and prose, *Elogio de la sombra* (1969, as *In Praise of Darkness,* 1974). "El etnógrafo" is a short (two-page) story in which the narrator recalls the fate of a doctoral student at a US university, whose name (he believes) was Fred Murdock. This "ordinary" young man has difficulties deciding on his research topic. So, one of the professors advises him to go live on the reservation of an indigenous tribe out west, to observe their rites and discover the secret that the medicine men reveal to the initiates. When he comes back he will have his dissertation, and the university will see to it that it is published. Murdock agrees and sets out on his mission, and as an exemplary anthropologist, lives for more than two years under strenuous conditions on the prairie, acquiring all the cultural habits of the indigenous population. He even comes to the point of dreaming in a language "that was not that of his fathers" (Borges 1998: 335) and thinking in a way that his previous logic rejected. After some time the tribe's spiritual leader tells him to remember his dreams, and the secret he has yearned for is, at last, revealed to him. But at the moment of initiation and acceptance, when Murdock is expected to have completed the successful immersion into indigenous otherness and literally to have become an Indian, he departs from the reservation without saying a word to anyone. Upon his return to the city, he visits the professor and tells him that he knew the secret and had resolved not to reveal it.

> "Are you bound by your oath?" the professor asked.
> "That's not the reason," Murdock replied. "I learned something out there that I can't express."

"The English language may not be able to communicate it," the professor suggested.

"That's not it, sir. Now that I possess the secret, I could tell it in a hundred different and even contradictory ways. I don't know how to tell you this, but the secret is beautiful, and science, *our* science, seems mere frivolity to me now." After a pause he added:

"And anyway, the secret is not as important as the paths that led me to it. Each person has to walk those paths himself" (Borges 1998: 335).

The professor then finally asks him if he plans to go back and live among the Indians. Murdock replies that what the men of the prairie taught him is valid anywhere and for any circumstances. The narrator laconically closes the story by noting "Fred married, divorced and is now one of the librarians at Yale" (Borges 1998: 335).

I spent five years recently struggling with the relation between fiction and truth—trying to solve the riddle of the seeming paradox, that fiction may be a way of getting at a certain truth—and this story was in a way what I finally arrived at, as a form of condensation and conclusion. I shall come back below to what it may imply. The subject of my research was the role of fiction—primarily prose literature but also, for example, film—in the transition processes of South Africa and Argentina (Hemer 2011, 2012a). The project was one of so-called *artistic research,* and it was from the outset my decisive intention to find a form that (1) to some extent is congenial with the subject matter of my investigation, and (2) transgresses the format of the conventional dissertation, yet fulfills all the criteria of academic research in terms of argument, transparence, referencing etc. The second point is crucial. The most congenial form might be a *novel*—or some kind of genre hybrid with fictional elements—that unsettles the very distinction between fiction and truth. Such text would indeed be an interesting challenge. (At least, it seemed like an intriguing possibility eight, nine years ago, when I started thinking about the project. Since then it has become a global fashion in literature to play in the borderland of fiction and fact.) But, such text would also be easily dismissed by academia as *fiction*—that is, as nonverifiable. Hence I decided to take on a much greater challenge—in fact, a mission impossible, or, what would turn out to be necessarily a compromise.

First of all, my approach to academia has been that of an outsider. I am a *writer.* I did not have an academic mother discipline—unless journalism is defined as an academic discipline, which it clearly is not. I never even regarded myself as a literary critic, although I have written hundreds of book reviews during more than twenty years as an arts journalist in different media. Writing is my profession—*and* my discipline, if you like. By writing, I am not referring to literary writing only, but journalism and academic writing as well.

Those are the three principal writing practices whose interrelations I have elsewhere illustrated with a like-sided triangle (Hemer 2005). I claim, hypothetically, that all forms of creative writing happen in the dynamic tension between these three poles, which are defined and regulated by certain clearly distinguishable traditions and genre conventions. In varying degrees, consciously or not, the novelist, the reporter, and the academic researcher all have to relate to the other two writing practices. But whereas writing style is crucial to both literature and journalism, it is strikingly subordinated in academia, as the supposedly neutral means of conveying the result of the research. Lack of style may sometimes even be regarded as a virtue, whereas good writing is met with suspicion, as if the eloquence were a way of concealing a meager academic content. Hence, according to this logic: the duller the text, the more significant the research behind it. This applies, not least, to anthropology. Think of Mary Louise Pratt's often-quoted exclamation: "How, one asks constantly, could such interesting people doing such interesting things produce such dull books?" (Pratt 1986: 33). Pratt's colleague and countryman, Vincent Crapanzano, explains this seeming paradox as a dissociation between the field experience—what he calls the ethnographic confrontation—and the writing: "Indeed, one could argue that at one level the writing of ethnography is an attempt to put a full-stop to the ethnographic confrontation, just as, so often in the history of civilization, writing has selectively embalmed reality rather than continuously explicating it" (Crapanzano 1977: 70).[1]

Please note that I am not trying to stage a conflict between literature and academia. Rather to the contrary. Most of the writers I interviewed for my thesis combine creative literary writing with more discursive forms. Ricardo Piglia, Carlos Gamerro, Martin Kohan in Argentina, and Bhekizizwe Peterson in South Africa are all academics besides being fiction writers. A better-known example would be JM Coetzee. He is not one of my interviewees, but one of the main references. Internationally, he is exclusively known as a novelist, but his work as a critic and essayist is as extensive as his fiction. And the question of fiction's relation to truth is a crucial concern, in his novels as well as in his nonfiction work. *Doubling the Point* (Coetzee 1992), which spans over two decades, from 1970 to 1990, is a key volume of essays interspersed with interviews, by the editor David Atwell, that deal with "the question of autobiography." When asked what it is that enables him to speak about the relationship between his critical activity and his fiction, Coetzee rephrases the question as one about *truth-telling* rather than autobiography. He distinguishes between two kinds of truth—the first truth to fact, the second to something beyond that, something that comes in—or from—the very process of writing. "… It is naïve to think that writing is a simple two-stage process: first you decide what you want to say, then you say it. On the contrary, as all of us know, you write because you do not know what you want to say. Writing reveals to you what you wanted to say in the first place. That is the sense in which one can say that writing writes us" (Coetzee 1992: 17–18). What does truth of this "higher" order imply? Is it a characteristic of fiction alone, something that only yields itself in the process of *literary* writing? The interviewer returns again and again to Coetzee's double perspective, as a critic and a fiction writer, and on the question of the novelist's relation with literary and critical *theory*, Coetzee quite frankly declares that he feels a greater freedom to follow where his thinking takes him when he is writing fiction. One reason is that he is not a trained philosopher, but another has to do precisely with the two discursive modes. Stories, he says, are defined by their irresponsibility—that is, "responsibility toward something that has not yet emerged, that lies somewhere at the end of the road" (Coetzee 1992: 246). When he writes criticism, on the other hand, he is always aware of responsibility toward a goal, set up not only by the argument, but also by the discourse of criticism itself. His concern is to write novels in which "he is not unduly handicapped (compared with the philosopher) when playing with ideas" (Coetzee 1992: 246). In his most recent work, from 1999 and onward, the two formerly separate yet communicating practices have been combined, and even fused, in more and less innovative ways.

My intent was, however, to become a researcher, in an academic meaning, yet retaining the perspective of the literary writer. The empirical material was gathered at several subsequent "field trips" in the years 2006 to 2008. I carried a suitcase with thirty kilos of books from Buenos Aires, and tapes with some ten hours of interviews, in addition to all the tapes and books and videos that I had brought from South Africa the year before. I had, in other words, more than enough material to work with, but I really did not know what to do with it. As time was ticking by, my desperation grew to find some kind of magic formula to address and arrange what seemed more and more unfathomable. Finally, or actually while I was still doing the arduous transcribing of the South African interviews, I simply decided to do what I know I'm quite good at: I started writing. My natural point of departure and first reference was the journey I had made to South Africa sixteen years earlier, in 1991, as a reporter for the daily newspaper that was my employer at the time,[2] precisely at the very beginning of the transition process that was the object of this new investigation. I decided that what I now set out to do was also a form of "essay reportage." But whereas my travel writing had, to a large extent, been improvised on location, finding its form and content during the course of the journey, I was now sitting with an already gathered collection of material that was, on the one hand, much more extensive than what I had brought back from any of my journalistic expeditions, and, on the other, only a fraction of the total amount of research that I would have to carry out. As a reporter, I could afford to be an impressionist and even to make a virtue of my tourist position, leaning on the dubious presumption that first impressions are always right. As a researcher, by contrast, I found myself in Borges's *garden of forking paths,*[3] where every reference led to another, and not necessarily ever back to the main track. The material not only grew in the process of writing; it gradually changed character. I am not sure how best to describe this ongoing knowledge process, but I know that it is intrinsically linked to the act of writing, and that it is fundamentally *intuitive.* In that sense, it resembles the literary writing process—even though it is disciplined by academic standards, and in English, at that, which was perhaps the greatest challenge of all.

My suggestion for the most congenial form hence turned out to be a basically discursive text that borders on both journalism and literature, incorporating reportage, essay, and memoir. Not fiction, for reasons that I have explained above. But I would be naïve to claim that there are no fictional elements. Memory belongs to that special category of "subjective truth," and when I recall experiences that I have previously used as material for my novels, the border between memory and fiction tends to become blurry. There is also a fictional element in the narrative structure, which follows the chronological timeline of my journeys and interviews, although most of the reading and research was actually conducted in between and after the "field trips." For example, I interviewed Carlos Gamerro before I had read any of his books. The interviews on the whole constituted a major challenge. In academia, the interview is principally a method to collect data—not a form or genre in itself, as in journalism. My interviews were not structured, in a strict academic sense; they were more like explorations by means of conversation with fellow writers. If I had integrated them into my own analysis, they would have been condensed down to just a few quotes, and I felt that the principal value of these talks would vanish in the process. So, I decided not to kill my darlings, but let them run in parallel, almost *in extenso,* sparsely edited, in a sort of dialogue with the body text, a bit in the same way that two different narrative registers—first person, third person, past tense, present tense—can be intertwined in a novel. And I really do regard my interviewees as co-authors rather than "informants"—although I am of course assuming the privileged position of editor.

But, if I claimed to be conducting academic research, what, then, would my academic subject matter be? Since "truth" primarily connotes philosophy, and "fiction" presumably has its natural counterpart in comparative literature, the theoretical and methodological foundation would appear to gravitate toward *literary aesthetics.* That was also my presumption. I plunged, with some enthusiasm, into what seemed to be a debate that had passed its momentum in the 1990s, and I soon realized that I was leading myself astray from where I had intended to go, and becoming further and further removed from the turbulent reality of political conflict and social transformation. I found a better match in the emerging field of "law and literature," which I came across in my readings on the South African *Truth and Reconciliation Commission*. But with no judicial background whatsoever I did not feel fully comfortable in that context either. Only at an advanced stage of the process, when I had already gathered all my "field" data, did I realize what I had known all the time, but not taken into consideration, possibly because it was so close at hand—namely, that there is another major academic tradition that approaches the issues of truth and fiction from a different angle than that of literary studies, and often with a more experimental, sometimes explicitly transgressive, purpose.

In the introduction to the fascinatingly far-seeing and highly influential—I dare say epoch-making—anthology *Writing Culture* (1986), one of the editors, James Clifford, describes ethnography as *hybrid textual activity,* traversing genres and disciplines (Clifford 2010: 2–3).[4] *Ethnographic writing,* in Clifford's generous understanding, which encompasses the historical predecessors of explorers' journals and travelers' reports, evidently borders on both journalism and literature. Ethnographers were, indeed, often the forerunners of colonial expansion, but they were also world reporters before the very notion of "foreign news." And many of them were certainly excellent writers. US American anthropologist icons Margaret Mead and Ruth Benedict both wrote poetry "on the side," while French ethnographer Michel Leiris was primarily a novelist, poet, and art critic. Leiris's first ethnographic expedition was the great *Dakar-Djibouti* mission in the 1930s to collect African art for French museums. His diary from the mission, *L'Afrique fantôme* (1934, *Phantom Africa*), is a partly hallucinatory and dreamlike record of the confrontation with the African reality. If Leiris is the surrealist poet-turned-ethnographer, Laura Bohannan is a cultural anthropologist-turned-novelist. In *Return to Laughter* (1954), she disclosed her fieldwork experience from Nigeria, disguised under the pen name Elizabeth Smith Bowen. Other prominent anthropologists such as Mary Douglas, Clifford Geertz, and Claude Lévi-Strauss stayed within the ethnographic writing genre, but they have, indeed, as Clifford puts it, "blurred the boundary separating art from science." (Lévi-Strauss's *Tristes tropiques,* first published in 1955, is possibly the most influential ethnographic work ever published—and definitely, by any standard, literature of highest quality.)

But what, exactly, is the "literariness" of ethnography, other than good writing and distinctive style? Clifford talks about ethnographies as *fictions,* to

underscore the *partiality* of cultural and historical truths: "Even the best ethnographic texts—serious, true fictions—are systems, or economies, of truth.
Power and history work through them, in ways their authors cannot fully
control" (Clifford 2010: 7). Replace "ethnographic" with "literary," and the
meaning will in my opinion be just as valid, although the notion of truth
may have slightly different connotations. The author is, in the two cases,
both interpreter and prisoner of his/her own time. Clifford's British colleague, Nigel Rapport, actually suggests that anthropology and literature
are *as one* "in their creative and imaginative writing of social reality" (Rapport 1994: 250).

The principal ethnographic method, participant observation, has also
been a favored journalistic and literary technique. In news journalism, the
combined presence and invisibility of the reporter is still an ideal, if not the
prevailing norm, and many literary writers, with the ambition to depict reality in a truthful way, strive to be like an all-seeing "fly-on-the-wall"—or, if not
stuck on the wall, flying around unnoticed in the field of action. In classical
ethnography, there was a sharp and absolute split between what one could
call "the ethnographic self" and "the personal self."[5] In the 1960s of decolonization, which entailed a moment of disciplinary crisis and self-examination,
this prevailing subjective/objective balance cracked, and an ethnographic
subgenre emerged; what Clifford calls the self-reflexive "fieldwork account,"
for which Leiris, Smith Bowen, and Lévi-Strauss were decisive predecessors
(Clifford 2010: 13–14). This happens more or less simultaneously with the
appearance of the "new novel" (*le noveau roman*)—Leiris is one of the admi-
rable models in Michel Butor's manifesto-like *Répertoire* (1960). Incidentally,
it also concurs with the renewal of the (political) chronicle or reportage,
when fiction writers descend from the ivory towers and turn into committed reporters, sometimes arguably even ethnographers. Rodolfo Walsh's *Operación Masacre* (1957), a precedent of "new journalism" by almost a decade,
and a classic in Argentinean political literature, is the pioneer example. In
other words, at a time when literature, on the one hand, aspires to becoming scientific and, on the other, reengages with social and political reality,
anthropology starts moving in the opposite direction—to the rhetoric of the
autobiography and the ironic self-portrait (Clifford 2010: 14). In the "fieldwork account," the ethnographer becomes a protagonist among others. His/
her voice is deprived of the pervasive authorial function it used to have in
traditional ethnography, whereas the other voices, which were previously
confined to the role of sources—"informants"—now may come forward as
co-authors. They may even express diverging opinions. This move from
"univocity" to "plurivocality"[6] rocks the foundation of scientific verification
and constitutes the most contested part of anthropology's "literary turn."[7]

Anthropology's courting of literature seems, however, to have remained unanswered or even dismissed. There has always been a certain highbrow arrogance from literature's side with regard to both journalism and academia. Good-writing anthropologists even used to be called "failed novelists."[8] And whereas many anthropologists of the post-80s clearly aspire to be regarded as writers also in a literary sense—and often rightfully, so—hardly any literary writer would aspire to being called ethnographer—that might even be taken as an insult—and very few have training in anthropology. There are, however, exceptions to the rule. Among Latin American writers, José María Arguedas, from Peru, and Darcy Ribeiro, from Brazil, were both ethnographers *and* novelists, and both have played very important roles in the formation of a Latin American cultural identity. Their US American colleague Tony Hillerman was an anthropologist of the Nevada desert who wrote detective novels with a Navajo Indian as the main character. And Kurt Vonnegut even had a novel—*Cat's Cradle* (1999 [1963])—accepted as a master's thesis at the University of Chicago in 1971. Vonnegut, who had been accepted as a graduate student already in 1945 and made several attempts at writing a more conventional thesis, but failed, defined cultural anthropology as "a science that is mostly poetry"—or "poetry which pretends to be scientific" (Whitlark 1989: 77). What is more, anthropologists as main protagonists in contemporary literature are rare—which makes Fred Murdoch even more exceptional. As Chilean literary scholar Idelber Avelar notes, everything impels us toward reading "The Ethnographer" as a parable, except that one is not quite sure of what it means (Avelar 2004: 55). For one thing, it is a story about anthropological legibility, which "depicts an encounter with otherness and the re-translation of that encounter back into the language of sameness" (Avelar 2004: 54). At the moment of initiation, the story seems to confirm the possibility that the other may turn out to be transparently legible. But, as the ending of the story makes clear, the immersion in the object also represented the retrospective implosion and dismantling of the research project. "The richness of the story stems from the fact that Borges suggests that [Murdock] never wrote the dissertation precisely *because* his experience as an anthropologist had been too perfect. In other words, Borges portrays anthropology's moment of perfection precisely as its moment of definitive collapse" (Avelar 2004: 55).

In order to decide *not* to write the dissertation, Murdock must be capable of doing it in the first place, and it has taken him several years of arduous work to arrive at that point. So, whereas "The Ethnographer" is certainly a critique of science, it is, at the same time, ascribing anthropology "the privileged space for that kind of interrogation to arise" (Avelar 2004: 57). Did Borges have an analogy with literary writing in mind? Most certainly, and if he didn't, it is still there, and that is perhaps even the crux of the story. One affinity lies in the shared paradox of the ultimate success that is also the ultimate failure. In order to exist as such, anthropology requires a certain degree of *imperfection*. If the ethnographer fully succeeds in literally becoming the other, he will not be able to retranslate that experience back into the language of his previous self. Full accomplishment, in that sense, would certainly also imply the collapse of art and literature. (There is a fine line here, to the domains of mysticism.) Another analogy, apparently banal but absolutely crucial, is in the very secret disclosed to Murdock that he decides *not* to reveal—and the lesson learned that he *does,* in fact, reveal; that the secret, itself, is not as valuable as the paths that led to it. What immediately comes to mind is the mystery and superstition surrounding the literary inspiration. But to Murdock, the secret is not an inspirational gift, it is something he has achieved in a long process, and it is this process that really matters. The secret could be told "in a hundred different and even contradictory ways"—although Murdock refrains from doing so—but the paths that led him to it—the creative knowledge process—are difficult, not to say impossible, to disclose, even in retrospect.

I had read most of Borges's *ficciones,* as he called his short stories, but for some reason I had missed "The Ethnographer." When I discovered it, by the end of my project, through Avelar's analysis, I recalled the conversation with one of my Argentinean interviewees, Horacio González, and a reflection that he had made, *en passant:* that one *almost* should not talk about fiction. Because "the ultimate investigation of it would be like revealing a very important secret about the world." I find this "almost" enormously intriguing. In a way this "almost" is what my whole thesis was about. Unlike Fred Murdock, I wrote my dissertation. And, if I did not have an academic mother discipline on the outset, I felt somehow that I found one in the end. I was very comfortable with anthropology as my subject—because it shares a very crucial feature with literature; it can encompass everything.

Moreover, another intriguing concept finally seemed to make sense: Borges's countryman and colleague Juan José Saer's suggested definition of fiction as *speculative anthropology*. In the key essay "El Concepto de Ficción" (1997 [1989]),[9] Saer points to fiction's constitutive dual character, which inevitably blends the empirical with the imaginary. The paradox of fiction, according to Saer, is that it takes refuge in the false in order to augment its credibility. This crucial "leap towards the unverifiable" is made, not to immaturely or irresponsibly circumvent the rigors of "truth," but precisely to demonstrate the complexity of the situation; a complexity that, if approached only from the perspective of the verifiable, would be abusively reduced and impoverished. Hence, the great literary works of our time—although asserting themselves as fiction—claim to be taken literally. However, and this is Saer's crucial point, *fiction does not solicit being believed as truth, but as fiction.*

> This wish is not an artist's whim but rather the primary condition for his existence, because only by accepting fiction as such can one understand that fiction is not a novelized statement of this or that ideology but a specific dealing with the world, inseparable from what it deals with. This is the crux of the entire problem and it must be kept in mind at all times if one wants to avoid the confusion of genres. Fiction keeps itself at a distance from both the truth prophets and the euphoric advocates of the false (Saer 1989: 12).[10]

To illustrate his argument Saer picks two diametrically opposed examples: in the one corner, representing the paradigm of truth: Alexander Solzhenitsyn. The "Finally-Prophesized-Truth" that Solzhenitsyn's writing claims to tell does not need to validate itself through fiction. Why write a novel on a subject matter about which one already knows everything beforehand? Documents and reports would have been sufficient. The opposite, and likewise negative, example is Umberto Eco, the Italian professor of semiology and specialist in medieval philology, who decides to write novels for amusement or, in Saer's scornful words, *entertainment for executives to read between airports.* While Solzhenitsyn proposes the grand revelation, Eco soothingly reassures that there is nothing new under the sun. Antiquity and modernity mingle; the detective story is transposed to the Middle Ages, which, in turn, become a metaphor for the present, and history is given meaning through an incredible conspiracy. This "apology of the false" seems in Saer's analysis far more despicable than Solzhenitzyn's prophetic claims.[11]

What Saer then finally arrives at is this tentative definition of fiction as a *speculative anthropology.* However, as if exhausted by the enormous intellectual effort, he never properly elaborates this captivating conclusion, but ends on a puzzling and somewhat disappointing note:

> Perhaps—I do not dare to assert it—this way of looking at fiction could neutralize the various reductionisms that, ever since the last century, have persistently lashed out at it. Through this lens, fiction might be able, not to ignore them, but to assimilate them, incorporating them to its own essence and stripping them of their pretensions of being absolute. Yet this subject is arduous, and it is better left for another time (Saer 1997: 16).

Unfortunately, this other occasion never occurs—so we can only speculate on the deeper implications, or see the concept as an open suggestion, to follow up on. The word *speculative* may of course sound derogatory. In academia it

is seldom if ever an asset to be speculative. You may make daring hypothe-
ses, but then you are supposed to find empirical evidence to support them,
whereas speculation is synonymous with gambling or talking off the top of
your head. But Saer quite obviously uses the word in an affirmative sense—
speculative as *uninhibited, unpredictable, transgressive.*

After five years of arduous academic discipline, it was a great relief to go
back to writing fiction. My latest project has been the completion of a major
literary endeavor, a novel trilogy, *Argentinatrilogin* (*The Argentina Trilogy*), consisting of the three novels *Cosmos & Aska* (2000), *Santiago* (2007), and *Misiones*
(2014).[12] I would not say that these projects have run in parallel, because I
can only be engaged in one major writing process at a time. But they have
certainly informed each other—and in retrospect I can clearly see how they
are really two different approaches to a common group of themes.

The title of the concluding part of the trilogy, *Misiones,* had been in the
back of my head ever since I wrote the second part, *Santiago,* or even earlier,
and I would certainly have written it a long time ago if the dissertation had
not come in between. But then, it would as certainly have become a quite
different novel. On the one hand, the systematic research into the ethnographic and historic material that I was beginning to explore in *Santiago*
provided my writing with a more solid ground. On the other, and more importantly, the subsequent greater confidence in my own authority enhanced
my ability and motivation to *invent* more freely.[13] For example, Misiones is a
province in northeastern Argentina with a fairly large and largely unknown
community of Swedish immigrants who arrived in the late nineteenth and
early twentieth centuries. I had been there twice, very briefly, and I was always planning to go back and do some proper ethnographic research for my
novel. But in the end I decided to write the novel first, completely based on
imagination and not making use of any of the "real" history.[14]

Hence, in the end, the *literariness* of my literary approach was actually
emphasized, and the distinction between the genres clarified rather than
blurred. So, what about *transgression?* To what extent do the ethnographic and
literary practices truly converge? Is it even desirable *that* they fuse into new
genres? These are questions that I am still struggling with. My dissertation
abided by the academic rules, but it actually also had "literary" offspring
in a hybrid text, "Hillbrow Blues," that was first written and published in
Swedish and later elaborated and published in English (Hemer 2012b). Its
background is that I was invited to contribute to a literary anthology. At first
I declined, explaining that I didn't have any material in store and no time to
produce new text, since I was immersed in my research project. But the editor was insistent, and I am happy that he was because it inspired me to write
something I most likely would not have produced without a sharp deadline.
The first Swedish version was written while I was working on the South Af-

rican material, more specifically on a chapter about "writing the city," that is, Johannesburg. So, it was a way of approaching the same material from a slightly different perspective. The English version, which is more than a mere translation, was also written in response to a call, for an anthology to celebrate the fifteenth anniversary of the yearly *Time of the Writer* Festival in Durban (in which I had participated in 2007). That was an even greater challenge; it is the first literary text I have written in English.

> It goes fast. Pretoria Street is shorter than he remembered it; he's looking for the hotel on the right side whose name he has repressed, no, simply forgotten, but he doesn't see any signs at all, nor any traces of bookshops, cafés, or lunch restaurants. Lots of people in the street, mostly young men, no suits or ties, a few older women, no commerce, shutters closed, the entire Carlton Hotel shut down like a ghost tower, the garage doors locked with chains, but no roadblocks or burning oil drums… "The Nigerians and the Zimbabweans have ruined the place," says the taxi driver with a matter-of-fact distaste that reminds him of his first taxi ride in Joburg fifteen years ago, that time with a white driver venting his contempt over the black hordes that had invaded the formerly secluded city. He stayed in the hotel whose name he doesn't remember, with a view to the street, noisy, without air conditioning, cockroaches in the bathroom but otherwise neat and tidy. Apartheid was already history, like communism in Eastern Europe, TV showed Hill Street Blues dubbed to seSotho (*he believes*), interspersed with commercials for Ohlsson's Lager, the beer for the New South Africa in the making. Double-deckers ran like shuttles along Hillbrow's busy artery, studded with shops, cinemas, bars, and restaurants where you could have breakfast at any time of the day; a block or two farther down were 24-hour cafés and bookshops, some of them amalgamated into book cafés. At Café Zurich, he had met Ivan Vladislavić, then in his early thirties, editor at the semi-clandestine Ravan Press and the author of a well-received collection of short stories. He retained the memory of Ivan's smile, leaning on the red PVC-coated sofa in the spacious venue. Café Zurich was to merge with nearby Café de Paris into the imaginary Café Europa, the center around which Hillbrow's and South Africa's transition evolves in the eyes and mind of retired proofreader Aubrey Tearle, the main protagonist of *The Restless Supermarket* (2001), a regular at the café and, in his own words, an incorrigible European, although he has never set foot outside South Africa.

As the opening paragraph above indicates, this is not an academic text. Yet, in bits and pieces it is identical with corresponding parts of my dissertation, which also has the literary elements of essay, reportage, and memoir. The difference is the component that would be defined as *fictional;* the stream of consciousness, the subjective distortion of reality—in the memory of the protagonist, the images of this taxi ride along Pretoria Street merge with other images into a slightly surreal cityscape—and, perhaps most importantly, the distancing device of the third person. That was something that I added in the English version, and I discovered that it really made a great difference. "He" is not "me." I'm not exactly sure who he is, where he comes from, or where he is going. So, it is a fiction. And it is ethnographic in the sense that it is conveying the experience of a real place; solemn as it may sound, even attempting to capture the spirit of this place. It's not one journey, but a condensation of many journeys, and with two registers in time, a now and a past; in this case, Johannesburg, South Africa, before and after the transition.

After the Hillbrow Blues, I have written a corresponding text about Bangalore, India, "Bengaluru Boogie" (Hemer 2015), and I am currently continuing these kind of transdisciplinary explorations that I, for lack of a sexier term, call *ethnographic fictions*. But what this tentative enterprise in the end may entail remains to be revealed.

Oscar Hemer is Professor of Journalistic and Literary Creation, founder of the Master's program in Communication for Development at Malmö University, and co-director of the binational research centre Ørecomm. He holds a D.Phil. degree in Social Anthropology from the University of Oslo. Recent work includes the monograph *Fiction and Truth in Transition: Writing the Present Past in South Africa and Argentina* (2012) and the novel *Misiones* (2014), which concludes his *Argentina Trilogy*.

NOTES

1. The short essay is a brilliant reflection on the act of writing as a complex act of communication between a self and an other. Borrowing Jean-Paul Sartre's description of Jean Genet's writing, Crapanzano suggests a definition of this act as *talking to oneself, though wanting to be heard,* with reference to Sartre (1964: 494).
2. *Sydsvenska Dagbladet.* I did several series of "essay reportages" from Africa, Latin America, and Asia during the 1990s. Some of them were eventually republished in the books *Andra Städer–3 essäreportage från Syd* (1993, *Other Cities–Three Essay Reportages from South*) and *Kuba & Kina–2 postkommunistiska reportage* (1996, *Cuba & China–Two Post-Communist Reportages*).
3. *El jardín de senderos que se bifurcan* was the title-story of Borges's first collection of short stories (1941), which was republished in its entirety in *Ficciones* (1944, in English in 1962). The story "The Garden of Forking Paths" was also the first of Borges's works to be translated into English, in *Ellery Queen's Mystery Magazine,* in August 1948.
4. He traces its tradition to Herodotus, on the one hand, and Montesquieu's Persian traveler on the other, hence inscribing the estrangement of fiction in its very origin.

5. It is symptomatic of this "split personality" that Laura Bohannan wrote the memoir of her fieldwork as a novel under a different name (Bruner 1993).

6. French Jesuit philosopher Michel de Certeau noted that the fictions of literary language were scientifically condemned (and aesthetically appreciated) for lacking *univocity,* the purportedly unambiguous accounting of natural science and professional history. Literary fiction, by contrast, is inherently unstable; "it narrates one thing in order to tell something else; it delineates itself in a language from which it continuously draws effects of meaning that cannot be circumscribed or checked" (De Certeau 1983: 128, quoted in Clifford 2010: 5). *Plurivocality* is defined by Russian literary theorist Michail Bachtin as one of the essential elements of the novel.

7. The experimental moment that reached momentum in the late 80s and early 90s is also known as the "postmodern turn." *Writing Culture* was indeed a product of the 80s, but its lasting importance cannot be overestimated. In a sense it came as a shock that anthropology still hasn't quite recovered from. A twenty-fifth anniversary edition was published in 2010, with a new foreword by Kim Fortun, a leading representative of the new generation of anthropologists that has been shaped by the *Writing Culture* critique.

8. The catchy concept *novelist manqué* is attributed to British anthropologist Edmund Leach, who quite unanimously is considered to have been one of the best writer-ethnographers in the English language.

9. This crucial text has given its title to an entire collection of essays (Saer 1997), ranging over three decades, from 1965 to 1996.

10. English translation by Paula Grossman and Alejandra Rogante.

11. The vehement contempt unleashed upon Eco is quite perplexing in the light of current tendencies in the global literary industry. One need not wonder what Saer would have thought of Dan Brown. What Saer suggests may in fact be that the worldwide success of Eco's *Il Nome della Rosa* (1981, *The Name of The Rose*) in a way paved the way for Brown and the like.

12. *Misiones* was published separately and with the two previous novels in one volume as an e-book, *Argentinarilogin.*

13. Ivan Vladislavić, one of my South African interviewees, suggested that there is not enough invention in literature and called for more writers who would simply make things up (Hemer 2012a: 96).

14. In fact, it is set in the near future, when intercontinental air traffic has been canceled, waves of refugees and other migrants are once again traveling by boat from the old to the new world, and Argentina appears at last to realize its enormous potential.

REFERENCES

Avelar, Idelber. 2004. *The Letter of Violence: Essays on Narrative, Ethics and Politics.* New York: Palgrave Macmillan.

Bohannan, Laura (alias *Elizabeth* Smith Bowen). 1964. *Return to Laughter*. New York: Anchor.

Borges, Jorge Luis. 1941. *El jardín de senderos que se bifurcan*. Buenos Aires: Emecé.

———. 1944. *Ficciones*. Buenos Aires: Emecé.

———. 1969. *Elogio de la sombra*. Buenos Aires: Emecé.

———. 1998. *Collected Fictions*. Trans. Andrew Hurley. London: Penguin.

Bruner, Edward M. 1993. "Introduction: The Ethnographic Self and the Personal Self." In *Anthropology and Literature*, ed. Paul Benson. Urbana: University of Illinois Press.

Butor, Michel. 1960. *Répertoire. I*. Paris: Éditions de Minuit.

Bystrom, Kerry. 2007. *Orphans and Origins: Family, Memory and Nation in Argentina and South Africa, 1983-2005*. Ph.D. diss. Princeton University.

Clifford, James, and George E. Marcus, eds. 2010 [1986]. *Writing Culture: The Poetics and Politics of Ethnography*. 25th anniversary ed. Berkeley: University of California Press.

Clifford, James. 2010 [1986]. "Introduction: Partial Truths." In *Writing Culture: The Poetics and Politics of Ethnography*. 25th anniversary ed., ed. James Clifford and George Marcus. Berkeley: University of California Press.

Coetzee, JM. 1992. *Doubling the Point: Essays and Interviews*, ed. David Attwell. Cambridge, MA: Harvard University Press.

Crapanzano, Vincent. 1977. "Communications: On the Writing of Ethnography." *Dialectical Anthropology*, vol. 2, nr. 1, February: 69–73

De Certeau, Michel. 1983. "History, Ethics, Science and Fiction." In *Social Science and Moral Inquiry*, ed. N. Hahn, R. Bellah, P. Rabinow, and W. Sullivan. New York: Columbia University Press.

Eco, Umberto. 1981. *Il Nome della Rosa*. Milano: Bompiani.

Hemer, Oscar. 1993. *Andra Städer: 3 Essäreportage från Syd*. Lund: Aegis.

———. 1996. *Kuba & Kina–2 postkommunistiska reportage*. Tollarp: Studiekamraten.

———. 2000. *Cosmos & Aska*. Stockholm: Atlantis.

———. 2005. "Writing the World." In *Media and Glocal Change: Rethinking Communication for Development*, ed. Oscar Hemer and Thomas Tufte. Buenos Aires: Clacso Books (Göteborg: Nordicom).

———. 2007. *Santiago. Historien om Gerardo K*. Umeå: H:ström.

———. 2011. *Writing Transition: Fiction and Truth in South Africa and Argentina*. Ph.D. diss. Department of Social Anthropology, University of Oslo.

———. 2012a. *Fiction and Truth in Transition: Writing the Present Past in South Africa and Argentina*. Berlin: Lit Verlag.

———. 2012b. "Hillbrow Blues." In *Africa Inside Out: Stories from The Time of The Writer*, ed. Michael Chapman. Scottville: University of KwaZulu-Natal Press.

———. 2014. *Misiones*. Stockholm: Vulkan.

———. 2015. "Bengaluru Boogie: Outlines for an Ethnographic Fiction." In *Memory on Trial: Media, Citizenship and Social Justice*, ed. Anders Høg Hansen, Oscar Hemer, and Thomas Tufte. Berlin: Lit Verlag.

Leiris, Michel. 1934. *L'Afrique Fantôme*. Paris: Gallimard.

Lévi-Strauss, Claude. 1955. *Tristes Tropiques*. Paris: Plon.

Pratt, Mary Louise. 1986. "Fieldwork in Common Places." In *Writing Culture: The Poetics and Politics of Ethnography,* ed. James Clifford and George Marcus. Berkeley: University of California Press.

Rapport, Nigel. 1994. *The Prose and the Passion: Anthropology, Literature and the Writing of E. M. Forster.* Manchester: Manchester University Press.

Saer, Juan José. 1997. *El Concepto de Ficción.* Buenos Aires: Seix Barral.

Sartre, Jean-Paul. 1964. *Saint Genet: Actor and Martyr.* New York: Mentor.

Vonnegut, Kurt 1999 [1963]. *Cat's Cradle.* London: Penguin.

Walsh, Rodolfo 1987 [1957]. *Operación Masacre.* Buenos Aires: Ediciones de la Flor.

Whitlark, James S. 1989. "Vonnegut's Anthropology Thesis." In *Literature and Anthropology,* ed. Philip A. Dennis and Wendy Aycock. Lubbock: Texas Tech University Press.

Chapter 12

Writing Together

Tensions and Joy between Scholars and Activists

**Eva-Maria Hardtmann, Vincent Manoharan, Urmila Devi,
Jussi Eskola, and Swarna Sabrina Francis**

We have since the time of Malinowski's fieldwork in the Trobriands, in the beginning of the twentieth century, seen many variations on the classic form of participant observation.[1] Anthropologists have studied "down, up, sideways, through, backward, forward, away and at home" (Hannerz 2006). Without doubt the anthropological field methods, the relation to the "subjects" and styles of writings, have been thoroughly discussed.

The same is also true regarding the relation between anthropologists and activists more specifically. In contemporary social movements and among many activists, the practice of ethnography has been integrated into the work as part of their activism, in what Holmes and Marcus (2008) term para-ethnography, speaking about contemporary fieldworks more generally. The activists are doing "superb ethnography in their own idioms" and anthropologists are not needed to add "critique, moral injunction, or higher meaning to these accounts" (Holmes and Marcus 2008: 84). At the same time a number of anthropologists take to activism and combine their roles as scholars and activists, for example Juris (2008), who argues in favor of a "militant ethnography." It seems, thus, that activists are now doing ethnography, carrying out the traditional tasks of the anthropologists, and anthropologists are, sometimes, taking to activism to combine it with their research.[2]

With the concept "militant ethnography," Juris (2008) refers to ethnographic research that is not only politically engaged, but also collaborative, and aims to break down the divide between researcher and practitioner during the moment of fieldwork. To understand activism, Juris uses his own body as a research tool to generate so-called "kinesthetic empathy" (Sklar 1994, referred to in Juris 2008: 21).[3] Even though the distinction between researcher and activist is broken down during fieldwork, Juris notes that, "the same cannot be said for the moment of writing and distribution, when one has to confront vastly different systems of standards, awards, selections and stylistic criteria" (2008: 21). In *Networking Futures,* a highly interesting volume with ethnography from among Barcelona-based activists in the Movement for Global Resistance, Juris describes how many of the ideas in his volume are developed with activists during the time of fieldwork in collective reflections, visioning, and analysis. These are integrated in the volume that also involves his own particular interpretation that is "offered back to activists, scholars and others for further reflection and debate" (2008: 23).

The idea of the writing project described in this chapter was different. It was to mutually share our understandings of the Global Justice Movement between scholars and activists, but also to explore how far a writing collaboration between us could possibly get. What could we learn by trying to break down the divide, not during fieldwork and after the writing was over, like Juris describes, but during a well-defined writing process?[4] This chapter will share the practical experiences related to a workshop in Kathmandu among scholars and activists with a common interest in the Global Justice Movement. For context there will, as a background, be a description of the workshop and preparations for it, but the main focus will be on the ups and downs of the writing that followed after the workshop, and some lengthy extracts from writings produced within the project. The anthropological framework in this article is written by me, Eva-Maria, as I am the "writing anthropologist" among us. I am also the one writing below, introducing the writings by the others and reflecting on our writing process at the end.

THE KATHMANDU WORKSHOP

At the World Social Forum (WSF) in Nairobi, in 2007, I carried out fieldwork among thirty Dalit[5] activists from India. This was a preparation for my research project focused on South Asia and activists in diverse transnational movements, which are part of the Global Justice Movement.[6] During the Forum I discussed the role of Dalit activists in the Global Justice Movement with Vincent Manoharan, lawyer and at the time the General Secretary of National Campaign on Dalit Human Rights (NCDHR). During these discussions we decided to prepare together for a small workshop in Kathmandu the following year. Our idea was to create a kind of collaboration, or far-going dialogues, between a small group of scholars and activists with the outcome of a small volume. The outline, design, and content of it was to be mutually decided between us and it was to be written in a true collaborative fashion, even though we expected that to take more time. Finally, it was also to be published and distributed in a way acceptable to both scholars and activists.[7]

Among activists there is certainly an "emphatic presumption of audiences," as Holmes and Marcus (2008) comment in a more general context, and the space of collaboration can be seen as having been created already before my arrival on the World Social Forum scene in Nairobi. In the words of Holmes and Marcus, "the ethnographer is a figure whose presence is anticipated" (2008: 86). Activists are to a large extent assuming intellectual partners with whom they can collaborate on their own terms and with their own agendas in mind.[8]

What followed after the WSF Nairobi was numerous and extended email exchanges between Vincent and me before the actual workshop could take place in Kathmandu. My suggestions for invitations were turned down, one after the other.[9] To be fair, I was also myself an obstacle to the decisions. I wanted to see Dalit participants from geographically different areas and related to activist networks focused on land, labor, feminism, media, sexual minorities, and art. My wishes to have Dalit diversity represented in the workshop were not easily realized. Finally, though, we came to an agreement on the participants.[10]

During the first day of the workshop we began by briefly presenting ourselves. We had invited eight participants in accordance with our budget, ten including ourselves.[11] From Nepal we had invited Suvash Darnal, a Dalit activist, journalist, and graduate in Mass Communication. Ayesha Singh was another invited Dalit activist from The Feminist Dalit Organization (FEDO) in Kathmandu. From India it was Urmila Devi, a Dalit activist as well as feminist with a master's in Social Work from Uttar Pradesh in the north. From south India, it was Sabrina Francis, Dalit activist and performer from Andhra Pradesh and Yashoda Puttappa, a feminist, Dalit activist, and postgraduate in sociology from Karnataka. From Sweden we invited Jussi Eskola, at the time a master's student in Religion, Conflict and Peace-Building. Two more invited participants could only participate partially due to other commitments.[12]

In the application for funding Vincent and I had settled on the framework for writing, and determined that the small volume *Dalits in the Global Justice Movement* would consist of three parts: My Story, Themes, and Reflections.[13] Now, during the workshop, we planned more in detail what kind of writing we would like to produce together. To prepare for the first part, "My Story," we interviewed each other in working couples during the late afternoon and sketched each other's life stories, also to show how each one of us had come to relate to the Global Justice Movement.[14]

During the second day we reorganized to have different working couples from the previous day. Ideally this would have been one scholar and one activist. However, the picture was more complex, and, again, several of the Dalit activists held master's degrees in different subjects. When the idea about the workshop came up in Nairobi, Vincent insisted that we not give the writing project the subtitle as "scholars and activists in dialogues," but "scholars/activists in dialogues," which generated long discussions between us.[15] We now identified four themes for the writing exercise and finally agreed to relate Dalits/Alliances/Global Justice Movement to: (1) Feminism,[16] (2) Cultural Activities, (3) Civil Society, and (4) Ambedkarism.[17] Finally, we discussed the third part of our writing. It would be reflections about our method of writing dialogically. To summarize, we thus attempted to write each other's life stories, four collaborative texts on our chosen themes in working couples, and finally, for those who wished, individual reflections on the writing process.

"My story" was completed within a year after the workshop. These stories were collaborative in the sense that we had interviewed each other, but when it came to writing, each life-story was written by the interviewer alone, mainly checking details over Internet with the counterpart. We successively realized that the themes were more difficult to complete. We struggled with a number of different problems. Language differences with participants speaking, for example, Hindi (north India) and Kannada (south India) made it more difficult to work together at a distance than face-to-face with a translator. Working constraints made it problematic for many of us to put time aside for the project. Suvash was, for example, deeply absorbed in the radical political changes taking place in Nepal and Yashoda in feminist struggle in Karnataka involving the protests against tax-free Special Economic Zones (SEZ). Aiyesha took on other commitments outside of FEDO and moved away from Kathmandu.

To some extent, tensions also seem to have grown out of the different audiences we had in mind, like activists, scholars, politicians, journalists, etc., and consequently we had different purposes and styles of writing. In drawn-out attempts we negotiated different formulations in the writing couples. It seems that we also lost the dynamics of writing when we tried to appear with one and the same voice in the text and thus as identical to each other. Instead of writing one text together on the themes, we decided after more than a year to rewrite our commonly written drafts, which were still quite messy and satisfied no one. We changed tactics and decided that each writing couple would instead write a common text in dialogical form.

WRITING COLLABORATION IN PRACTICE

Writing in our diverse personal styles but in a dialogical form was easier, and it also allowed each of us to share personal experiences in a way that the single-voiced and commonly written text did not allow for. In the end, we all found this way of writing more satisfying than negotiating common formulations. To give an idea of our common efforts, some writings will follow. The first one is by Vincent and is part of a dialogue on the theme of BR Ambedkar. He puts the ideas of Ambedkar (1891–1956), the role model in the Dalit movement, in the context of the contemporary Global Justice Movement (GJM). Next, Urmila offers thoughts about the Dalit feminist perspective, which provides an insight into the content of discussions in our workshop. Finally, the writing by Sabrina and Jussi on Dalit cultural activities exemplifies the form of writing dialogically together, as an alternative to the single-voiced commonly written text, and I comment on this form at the end.[18]

DR. AMBEDKAR AND THE GLOBAL JUSTICE MOVEMENT

by Vincent Manoharan

The Charter of Principles evolved in the First World Social Forum (WSF) held in Porto Alegre in Brazil in 2001 with the slogan "Another World is Possible" and counts fourteen important principles. The crux of the principles include "the principle of open space" for the affected, victimized, and marginalized communities and sectors to come for discussions, exchanging views, and forging alliances within themselves.[19] Of late, this decade-old initiative of the WSF evokes critical comments on the whole exercise and outcome of this global move. In this situation, looking at the Global Justice Movement (GJM) with the perspective of Dr. Ambedkar is timely, significant, and essential.[20]

Ambedkar believed in inclusiveness, which means he never accepted the caste system, untouchability, or the notion of Brahmanism, which does not allow all human beings to be equal or to enjoy equal rights and privileges, share, and mingle with one another in the same plane (Keer 2005: 60; Iyer 1990: 38f.; Ambedkar 1989b: 46–48).[21] Ambedkar objected throughout his life to the principles of exclusion and segregation and fought for equality, the "right to touch and to be touched," and to mingle with each other. This very much correlates to the "open space" principle of the WSF, which holds that all have a right to meet together on an equal footing to share their experiences, views, and programs. No one is above another.

Equally, Ambedkar was against any kind of monopoly, whether social, economic, or political. While opposing caste, which is a social phenomenon, equally he opposed class domination and economic exploitation (Ambedkar 1994: 9; Jadhav 1993: 77–83). He condemned both Brahmanism and capitalism as a source for exclusion and exploitation (Omvedt 2007: 165–167). This position of Ambedkar draws a parallel to the charter of the GJM, as well, which stands against the dominance and monopoly of multinational corporations and the support that they enjoy from International Financial Institutions (IFIs) and capitalist, imperialist governments.

Ambedkar was known to fight for the rights of the discriminated against, women, and the marginalized, and especially against exclusion by caste in the Indian context (Ambedkar 2003: 282–283). He was well aware of racism and also slavery (Ambedkar 1987: 419). However, he found casteism to be worse than slavery, since a slave could be freed and allowed to enjoy freedom but a person born in a caste cannot come out of it (Ambedkar 1989a: 15–17). This position of Ambedkar is relevant to the charter of the GJM, which condemns any forms of exclusion. Along with that, as a person primarily committed to the cause of social equality he would definitely also try to include the oppressiveness of "casteism, racism and patriarchy" as something to be challenged and rooted out.

His last clarion call was to "educate, agitate and organize." This slogan very much offers the basis for the slogan of the GJM: "Another world is possible." Therefore, if Ambedkar were alive today, certainly he would support the initiative of the WSF and the promotion of the GJM to challenge the oppressive economic system—the neoliberalism of today. His philosophy and strategy has the essence for the formation of another world to ensure equality, justice, and peace with human dignity!

MY INVOLVEMENT IN THE WSF

I had the privilege to be one among the 4,700 delegates out of around 20,000 participants who attended the first WSF in 2001 in Porto Alegre, Brazil. It was activists from all over the world who joined and discussed the need for, as well as the charter of principles of, the GJM. From India, however, we were only a few and from the Dalit sector, it was only me and another activist from Karnataka. When I went there representing the National Campaign on Dalit Human Rights, I never thought that it would emerge as a strong "Global Open Space" for a wide range of people's networks, movements, trade unions, and civil society and human rights organizations to raise their voice against the Davos-based World Economic Forum, which was masterminded by multinational corporations, supported by world capitalistic governments, and strengthened by the Unholy Trio—the World Bank, International Monetary Fund, and World Trade Organization.

I have used several platforms to highlight the issue of caste and the plight of 260 million Dalits who struggle in South Asia in regaining their human dignity, their right to life and livelihood. Our lives and rights have further been pushed back even from "periphery" to "no person's land" by the ill-designs of neoliberalism. Later I participated in the WSFs in Porto Alegre (2003 and 2005); in Mumbai (2004), where I served as one of its Organizing Committee members; and also in Nairobi (2007). I contributed to organizing the Asian Social Forum that we held in Hyderabad (2003), and to the Indian Social Forum in New Delhi (2006). At the international level, I had the opportunity of attending a few International Council meetings of the WSF, like in Miami (2003). I attended a couple of European Social Forums, one in France and the other in the UK, and also the first planning meeting for the promotion of the US Social Forum held in Detroit. In fact, participation in all these WSFs, ESFs, and other Council meetings has helped me to widen my world-view, perspectives, dynamics, and strategies, besides establishing contacts with other peoples movements.

RESILIENCE—DALIT WOMEN

by Urmila Devi

PRESENT STATUS OF DALIT WOMEN

Placed at the bottom of India's class, caste, and gender hierarchy, Dalit women experience endemic gender, caste, and economic discrimination. Dalit women are seen as available and affordable for Dalit and non-Dalit men and for cheap labor. The majority of the Dalit women are found in the field doing backbreaking jobs like plantation, harvesting, cutting the grass for domestic animals and feeding them, working at construction sites, carrying loads, and cleaning the roads. They are found in their landlord's house conducting delivery as midwives—giving life to the newborn baby and the mother. They are found at home, getting up 4:00 A.M. and doing all the household work, rearing the children, caring for the husband and all the other members of the family, and then going for work, coming back in the evening again to do all the work at home—taking care of the children, cooking, feeding everyone in the house, making sure that everyone has their place for rest and then eating what is leftover and going to bed by 10:00 P.M. or even later. They are the first ones to get up and last ones to go to rest and throughout the day they are at work. Dalit women are not a homogeneous group, but they are homogeneous in pain and suffering.

DALIT WOMEN'S STRUGGLE TO FORM AN IDENTITY

M. Swathy Margaret, a Dalit woman intellectual says, "If we do not define ourselves for ourselves, we will be defined by others – for their use and to our detriment" (Margaret 2005). I would like to illustrate one among many stories of Dalit women's struggle to build their own identity with one small story told to me by Usha.

Usha experienced discrimination personally by the caste Hindus and heard the story of their oppression by her grandmother as a child. This experience and stories made her take revenge even as a child. Since she was very small, and thus physically too weak to fight against giants (in the caste system), at night with her friends she used to destroy the perpetrators' crops. She said: "Since I could not beat them, I used to take my other friends to high caste's field at nights and cut their crops and give to our domestic animals. I made everything clean as even house people should not know, because once they would come to know they would scold me and due to fear prevent me from doing so." In school she once organized her Dalit girl-friends to beat the high-caste girls on the way back home as they wouldn't allow the Dalit girls to sit in the front row during class. The complaint went to the teacher and to her home, but still she dared to question the teacher about discrimination in the school. She is not afraid of anything or any-body—so courageous is she.

DALIT WOMEN WITHIN THE GLOBAL JUSTICE MOVEMENTS

Still, in India, the women's movement leaders are from upper castes and the masses are lower-caste women. In such movements the Dalit women leaders have no space and non-Dalit leaders generalize the issue as one of patriarchy and not of caste. Similarly, the Dalit movements do not allow space for Dalit women in leadership positions. But today the Dalit women's movements are challenging the women's movements as well as the Dalit movements to get their due place in leadership roles. Dalit women are elected as members in local governance and through that they are making plans for their village and society. This has identified a lot of Dalit women intellectuals and brought them to one platform. Dalit women are now working as catalysts in different movements, sensitizing the civil society, government, and movement people.

In the World Social Forum in Mumbai in 2004, NCDHR had planned a nationwide Swadhikar Rally to mobilize the Dalit community of the country. This rally took up four routes: Budh Marg, Bhim Marg, Kalinga Marg, and Trivelure Marg. I led the Route of Budh Marg—from Delhi to Mumbai—for forty days, where we mobilized the Dalit community in the villages and cities and then participated in the World Social Forum.

[This was the end of Urmila's writings.]

A DIALOGICAL EXAMPLE

Below is the writing by Sabrina Francis, activist and performer in *Chindu*, a Dalit cultural resource center in Hyderabad, India, and Jussi Eskola, at the time a master's student in Uppsala, Sweden.[22] The short dialogue *Dappu—A Cultural Weapon of Dalits*, was deliberately planned to be in the form of a combined essay/email exchange. It begins with a text by Francis, followed by Eskola's shorter comment. Francis finally gives half a page of response to Eskola.[23] To be clear, the experimental aspect of our project has nothing to do with the communication taking place over the Internet, but rather, as mentioned, with exploring how far a writing collaboration between scholars and activists can get with the purpose of exploring our own positions in relation to what is called militant ethnography (from the scholar's point of view) and in relation to academic writing (from the activist's point of view).

DAPPU—A CULTURAL WEAPON OF DALITS

A dialogue by Swarna Sabrina Francis and Jussi Eskola

DAPPU

Dalits have a belief that the Dappu (drum) was used as a powerful communicator in the society where and when there was no language among humans. It was used to protect the people from the wild animals by dispersing them. Many acknowledge it as one of the first musical instruments of human beings. At one stage it was used to inform Chathurvarna (Brahmins, Kshatriyas, Vysyas, and Backward castes) that untouchables were on the streets, so that dominant caste people would take care and not get polluted by seeing them. But as artists and social activists, Dalits have developed the Dappu creatively as a social instrument. The Dappu leads many occasions such as celebrations, festivals, marriages, and occasions of birth and death. Politically, it has become a necessary tool for all parties and movements irrespective of ideology. It is a collective art form that involves no line between audience and performers. It is a community effort and education where there will be no teaching.

FORM OF DAPPU

The Dappu consists of a round rim, carved out from a tree, in which three to four types of wood are used. One face of it is covered by a tightly drawn and cured calfskin. The skin is processed with skill and care and fastened onto the rim with leather strips.

CONTENT OF DAPPU

The Dalit habitations reverberate with the many beats and rhythms of Dappu—the drum. There are many rhythms, accompanying different rituals, festivals, celebrations, and routine functions. It elicits rouses, evokes, stimulates, mesmerizes, celebrates, and captivates in a sense that is invitational to and affirming of Dalits. As an art form Dappu has within itself the ability to unite people through its sway over them. As the drum is played and the community gets lost in it by losing all forms of inhibition they join together in a corporate dance or swing or song. In the process the conflicts are resolved, wounds are healed, and a reconciled community is born anew. One of the ways by which the individual and the community cope with the brunt of their suffering is by playing the drum. As the drum is played an individual pours out his anger, anguish, and deep feelings of pain. In this process catharsis takes place and the individual is all set to face the routine of the day. It also evokes faithfulness in relationship between the performers and the audience. In the beat of Dappu one can notice the pathos, protest, and the hope of the Dalit community.

IDENTITY OF DAPPU

Yesterday Dappu was the symbol of shame and subjugation.
Today it is the symbol of assertion and struggle.
Tomorrow it will be the symbol of celebration and liberation.

RHYTHM OF DAPPU

It's a rhythm of the blood
It's a Fire of anger coming out from our wounds of experience
It's a dancing song of "untouchables" that touches the heart of human beings
It's a sound recollecting and reminding the broken dreams of our elders
It's the anguish of our children who are going to win this caste world
It's the power of the oppressed masses who have nothing to lose

(Poem by Suresh Lelle, *Chindu*, Hyderabad, 2008).

CULTURAL POLITICS

The state, which serves the interests of the dominant communities, often makes use of the Dalit culture as a showpiece and reduces the culture to art forms by patronizing the performance. The cultural art forms of Dalits are graded as entertainment and also degraded as symbols of untouchability and victimization. Many intellectuals are interpreting the understanding of Dalit cultural art forms as a counterculture to Brahminic cultural art forms. This understanding will not prove Dalit culture as an alternative. It also restricts the Dalit culture and art in exploring and experiencing new forms and content. The influence of Brahmanism, patriarchy, Sanskritization, and hybridization is often manifested in Dalit communities and their art forms. The Dalit life, which has undergone continuous and consistent oppression for many centuries, has also internalized many elements of oppressive value systems and cultures.

MY PERSONAL EXPERIENCES IN PLAYING THE DRUM
AT LOCAL AND GLOBAL LEVELS

I am neither trained nor do I have an inborn talent. But my passion for dance and music keeps me vibrant every time I play the Dappu. I am the only woman performer in my team of twenty-five to thirty men but yet I enjoy the dance and the music. Since 2002 I have been performing both theater and Dappu dance and most of them are indoor performances. In the Asian Social Forum held in 2003 at Hyderabad, where people gathered from different parts of Asia, the *Chindu* team was given the honor of inaugurating the Asian Social Forum program. My first international performance outside of Asia was the marching in the World Social Forum held in 2005 at Porto Alegre, Brazil. We joined along with the cultural events with people from different countries, and played the Dappu as we walked toward the venue in the bright hot burning sun. For the first time I experienced the Dappu as a universal phenomenon that provokes and stimulates anyone to its tunes. People who are not very familiar with dance and music were also able to easily get into the mood and tunes of the Dappu. I also observed that language is not a barrier or necessary to communicate. People could easily understand the message through the different patterns of Dappu beat.

Dear Sabrina,

It is of course alarming that the deep impact of Dalit culture on India's history is not taken as a genuine national treasure. Obviously the positive values of an alternative tradition are dismissed and the entire concept of Dalit folk art seems to incarnate a lot of preconditional views. Either fazed as a counterculture to Brahminical domination or unfairly domesticated and misused as a cheap and "dirty" image of the ancient Hindu culture, the spirit of Dalit folk art has until this day not been given credit on its own. This shows a serious lack of ethics and reveals the absence of an open public sphere in India where different traditions can venture into dialogue and possibly interlink. Since this also is a case of cultural freedom, let me remind you of Amartya Sen's argument on this issue, namely, that: "to plead for cultural diversity on the grounds that this is what the different groups of people have inherited is clearly not an argument based on cultural liberty. […] Just as social suppression can be a denial of cultural freedom, the violation of freedom can also come from the tyranny of conformism" (Sen 2007: 116f.).

You make important observations concerning the dilemma facing Dalit communities in India.

When it comes to the Dalit art forms and cultural expressions, you give a twofold perspective: first, we really need to understand and value all the powerful signs of a culturally vibrant Dalit identity. Second, we should still not forget that these resources construct a "hidden culture" in the shadow of the Brahminic hegemony. I reckon that this echoes Ambedkar's assertion that "caste has killed public spirit" by revealing the absence of a meaningful public sphere (or cultural space) (Ambedkar 1979 [1936]).[24]

Still the history of India shows how the structure of power (the logic of caste) has with countless methods organized the cultural preferences in the society. Therefore the assertion of Dalit pride and self-respect includes a tough pedagogical burden: it should attach importance to, and go along with, the understanding of the psychological roots of an intrusive and effective negation of certain cultural values. Jyoti Sahi gives the following description of this scenario, analyzing the tragic high-caste fear of the Panchama-Dalit: "… the pathology which makes the literate, so-called educated person, not only reject the craftsperson, but deep down even fear those who have a direct experience of life. The fear of the Panchama as being in some way polluting, arises, clearly from a deep sense of insecurity in the culture which has arisen out of a rejection of, and alienation from, the sensual or physical" (Sahi 2000: 3).

This brings me to my final thoughts concerning Dalit arts: I realize, once again, that the Dalits have a lot of glorious elements in their culture. This message is made visible by various Dalit artists—and you are definitely one of them! To form the basis of a comprehensive Dalit culture, inspiration can be drawn from local Indian roots as well as from cultural protest trends globally. I believe that you agree with Debi Chatterjee's words "that little headway can be made towards engineering social change without developing an alternative cultural milieu capable of challenging the basic tenets of the Brahminical cultural ethos" (Chatterjee 2004: 198).

In all this I experience a powerful assertion of human dignity. There are many verifiable signs of the lack of human rights that affects all public life in India. But I am encouraged to believe that Dalit art forms—as signs of creative capacity—are remarkable assets for human rights and strong tools for change.

Yours sincerely,
Jussi

Dear Jussi,

Thank you very much for your thought-provoking reflections. Your connections and exploration of the conceptual links from different cultural experts are useful for me to further my work in the area of Dalit culture.

I would like to share with you a few points in this regard.

I agree that Dalits have powerful cultural expressions that are used differently in two ways. One is to work for dominant caste people for their rituals and entertainment. Irrespective of the purpose, the dominant caste people treat them with the air of untouchability and using the notion of victimization. Dalits are culturally (physically) used up to the caste outer boundaries and thrown back within the Dalit boundaries once the job is finished. Psychologically the dominant caste always forces Dalits to be victims even within their own boundaries. This is the indirect caste invasion on the Dalit mind.

The other is that Dalits are using their art forms for their joy and celebration. This experience makes Dalits wholeheartedly connect to the self as well as to the outer world. They create public space, own the public, and assert themselves with great confidence. They forget the caste boundaries and create new shades of their life expressions. New thoughts join to the Dalit mind like Dalit music. When the music stops the thought goes unconscious.

The challenge is to explore the Dalit unconscious and make it a song of Dalit dream. This song creates Dalit identity with new meanings.

For the time being I remain with these thoughts.

Warm regards,
Sabrina

[This was the end of the dialogue between Sabrina and Jussi.]

THE TENSIONS AND JOY OF WRITING TOGETHER

The people among whom we carry out fieldwork are not simply responding to and tolerating the ethnographer's overt agendas, as Holmes and Marcus (2008: 85) have noted. This is certainly the case regarding activists, who may be performers, journalists, authors, scholars, or lawyers lobbying within the United Nations. The rules of collaboration have to be renegotiated. In the planning of our writing project and at the time of our workshop we shared analytically and reflexively our expertise between us and also collaboratively defined the issues at stake as well as the means by which to explore them, as discussed by Holmes and Marcus (2008: 86). By that point we had not faced any serious problems.

The tensions arose when we practically endeavored to write a single-voiced text collaboratively. No one was ready to give up his or her own ideas about what the writing was all about. It became a kind of embodied collaborative writing involving a lot of emotions. That is not to say that we were rigid and nonflexible, and we were certainly ready to sacrifice some of our convictions. We had foreseen this difficulty during the workshop, and discussed it in terms of how we wanted to reach out—publishing with a Dalit organization in Nepal, a small scholarly publishing house in India, Indymedia, or print-on-demand.

It may seem obvious that it is a qualitative difference between, on the one hand, writing a text on a theme with one and the same voice, and, on the other hand, writing a co-authored text, in which you could clearly recognize the different authors of the different parts. For most anthropologists and activists this never becomes an issue at all, as they never wish or attempt to write a text together. I find it, however, to be a matter well worth exploring further. This is not only because the gap between anthropologists and activists has narrowed, or for activist-scholars at times even ceased to exist, but because I think it will tell us something more generally about the sociability of our writing.

For simplicity, I will refer to the collaborative single-voiced text as "collaborative" and the text in which you can differentiate between the authors as "dialogical." In the collaborative (single-voiced) text we have to play down the differences between us as authors and negotiate, to the extent of coming to a total agreement, in relation to the reader. This is regarding both content and writing style, as done by Smith et al. (2008) in the fascinating volume *Global Democracy and the World Social Forums.*[25] Let me reflect on the writing by Francis and Eskola above, as they seem to have come as far as they possibly could with respect to a common ground for a dialogue. When it comes to style, Francis is writing as an activist with an academic audience in mind and Eskola, a master's student at the time, as a scholar with the activists in mind. In format, Francis is writing without references, except for the poem by Suresh Lelle, not published before. Eskola has chosen to write only with references taken from India, including combined activists/ scholars like Ambedkar, well known in Dalit activist circles.

Francis and Eskola have managed to find a common ground for their dialogue, and for the rest of our article I agree with one of the earlier reviewers of the chapter, saying that "the individual writings don't really sit well with each other, except for sharing some common thematics." In the sense of the final product being a smooth text, it may be seen as a failure. However, agreeing with each other and fitting everything neatly together was never our goal and it is reflected in this piece. The text arose out of heated debates and individual opinions and the end-product has only been secondary to the learning process. We may rather look at the text, maybe not as a failure or success, but as the materialization of a tense and enjoyable writing exercise.

So, what have we learned from our workshop in Kathmandu and the writing process so far? Did the text by Francis and Eskola benefit from being written in dialogical form? What is gained compared to a text written by a sole, combined activist-scholar like Juris, or compared to a collaboratively written text—in which you cannot make out the difference between the authors—like in the volume by Smith et al. (2008)? There seem actually to be some advantages to the dialogical text. The dialogical text appears at first sight to be a text in which the authors only address each other while the collaborative text seems to directly address us as readers. I will explore these two forms more closely below and argue that it seems rather to be the other way around. The dialogical text may pride itself on inviting the reader and being welcoming in a way that the collaborative single-voiced text does not, in the end.

To begin with, Francis and Eskola have the possibility of addressing each other and in this way conveying to the reader what they learn in the process, in a way that is not possible in a single-voiced text (by a sole author or collaboratively written). They have the chance to confirm each other's writings and when they wish also to slightly correct each other. The writing form allows for differences. We could also track how they, by writing on a common theme, introduce each other to new ideas and networks.

The same kind of social and intellectual exchange certainly happens between authors in a collaborative single-voiced text, but the final product is to a larger extent introverted in relation to the reader. The writing process is hidden to us, and becomes the tacit knowledge shared solely among the authors. In the collaborative text the reader is not invited to share the differences and tensions among the writers, which no doubt must exist. We are not invited to take part in the process, but are only presented the final neat and well-structured result. The authors of the collaborative text are not exposing the diversities but the ideal is rather to forget or downplay differences among themselves and to hide these divergences in relation to others. In this case "the others" will be us, the readers of the book.

Finally, if our ideal is that activists and scholars should be looked at as being equal knowledge producers, rather than scholars being the sole "arbiter of 'truth'" (Juris and Khasnabish 2013: 370; see also Eyerman and Jamison 1991; Edelman 2009; Casas-Cortés, Osterweil, and Powell 2013: 199ff.; Conway 2013) the dialogical text is to be preferred. In the collaborative text we are not supposed to follow how knowledge producers differ and interact in the exciting process when new knowledge emerges. We are not given the possibility, as readers, to find out for ourselves what happened in the process. This is not to say that this is obvious in the dialogical text either, but it is at least an ideal to aim at.

The dialogical text is thus more welcoming, as we are invited by the authors, who openly share their learning process, as well as the positive and negative dynamics taking place among them, in the process of producing new knowledge. It may be seen as more inviting as it also shares its shortcomings with the reader. The ideal in the dialogical text is not to downplay differences in relation to each other and the reader, but rather to allow for and accept differences as a creative source in the writing process.

In summary, the simple point is that there are constructive sides to the co-authored dialogical text in which you can differentiate between the writers, both in the production of the text and in the final result, which are lost in the single-voiced collaborative text as well as in the text written by a sole author.

What about the moment of publishing and distribution in our project? The solution is now to break up our writings and bring them out through different sources, to satisfy varied needs. This chapter is our first attempt. When it comes to "My Story," we may update and get it published, maybe translated, and distributed by *Samata Foundation* in Kathmandu, founded by Suvash Darnal, who participated in our workshop. It will then be available to people in Nepal and India and the price of it will be reasonable, as emphasized during our workshop.[26]

It may happen that the activist and scholar are combined in one and the same person, as was the case among participants in our workshop. But scholars and activists often differ regarding the purposes of writing, have different audiences in mind, and thus prefer different styles of writings. However, activists sometimes want to reach out to scholars, and scholars wish to get in touch with circles of activists.

The chapter now coming to an end has been an attempt by Francis, a Dalit activist and performer, by Eskola, with an M.A. in Religion, Conflict and Peace-Building, by Devi, a Dalit feminist with a master's degree in Social Work, by Manoharan, a Dalit activist-scholar and lawyer, and by Hardtmann, a social anthropologist, to share with the reader one specific common experience of writing. Our identities and roles as scholars and Dalit activists as well as scholar-activists have probably been slightly changed and transformed during the process of writing together. It has been a kind of shared joy recognizing differences.

In memory of our friend Suvash Darnal. Suvash, who was thirty-one years old, passed away unexpectedly on 15 August 2011 at around 7:30 A.M. He was traveling in a shuttle bus from Washington Dulles International Airport when the bus hit the New Jersey wall and met with an accident. Suvash Darnal was a founder of Jagaran Media Center (JMC–the producer of Dalan tele-serial), the President of the Samata Foundation, and President of COCAP (Collective Campaign for Peace).

Urmila Devi received her Master in social work from Mumbai in North India. She is a Dalit activist and feminist based in rural Buxar in Bihar, India. She has got 25 years of grassroots experiences of working with Dalit women.

For the volume *Violence against Dalit Women in India* (2006) she identified and interviewed survivors in Bihar. She has been the national monitoring secretary of National Campaign on Dalit Human Rights (NCDHR) and participated in the World Social Forum in India.

Jussi Eskola received his M.A. in Religion, Conflict and Peace-building at Uppsala University. His master thesis *Dalit Dynamics in South India: Culture as a tool for Emancipation* is based on fieldwork in India and explores the changing perception of Dalit identity steered by new possibilities of self-assertion. He is currently involved in an exhibition-project making Dalit art and poetry known to a wider audience.

Swarna Sabrina Francis is the Director of Chindu, a cultural resource centre based in Hyderabad, India. She is a trained theatre artist and has given performances at national and international events, including the World Social Forums in India and Brazil. Her performances of *Dalit women, Dark Moon* and *Dark & Dreary* have been described as exceptional and emotional. Since ten years she is directing theatre groups and holding leadership workshops.

Eva-Maria Hardtmann is Lecturer in Anthropology in the Department of Cultural Anthropology and Ethnology at Uppsala University, Sweden. She received her PhD in Social Anthropology at Stockholm University and is the author of *The Dalit Movement in India: Local Practice and Global Connections* (2009) and *South Asian Activists in the Global Justice Movement* (2016, forthcoming).

Vincent Manoharan is a Dalit human rights activist and lawyer based in Tamil Nadu, India. He received his PhD in Dalit theology at the College of Arts and Law at University of Birmingham. Manoharan is the chair of the National Federation of Dalit Land Rights Movement (NFDLR) and co-founder of the National Campaign on Dalit Human Rights (NCDHR) in India. He was an India organizing committee member in the World Social Forum (WSF) in Mumbai and participated in the preparatory WSF International Council meeting in Miami.

NOTES

1. We have seen "observant participation" and discussions about "halfies" (Abu-Lughod 1991, with a concept borrowed from Kirin Narayan 1989). Further, we have "embodied ethnographic praxis" (Wacquant 2004), "collaborative ethnog-

raphy" (Lassiter 2005; Holmes and Marcus 2005), as well as an engaged "public ethnography" (Lassiter 2008). Another concept is "performative ethnography," and ethnography has also been discussed as shifting forms of connectivity (Faubion 2009). Holmes and Marcus (2008: 82) write about a "para-ethnography" and have arranged "dialogical writings" in which nonanthropologists are brought into research projects and asked to "exercise something like an ethnographic sensibility" (see also Marcus 1993–2000 and Holmes and Marcus 2008).

2. Examples of anthropologists cum activists in relation to the Global Justice Movement and the Occupy movement include Alvarez (2009), Escobar (2009), Graeber (2009), Juris and Razsa (2012), Desai (2013), and Routledge (2013). See Eschle and Maiguashca (2010) and Conway (2013) for more about feminism within the Global Justice Movement in the context of South Asia. Edelman (2009) has in detail discussed the complex relation between activists and scholars and the sometimes blurred boundaries, the synergies and tensions. Related discussions are also found in Kunnath (2012, 2013).

3. For more about how to use the body as a research tool, see, for example, Wacquant (2004). For an elaboration on the concept "kinesthetic empathy," in another kind of anthropological field, see for example Wulff (1998).

4. To make it clear, I have not practiced "militant ethnography" during my own field studies among activists. Still though, I have taken part in demonstrations in India and Nepal and probably even experienced "kinesthetic empathy" by participating in the emotionally overwhelming Mumbai World Social Forum in 2004.

5. Dalit is an emic concept, used by activists among the so-called untouchables— who mobilize against caste discrimination, which is still widespread in India in spite of the laws. With the Dalit Panthers in the 1970s, inspired by the Black Panthers in the United States, the concept of Dalit, "oppressed," was transformed to signal self-respect and strength.

6. I was familiar with the field, since I had earlier worked among activists in the Dalit movement in India and Great Britain (Hardtmann 2009) and was also part of the preparatory discussions over the Internet among the Dalit activists traveling to the WSF in Nairobi.

7. I had collaborated before in writing with Dalit scholars, activists, authors, poets, and artists. (Hardtmann and Thorat 2006a, 2006b). The writing project described in this essay was different, as the idea to explore the collaborative writing possibilities between scholars and activists was, as mentioned, an explicit purpose on its own.

8. The same could be said about media and journalists present at demonstrations and at World Social Forums, who are highly valued as interlocutors and "appropriated" by the activists.

9. My idea to invite two European professors of Social Anthropology as well as two prominent senior Dalit feminists from India and Nepal was, for example, severely questioned. The first two were rejected, by Vincent, with the argument that it would create an uneven power balance in status between the Indian activ-

ists and the European professors and the activists would be less inclined to take part in the discussions. We took advice from some younger activists, who were not in favor of including the two suggested senior Dalit feminists from India and Nepal. Time has passed, they argued, and younger Dalit feminists should now replace the seniors with the ideas and energy of the new generation.

10. We further discussed the platform where the workshop should take place in some drawn-out email correspondence. Neither a university in Kathmandu nor the office of a Dalit organization were seen as options. Finally we decided to get together for the workshop in a neutral small family-run hotel, with a conference room, on the outskirts of Kathmandu. We had some of the different interests represented according to my wishes in the workshop, as well as representation from different geographical areas. We choose to invite some younger Dalit feminists, and in the end no professors participated.

11. The workshop was financed by the Swedish South Asian Studies Network (SAS-NET), Lund University www.sasnet.lu.se/.

12. One of them was a social anthropologist from London, with an expertise in Nepal society and activism and the other one was a woman from Osaka in Japan, involved in an exchange program between Dalit women in Nepal and Burakumin women from Japan. (Burakumin is the largest minority in Japan, who experience a similar kind of caste discrimination as Dalits in South Asia.) At the time of the workshop they were both living in Kathmandu.

13. Vincent gave a background of the World Social Forum, describing an economic neoliberal globalization out of which protests had grown across the world. We read the Declaration of Principles for the World Social Forum together and discussed critically, in detail, each one of the principles. We discussed the purpose of the World Social Forum, using as a point of departure a debate between Chico Whitaker and Walden Bello (http://www.openspaceforum.net/twiki/tiki-read_article.php?articleId=418) and also discussed it in relation to the feminist critique of the WSF being patriarchal in spite of its ideals.

14. During the workshop Sabrina Francis translated between Hindi, English, and Kannada.

15. Our original title of this chapter was shortened in agreement with the editor to better fit the format of this volume, but it originally differentiated between scholars, activists, and activist-scholars.

16. For more about Dalit feminism, see for example Moon and Pawar (2006), Rege (2006) and Ciotti (2014). For Dalit feminism in the broader context of South Asian feminism, see, for example Loomba and Lukose (2012). For Dalit feminism in the context of the Global Justice Movement, see Eschle and Maiguashca (2010), Conway (2013) and Hardtmann (2016, forthcoming).

17. We discussed briefly in the group what to cover under each of the themes. In working couples we made a first sketch of our respective themes. The couples returned to the group, presented their rough outlines, noted the group's reactions, and returned in couples to revise the outlines to include the new ideas from the group.

18. We have discussed what extracts should be included and some of the authors have made small adjustments in order for their writings to fit this chapter.

19. It also includes the principles of opposing economic globalization (neoliberalism) by challenging multinational corporations, the International Financial Institutions, and the governments supporting such corporations; respecting diversity, multiculture, democracy, social justice, equality, gender rights, and human rights; opposing exclusion of any sort and form; and claiming no representation as a global body for networks, organizations, NGOs, and civil society organizations, etc.

20. www.forumsocialmundial.org.br.

21. For example, interdining, intercaste marriage, common worship, sharing cemeteries, availing common resources, assembling all in a common place, education to all, property to all, and equality for women were prohibited by Brahmanism. (Sakshi, Human Rights Watch, Special Survey and Report, Hyderabad, India, 2006.)

22. Eskola also collaborated after the workshop in Nepal with Francis, and went to India for fieldwork related to his M.A. thesis on the Dappu (see Eskola 2010).

23. The original length of the text is 3,550 words (2,000 + 1,300 + 250). The texts of Devi and Manoharan have also been shortened, after discussions, for the purpose of this article.

24. Ambedkar says that a Hindu's public is his caste.

25. In this 150-page volume twelve scholars, experts on the Global Justice Movement, have written collectively in such a way that you cannot tell the different authors apart. Even though I have discussed the working procedure and the format of the book with Jackie Smith, one of the contributors, I am still intrigued by the fact that as many as twelve people managed to collaborate to produce one volume with one and the same voice. For another example of a collaborative writing between an anthropologist and activist, see, for example, Razsa and Kurnik 2012.

26. Darnal has written *A Land of Our Own* (2009), in which he presents the personal stories of eighteen Dalit members in the Nepalese Constituent Assembly.

REFERENCES

Abu-Lughod, Lila. 1991. "Writing against Culture." In *Recapturing Anthropology: Working in the Present,* ed. Richard G. Fox. Santa Fé: School of American Research Press.

Alvarez, Sonia E., with Nalu Faria and Miriam Nobre. 2009. "Another (Also Feminist) World is Possible." In *World Social Forum: Challenging Empires,* ed. Jai Sen and Peter Waterman. Montreal: Black Rose Books.

Ambedkar, BR. 1979 [1936]. *Dr. Babasaheb Ambedkar, Writings and Speeches, Vol 1. The Annihilation of Caste.* (Compiled by Vasant Moon.) Bombay: Education Department, Government of Maharashtra.

———. 1987. *Dr. Babasaheb Ambedkar, Writings and Speeches, Vol 3. Unpublished Writings.* (Compiled by Vasant Moon.) Bombay: Education Department, Government of Maharashtra.

———. 1989a. *Dr. Babasaheb Ambedkar, Writings and Speeches, Vol 5. Unpublished Writings.* (Compiled by Vasant Moon.) Bombay: Education Department, Government of Maharashtra.

———. 1989b. *Dr. Babasaheb Ambedkar, Writings and Speeches, Vol. 6. On Economics.* (Compiled by Vasant Moon.) Bombay: Education Department, Government of Maharashtra.

———. 1994. *Dr. Babasaheb Ambedkar, Writings and Speeches, Vol 13. Dr. Ambedkar–The Principal Architect of the Constitution of India.* (Compiled by Vasant Moon.) Bombay: Education Department, Government of Maharashtra.

———. 2003. *Dr. Babasaheb Ambedkar, Writings and Speeches, Vol 17 (III). Dr. BR Ambedkar and his Egalitarian Revolution.* Bombay: Education Department, Government of Maharashtra.

Casas-Cortés, Maribel, Michal Osterweil, and Dana E. Powell. 2013. "Transformation in Engaged Ethnography." In *Insurgent Encounters: Transnational Activism, Ethnography, and the Political,* ed. Jeffrey S. Juris and Alex Khasnabish. 2013. Durham: Duke University Press.

Chatterjee, Debi. 2004. *Up Against Caste–Comparative Study of Ambedkar and Periyar.* New Delhi: Rawat Publications.

Ciotti, Manuela. 2014. "Dalit women between social and analytical alterity. Rethinking the 'quintessentially marginal.'" In L. Fernandes (ed.). *Handbook of gender in South Asia.* London, New York: Routledge.

Conway, Janet M. 2013. *Edges of Global Justice: The World Social Forum and Its "Others".* New York: Routledge.

Darnal, Suvash. 2009. *A Land of Our Own: Conversations with Dalit Members in the Constituent Assembly.* Kathmandu: Samata Foundation and Jagaran Media Centre.

Desai, Manisha. 2013. "The Possibilities and Perils for Scholar-Activists and Activists-Scholars: Reflections on the Feminist Dialogues." In *Insurgent Encounters: Transnational Activism, Ethnography, and the Political,* ed. Jeffrey S. Juris and Alex Khasnabish. Durham: Duke University Press.

Edelman, Marc. 2009. "Synergies and Tensions between Rural Social Movements and Professional Researchers." *The Journal of Peasant Studies* 36, no. 1, 245–265.

Eschle, Catherine, and Bice Maiguashca. 2010. *Making Feminist Sense of the Global Justice Movement.* Lanham: Rowman and Littlefield Publishers.

Escobar, Arturo. 2009. "Other Worlds are (Already) Possible: Self-organisation, Complexity, and Post-Capitalist Cultures." In *World Social Forum: Challenging Empires,* ed. Jai Sen and Peter Waterman. Montreal: Black Rose Books.

Eskola, Jussi. 2010. *Dalit Dynamics in South India: Culture as a Tool for Emancipation.* Master's thesis. Uppsala: Department of Theology, Religion in Conflict and Peace-Building.

Eyerman, Ron, and Andrew Jamison. 1991. *Social Movements: A Cognitive Approach.* Cambridge: Polity Press.

Faubion, James D. 2009. "The Ethics of Fieldwork as an Ethics of Connectivity, or The Good Anthropologist (Isn't What She Used to Be)." In *Fieldwork Is Not What It Used to Be: Learning Anthropology's Method in a Time of Transition,* ed. James D. Faubion and George E. Marcus. Ithaca: Cornell University Press.

Faubion, James D., and George E. Marcus, eds. 2009. *Fieldwork Is Not What It Used to Be: Learning Anthropology's Method in a Time of Transition.* Ithaca: Cornell University Press.

Graeber, David. 2009. *Direct Action: An Ethnography.* Edinburgh: AK Press.

Hannerz, Ulf. 2006. "Studying Down, Up, Sideways, Through, Backwards, Forwards, Away and at Home: Reflections on the Field Worries of an Expansive Discipline." In *Locating the Field,* ed. Simon Michael Coleman and Peter Collins. London: Berg/Bloomsbury.

Hardtmann, Eva-Maria. 2009. *The Dalit Movement in India: Local Practices, Global Connections.* New Delhi: Oxford University Press.

———. 2016, forthcoming. *South Asian Activists in the Global Justice Movement.* New Delhi: Oxford University Press.

Hardtmann, Eva-Maria, and Vimal Thorat, eds. (in collaboration with the Indian Library). 2006a. *Berättelsen på min Rygg: Indiens Daliter i Uppror mot Kastsystemet: Prosa, Essäer, Dokument.* (*The Epic Inscribed on my Back: Indian Dalit Uprising against the Caste System.*) Stockholm: Ordfront.

Hardtmann, Eva-Maria, and Vimal Thorat (in collaboration with the Indian Library). 2006b. *Detta Land som aldrig var vår Moder: Dikter av Indiska Dalitpoeter och Bilder av Savi Sawarkar.* (*This Land Which Was Never Mother to Us: Poetry by Indian Dalit Poets and Paintings by Savi Sawarkar.*) Stockholm: Tranan.

Holmes, Douglas, and George E. Marcus. 2005. "Refunctioning Ethnography: The Challenge of an Anthropology of the Contemporary." In *Handbook of Qualitative Research,* ed. Norman Denzin and Yvonna Lincoln. Thousand Oaks, CA: Sage.

Holmes, Douglas, and George E. Marcus. 2008. "Collaboration Today and Re-Imagination of the Classic Scene of Fieldwork Encounter." *Collaborative Anthropologies* 1: 81–101.

Iyer, VR Krishna. 1990. *Dr. Ambedkar and the Dalit Future.* Delhi: BR Publishing Corporation.

Jadhav, Narendra. 1993. *Dr. Ambedkar's Economic Thought and Philosophy.* Bombay: Popular Prakashan,

Juris, Jeffrey S. 2008. *Networking Futures–The Movements against Corporate Globalization.* Durham: Duke University Press.

Juris, Jeffrey, and Maple Razsa. 2012. "Occupy, Anthropology, and the 2011 Global Uprisings." *Fieldsights–Hot Spots, Cultural Anthropology Online.* 27 July. http://www.culanth.org/fieldsights/63-occupy-anthropology-and-the-2011-global-uprisings.

Juris, Jeffrey S., and Alex Khasnabish, eds. 2013. *Insurgent Encounters: Transnational Activism, Ethnography, and the Political.* Durham: Duke University Press.

Juris, Jeffrey S., and Alex Khasnabish. 2013. "Conclusion." In *Insurgent Encounters:*

Transnational Activism, Ethnography, and the Political, ed. Juris, Jeffrey S. and Alex Khasnabish. Durham: Duke University Press.

Keer, Dhananjay. 2005 [1990]. *Dr. Ambedkar: Life and Mission.* Mumbai: Popular Prakashan.

Kunnath, George J. 2012. *Rebels from the Mud Houses: Dalits and the Making of the Maoist Revolution in Bihar.* New Delhi: Social Science Press.

——. 2013. "Anthropology's Ethical Dilemmas: Reflections from the Maoist Fields of India." *Current Anthropology* Volume 54, Number 6, December.

Larbeer, Mohan, and V. Alexander, eds. 2000. *The Colors of Liberation.* Madurai: Dalit Resource Centre.

Lassiter, Luke Eric. 2005. *The Chicago Guide to Collaborative Ethnography.* Chicago: Chicago University Press.

——. 2008. "Moving Past Public Anthropology and doing Collaborative Research." In *Annals of Anthropological Practice.* Vol. 29, Issue 1 (March): 70–86.

Loomba, Ania and Ritty A. Lukose (eds). 2012. *South Asian Feminisms.* Durham and London: Duke University Press.

Marcus, George E., ed. 1993–2000. *The Late Editions Series, Vol 1- 8: Cultural Studies for the End of the Century.* Chicago: Chicago University Press.

Margaret, M. Swathy. 2005. "Dalit Feminism." *Countercurrents.* 3 June. http://www .countercurrents.org/feminism-margaret030605.htm.

Moon, Meenakshi and Urmila Pawar. 2006. *We also made History: Women in the Ambedkarite Movement.* New Delhi: Zubaan Books, an imprint of Kali for Women.

Narayan, Kirin. 1989. *Saints, Scoundrels and Storytellers.* Philadelphia: University of Pennsylvania Press.

Omvedt, Gail. 2007. *Dalits and the Democratic Revolution: Dr. Ambedkar and the Dalit Movement in Colonial India.* New Delhi: Sage.

Razsa, Maple, and Andrej Kurnik. 2012. "The Occupy Movement in Zizek's Home Town: Direct Democracy and a Politics of Becoming." *American Ethnologist* 39, no. 2: 238–258.

Rege, Sharmila. 2006. *Writing Caste/Writing Gender – Narrating Dalit Women's Testimonies.* New Delhi: Zubaan, an imprint of Kali for Women.

Routledge, Paul. 2013. "Activist Ethnography and Translocal Solidarity." In *Insurgent Encounters: Transnational Activism, Ethnography, and the Political,* ed. Jeffrey S. Juris and Alex Khasnabish. Durham: Duke University Press.

Sahi, Jyoti. "Dalit as a Cultural Memory: The Creative Language of the 'Panchamama.'" In Larbeer, Mohan, and V. Alexander, ed. 2000.

Sen, Amartya. 2007. *Identity and Violence: The Illusion of Destiny.* New York: WW Norton & Company.

Sklar, Deidre. 1994. "Can Bodylore Be Brought to Its Senses?" *Journal of American Folklore* 107, no. 423: 9–22.

Smith, Jackie, Marina Karides, Marc Becker, Dorval Brunelle, Christopher Chase-Dunn, Donatella della Porta, Rosalba Icaza Garza, Jeffrey S. Juris, Lorenza Mosca, Ellen Reese, Peter (Jay) Smith, Roland Vázquez. 2008. *Global Democracy and the World Social Forums.* Boulder: Paradigm Press.

Wacquant, Louïs. 2004. *Body and Soul: Notebooks of an Apprentice Boxer.* New York: Oxford University Press.

Wulff, Helena. 1998. *Ballet across Borders: Career and Culture in the World of Dancers.* London: Berg/Bloomsbury.

IV.

Writing across Genres

Chapter 13

Fiction and Anthropological Understanding

A Cosmopolitan Vision

Nigel Rapport

THE "LITERARY" AND THE "ANTHROPOLOGICAL"

Let me begin with two themes. The first is that fiction—the novel in particular—has prided itself on the respect it has had for, and the attention it has paid to, the human individual. A critical study of literature affords a reliable antidote to any attempt at a mass description of humanity and a mass solution to its problems, according to Joseph Brodsky (1988: G2). Or in the words of novelist EM Forster (1972: 66): "I have no mystic faith in the people. I have in the individual. He seems to me a divine achievement and I mistrust any view which belittles him." Literature fosters a sense of individual uniqueness and separateness, experiential authenticity and integrity, providing testimony to human diversity and perversity.

The second theme is that since an individual human life is *sui generis,* it cannot be treated systematically. Individual identity can neither be represented in symbolic terms nor translated from one consciousness to another because subjectivity, the qualia of consciousness, cannot be generalized upon or objectified. "Subjectivity is truth, subjectivity is reality," as Søren Kierkegaard summed up (1941: 118), for only living is like living. "Shut in a bone box," in novelist William Golding's words (1962: 7–10), communication is "our passion and our despair": "living is like nothing because it is everything."

Taken together, these two ideas can be said to constitute the problematic of my personal anthropology. I would write so as to provide testimony for individual uniqueness and to do justice to the individuality of human identity and experience. On the face of it I recognize that this is a paradoxical project, counterintuitive, contrarian. Is not this the self-proclaimed territory of literary fiction? Is not the project a scientific impossibility—hence "fictional"? Should not anthropology concentrate on social-scientific concerns that are distinctively its own: social structure, cultural pattern, determinations of identity that may or may not be individual?

One faces, in short, a disciplinary divide, recognized by exponents on both sides, which demands that differences of genre, institutionality, and social engagement between anthropology and literary fiction are their outstanding and abiding characteristics. The "literary," then, Eric Auerbach (1974: 538) explains, revokes the hegemony of exterior events so that inner processes of consciousness can be made focal. "Literature," David Lodge (1977: 1) elaborates, entails language being aesthetically pleasing, calling attention to itself as a medium beyond what it appears superficially to be describing. The literary text is indirect and selective: introverted and self-oriented, it would rivet attention on itself. Literature takes cultural matériel and transforms it, exploits it, into the might-have-been, the should-be, the could-well-be, the would-never-be. The "anthropological" text, by contrast, is ideally referential and based on the descriptive honesty of ethnography: a dedication to fact, not to the satisfaction of artistry; an honest depiction of actual happenings in genuine settings not an impressionistic fusion of idea and reality (Watt 1964: 306–308). Realism of anthropological content is part-and-parcel of a methodological rigor that includes the painstaking revelation of the logic in associations and extrapolations behind arguments made and conclusions reached. In short, as Clifford Geertz (1988) reported amid the "Writing Culture" debate, anthropology would resist seeing its studies as in any way fictional or imaginative: speculative, maybe, inductive probably, but always true, and directly relatable to the stimuli of an externally met world. Anthropology produces plain texts in no wise overdetermined by rhetoric or style. Hence, Geertz (1988: 141–142) distances the "mythopoetic treatments" of literature, and the "make-believe" it concerns, from the anthropological logic that delivers convincing accounts of how real others really lived.

In short, a disciplinary divide mutually distinguishes the "anthropological" and the "literary" as projects properly defined through their binary opposition. If symbolic realities are founded upon dialectical relations (Leach 1976: 33–34), so that things are epiphenomena of the perceived discontinuities and differences between them, then this will include intellectual disciplines. It might come as no surprise, then, should the title of this chapter,

"Fiction and Anthropological Understanding," translate into a review of those ways in which two discrete genres (or genre-systems) have related to one other by way of partial overlaps and oppositions, partial samenesses and differences. To go beyond this—to say, perhaps, that "Fiction and Anthropological Understanding" portends the fictional nature of anthropological understanding as such—is surely to be contrarian, unnecessarily counterintuitive. Is not a conception of anthropology *as* literature, *as* fiction, a surrendering of ground, a conflation with an antithesis? Should not anthropologists resist a "literary turn" if this is taken to mean so radical a change to their disciplinary tradition, their "culture," as to enter the territory of fiction—to give testimony to the individuality of consciousness and experience?

AN INCLUSIVE "COSMOPOLITAN" ANTHROPOLOGY

It is the case, to be sure, that one does not have to be contrarian. Before the "Writing Culture," debate as well as since, "Fiction and Anthropological Understanding" can be seen to have entailed a range of insightful explorations of *fiction as local practice,* in a manner similar to how anthropology has explored kinship or politics or ritual or dance, as local traditions of expression and action. One includes here work by the likes of Ruth Finnegan (1967), Brian Street (1975), Victor Turner (1976), Bill Watson (1995), Michael Herzfeld (1997), Karin Barber (2003), and Helena Wulff (2012) on the insights fiction gives into local structures of power, cognition, socialization, imagination, aesthetics, and ritual. Richard Handler and Dan Segal (1990), again, find in the fiction of Jane Austen what they call "alter-cultural action." Social conventions need not be seen as finite sets of rules that determine behavior but as complex metaphors that encourage creative negotiation of social relations. Austen's heroic characters are those who most creatively comment upon, invert, and, indeed, implement a pragmatic understanding of the rules of etiquette and do not naively reproduce a standardized version of their society. The expression of a social aesthetic consolidates an individual identity (cf. Wulff 2002).

Equally, "Fiction and Anthropological Understanding" can encompass a variety of explorations concerning how a *contrastive comparison* of the different generic histories, practices, and intentionalities of anthropology and literature might elucidate and advance the distinctive projects of each. One recalls, here, the incisive contributions of James Boon (1973), Paul Rabinow (1977), Mary Louise Pratt (1992), Vincent Crapanzano (2003), among others. In *The Prose and the Passion* (Rapport 1994), I read my ethnography of the English village of Wanet through the novels of EM Forster—how would it be to regard Forster as a fellow-ethnographer of English twentieth-century social life?—and also vice versa—how would it be to regard Forster as informant and his novels as his world-view, alongside the other world-views of English informants I was intending to decipher? To compare across the boundary between social novelist and social anthropologist, I concluded, is to be delivered of deeper insights into the nature of writing self and society, of individuality and creativity, of belonging and community, of the way in which the individual narration of world-view is a constant human practice. I argued for "the zigzag" as method and ethos. To zigzag between the genres of ethnography and novel, between Forsterian characters and my informants, between the moral and psychological insights of any individual writers of social life, is to set up kinds of partial connection. Zigzagging between different phenomena, intent on experiencing each in its turn, is to be delivered of comparative truths while still maintaining a sense of the integrity and individuality of each phenomenology. To compare across disciplinary boundaries in this way is, to adapt an argument of George Devereux's (1978: 1), to honor the complex reality of the phenomena under review. Knowledge is revealed as itself a form of movement.

Finally, "Fiction and Anthropological Understanding" can be understood to include those attempts by anthropologists to be *writers of fiction themselves*. One turns to the fictional to better express truths of fieldwork that one deems cannot be formulated in conventional ethnographic genres. One includes here works that have garnered critical reaction as aesthetic achievements in their own right (Briggs 1970; Wilmsen 1999; Jackson 2004, 2013; Narayan 2012). Oliver La Farge won a Pulitzer prize for *Laughing Boy: A Navajo Love-Story* (1929). At a ceremonial dance in 1915, the young, earnest silversmith "Laughing Boy" falls in love with "Slim Girl," a beautiful but elusive "American-educated" Navajo: against the background of the changing cultures of the American Southwest, Laughing Boy and Slim Girl's conflicted way of life brings tragic consequences. In *Return to Laughter: An Anthropological Novel* (1954), again, Laura Bohannon, writing under the pseudonym Elenore Smith Bowen, revisits her fieldwork experiences in Nigeria among the Tiv. Witch trials and a smallpox epidemic provide the dramatic context for an exposé of the ethical ambiguities facing a neophytic anthropologist as ideals and unconscious assumptions meet the reality of living in an alien setting.

But what if, by "Fiction and Anthropological Understanding," one wished to imply something else again, distinct from the above three practices, more subversive of disciplinary boundaries? I have been very taken by a passage from EM Forster where he reflects on the novelist's art. "We cannot understand each other except in a rough and ready way," Forster begins (1984: 69), "we cannot reveal ourselves, even when we want to; what we call intimacy is only a makeshift; perfect knowledge is an illusion. But in the novel," he concludes, "we can know people perfectly, and ... we can find here a compensation for their dimness in life." For this reason Forster would describe fiction as "truer" than the human sciences. It may go beyond the evidence provided by word and act, but then each of us knows from experience how much of human significance *does* lie beyond. While concerned with characterizing the human condition, the human scientist has nevertheless appeared content to treat only the surfaces of social life and with what can be deduced from the forms of life, the external signs. Only the novelist has revealed characters' inner and outer lives, their self-communings and subconscious musings alongside what is evident: the novelist alone has taken the opportunity to provide testimony of "the hidden life at its source" (Forster 1984: 55–56).

I am taken by Forster's vision of a true human accounting but I am loath to accept his dichotomy. I would like an anthropological science, too, to account for all of human experience: for individuality, subjectivity, interiority, as well as the formal coming together of individuals in social relations (Cohen and Rapport 1995; Rapport 2003). If, as Kierkegaard put it, "subjectivity is the truth," then I would like to envisage a kind of *scientific* evidencing that is based in experience and interpretation, however "fictional." (I recall Clifford Geertz's (1988: 141) term "faction" for a kind of anthropology in search of meaning not mechanical laws. Faction entailed an imaginative writing about real people in real places at real times; where "imaginative" and "imagined" need not be confused with "imaginary," where "fictional" need not equate to the "false," nor the "made-out" to the "made-up.")

It might be said that anthropology has, indeed, increasingly admitted fiction into its genre-system. Luminaries such as Geertz have welcomed it; Rodney Needham (1978: 75–76) counseled anthropology to aspire to the "humane significance" of great art precisely by writing with the "acuity" and "penetration" of a George Eliot, a Fyodor Dostoevsky, or a Virginia Woolf; Edmund Leach (1982: 52–53) challenged anthropologists to be more than "bad novelists" by realizing their own capacities, and duty, to provide the "deep understanding" and "insight" found in the work of "great artists."

But then if the novelist (George Eliot, EM Forster) has traditionally privileged the individual, and if literary modernists (Virginia Woolf, William Golding) have earned their reputations through endeavoring to represent the subjective and inchoate nature of consciousness and the ambiguous, individual connections to social life, then how and why might this be improved upon by the anthropologist? The key, I suggest, lies in anthropology's dual or hybrid status as both science and humanity. "Born omniform," was Geertz's (1983: 21) depiction of anthropology's disciplinarity, intent on transcending boundaries between kinds of knowledge. Similarly for Gregory Bateson (1959: 296), only the holistic approach of a nonspecialist, "interdisciplinary discipline," however apparently amateurish, could hope to tackle the vast intricacies of human experience. Being both science and humanity I would designate anthropology's project as *at once* an elucidation of human truths—the facts of the human condition—*and* a concern with appropriate representation, with aesthetics, *and* a concern with right, with justice. *Anthropology adds to the literary endeavor of giving faithful testimony to the individual case and of representing a subjective consciousness by placing these in the context of a scientific rationality and a moral philosophy.* Alongside the representation of consciousness, anthropology intends to disclose the objectivity of human subjectivity and engender the expression of human individuality as a universal right.

I might call this vision for anthropology a "cosmopolitan" one, borrowing from the conceptualization by Kant (and concomitant, significantly, with his conceptualization of "anthropology," the first in modern times). Kant envisioned "cosmopolitanism" as a bringing together of the two poles of human existence in a dialectical tension. At one pole lay "*cosmos*," the human whole or species, the universal human condition. At the other pole lay "*polis*," the individual particular: the specific embodiment of the human condition in an individual life. Cosmo-politanism claimed that these two have always to be understood in relation to each other. Humanity manifested itself only in particular individual lives: each individual life was an embodiment of universal human capabilities and liabilities.

The dualistic or dialectical formulation of the one and the many, of unity in diversity, gave rise to an enterprise that, according to Kant, was tripartite. Cosmopolitanism was a scientific endeavor, concerned with ontology: one would *know* the human whole by accumulating knowledge on its individual particulars, on the specificities of individual lives locally practiced. In addition, cosmopolitanism was a moral endeavor: one would *improve* the human lot by applying scientific knowledge to the conditions of social life and exchange and working to secure the better fulfillment of all human individuals. And in addition, cosmopolitanism was a methodological endeavor: one would search out ways best to *represent* the specific contents and contexts of individual lives, and species-wide capacities.

It is because I would (again) imbue anthropology with a Kantian, cosmopolitan purpose—science married to aesthetics married to morality—that I would delineate its project in the seemingly paradoxical terms of including the literary-fictional other: intending testimony of individual uniqueness and attempting to do justice to the individuality of experience. Individual and species are the ontological poles of the human condition: in every *individual* life is embodied a *human* exemplar. Anthropology is to write the human—accumulatively to secure knowledge and a moral awareness and an aesthetic sense of the human condition—by knowing that there is a potential sameness to every individual life. Beyond the contingencies of time and place, beyond accidents of birth, beyond rhetorical-cum-symbolic classifications of individuals into membership of societies and cultures, communities, nations, religions, ethnicities, and classes, there exist the abiding and concrete and overriding realities of individual and species. It is to these realities that a cosmopolitan anthropology attends, scientifically, morally, and aesthetically.

The cosmopolitan vision has not been better phrased than in Martha Nussbaum's (1996) latter-day Kantian summary. "Any human being might have been born in any nation"; the cosmopolitan duty is to "recognise humanity wherever it occurs, and give its fundamental ingredients, reason and moral capacity, our first allegiance and respect" (Nussbaum 1996: 7). A cosmopolitan allegiance is to no social structure or system of government, no classificatory identity (concerning societies and cultures, communities, nations, religions, ethnicities, and classes), but to the worldwide commonality comprising the humanity of all human beings. Here is a virtual commonwealth (Kant named it the "kingdom of ends") whose constituents or citizens are human individuals anywhere and everywhere. As Nussbaum (1996: 133, 136) concludes:

> Whatever else we are bound by and pursue, we should recognize, at whatever personal or social cost, that each human being is human and counts as the moral equal of every other. ... The accident of being born a Sri Lankan, or a Jew, or a female, or an African-American, or a poor person, is just that—an accident of birth. It is not and should not be taken as a determinant of moral worth. Human personhood, by which I mean the possession of practical reason and other basic moral capacities, is the source of our moral worth, and this worth is equal. ... Make liberty of choice the benchmark of any just constitutional order, and refuse to compromise this principle in favour of any particular tradition or religion.

Cosmopolitanism is an emancipatory project. It would improve the conditions of human life by freeing both species and individual from that which would hinder the potential for fulfillment. One considers here not only the "despotism" of famine and disease but also the despotism of ignorance, of tyranny, and of lives circumscribed by narrow limits of merely local conventionalism ("What ever crushes individuality is despotism, by whatever name it may be called, and whether it professes to be the will of God or the injunctions of men" (John Stuart Mill 1963: 188)). Cosmopolitanism opens up individual lives to global expectations, just as it celebrates any freely chosen local life-project as a respectable and rightful manifestation of global human potential. A cosmopolitan anthropology sees in the individual "*Anyone,*" the global human actor (Rapport 2010a, 2010b).

"FICTIONAL TRUTH," "VITAL TRUTH"

Let me return to the two themes with which I began and that I said consti-tuted the problematic of my anthropology. Literary fiction prides itself on the respectful attention it gives to individual identity, experiential authentic-ity, and integrity. Here is a uniqueness that cannot be treated systematically or generalized upon. And yet there is a universality of human condition also contained here that a cosmopolitan anthropology would objectively know, morally secure, and aesthetically celebrate. With a foot in the sciences and the humanities alike, it would appear that anthropology demands of and for itself a particular and novel kind of truth: one might name it "fictional truth."

Nor need one be loath to extend or multiply the notion of "truth" in this way. Truth can retain its essential fixity, John Stuart Mill counseled (1963: 160), even as one recognizes that the kind of *certainty* humanly reach-able differs depending on the complexity of the subject-matter under re-view. The truth that is attainable in mathematics, then, is different from that of natural sciences, which is different again from truth in the domains of politics or philosophy where different argumentational matrices or ide-ologies can be brought to bear, and different again from religious or poetic domains where experiential judgments can remain incommensurate. More radically, Patrick Baert (2005) argues recently that no one *logic* of inquiry need even guide all science: no one method or set of procedures, and no unchangeable foundations to "knowledge." The living nature of the sub-ject-matter of biology, for instance, excludes it from too determinate and law-governed a structuration: "biological complexity surpasses our compu-tational and cognitive capabilities so that a complete account cannot be ac-complished" (Baert 2005: 192). The scientist must be more pragmatic and instrumental than systematic, suiting guidelines and frames of reference to research objectives.

A formulation of TS Eliot's (1917: 9) resonates here: "Any vital truth is incapable of being applied to another case: the essential is unique. Perhaps that is why it is so neglected: because it is useless." The formulation comes from the short story, "Eeldrop and Appleplex" (the only one that the poet and critic had published), in which Eliot fictionalizes a conversation between himself and Ezra Pound (possibly) concerning the "concrete individuality of the human soul" and how this phenomenon is hidden and lost in a public language of ubiquitous generalization, classification, and labeling. Eeldrop's (Eliot's) conclusion, nevertheless, is that while apparently useless—seeming not to refer to anything beyond itself—and neglected, the truth of individuality is still vital, still essential. Hence, Eeldrop (Eliot) will determine to keep on philosophizing from a particular, individual point of view and refuse labels so far as possible (the key being, he feels, to eschew self-consciousness and a language that calls attention to itself as language).

Eliot, however, was content to write in an aesthetic discourse alone: poetry, criticism, occasional fiction. What might be the key to conceptualizing and effecting a new kind of fictional, vital truth that aspires to know an essential individuality not only aesthetically but also scientifically and morally? In line with the tripartite character of the cosmopolitan enterprise, the fictional-cum-vital truth associated with its anthropology would, I suggest, have the following components. *First,* anthropology must discern the (scientific) truths surrounding the capabilities and liabilities of human being. One does not limit study to the "accident" of current customary behaviors and conventions but seeks to discover, as if an abstraction or a potentiality, all that human individuals might be capable of achieving and might be liable to suffer. One builds up one's knowledge from present and past manifestations of human circumstance but one recognizes that human-individual capacities exceed all that has so far filled human history: intrinsic to the human is the capacity to create, to mutate, and to transform (Rapport 2010c). *Second,* anthropology must determine the (moral) truths that surround the expression of human capabilities and liabilities and the fulfillment of individual lives. To fulfill one's potential is to be deemed a universal human right, while "the despotism of custom is everywhere the standing hindrance to human advancement" (Mill 1963: 194). At the same time, if one is to universalize the right to fashion a life-project that accords with world-views of one's own personal construction, interpretation, and narration, then an ethos of mannerly exchange and schema of public politeness is instituted. To right the hindrances to free expression is also to write a social program of global citizenship (Amit and Rapport 2012). *Third,* anthropology must determine the (aesthetic) truths that surround gaining access to, and providing representation of, human-individual life-projects and world-views. One hopes to know and to show the individual beyond the role-player, the individual beyond the public figure, and the individual beyond the contingencies of historical circumstance. One reaches for the individual as human being, instantiation in his or her very bodily specificity of the universality of species (Rapport 1997).

CASE-STUDY: "FRANCESCA"

The ambition of the above "cosmopolitan" program is not gratuitous. Its anthropological focus on individuality is justified inasmuch as the individual self represents, in Anthony Cohen's (1994: 50) phrasing, "the essential dynamo of social process." A culture, as a fund of symbolic forms, is maintained to the extent that it provides the vehicles of conception and expression, the meaning-making tools, of interpretative individuals; a society, as a set of institutions, remains a collective of members by virtue of self-conscious individuals. The individual is, in short, "the site where life is lived" (Jackson 1996: 22).

In elaboration of this point let me, finally, change register and recall the plot of the novel, *The Bridges of Madison County*, by Robert James Waller (1992), better known perhaps in the film version with Clint Eastwood and Meryl Streep (1995). At their mother Francesca's death, Michael Johnson and his sister Carolyn find that a strange request had been conveyed to her attorney: their mother's remains are to be cremated, and the ashes scattered at Roseman Covered Bridge. Cremation itself was an unusual practice in this part of America and the request engenders gossip. Her children carry out their mother's instructions but still wonder why their "rather sensible" mother should behave in such an "enigmatic" way, not wanting to be buried beside their father as was customary. The contents of a safe deposit box, plus their mother's journals and a sealed envelope to "Carolyn or Michael" gradually bring to light things that had remained their mother's secrets for over twenty years.

Much of the architecture of the novel is concerned with how that secret— in effect, Francesca Johnson's inner life—comes to be feasibly made public. The key artifact is the sealed letter, and its revelation of a story whose details are delicate but remarkable, of Madison County, Iowa, in the summer of 1965, and the meeting between Francesca and one Robert L. Kincaid. The drama of the story concerns the distance between the private truths of Francesca's life and the conventional, surface calm of rural farm life that went on undisturbed for decades.

Francesca writes the letter, she explains, to set her affairs in final order. The children have married and moved away; her husband Richard (their father) has died. If her children are to know who their mother really was, then even at the risk of spoiling their memories of her, there is a matter too important, and beautiful, for them to remain ignorant of. During four summer days long ago, when her husband and children had traveled to the Illinois State Fair, Francesca had met and fallen in love with Robert Kincaid, a photographer contracted by *National Geographic* magazine to document the wooden, covered bridges of Madison County. They had met by chance when he stopped at the farmhouse to ask for directions. She accompanied him to Roseman Bridge, but soon she found herself drawn further: toward a peregrine, unearthly quality of his that she found irresistible.

Francesca found, too, her Iowa life being brought into sudden clear focus. She had come from Europe as a war-bride, content to enter America and escape war-torn Italy. Richard Johnson had provided her with sturdy kindness: steady ways, and an even life of safe, caring friendship. For twenty years she had accepted the circumscriptions of rural Iowa, rebelling only silently against the triviality, the fear of change, the suspicion of openness. But her relationship with Richard, she now saw, was more a partnership—familial and business—than an emotional or even physical sharing. And this was not her dream.

What was she to do? Robert Kincaid begged her to go with him; Francesca knew herself ready to go. But her duty lay elsewhere. Her husband's character—his remoteness from passion and magic—did not make him an inferior person. He had been good to her, and given her children she treasured. Her leaving might well destroy him; her teenaged children would experience, too, the pity and whispering of their neighbors. Francesca concluded that she could not tear herself away from these responsibilities. It was likely, also, that living with her irresponsibility would change her from the woman Robert had met and loved; while if she were to leave with Robert, his otherworldliness might become restrained—something that she loved him too much to risk.

Her decision made, it had been respected by Robert. He had departed before her family returned from the fair and had not tried to intervene again in her life. Over the years, she had collected clippings of his articles in *National Geographic,* and had lived with her memories. After her husband Richard's death and her children's moving away Francesca had tried to contact Robert again, but without success. Then, a package had finally arrived from Washington State and Robert Kincaid's executors: his earthly effects, a handwritten letter, and the information that the ashes of his cremated remains had recently been scattered at Roseman Bridge. Hence, the final denouement of Francesca's posthumous letter to her children:

> The paradox is this: If it hadn't been for Robert Kincaid, I'm not sure I could have stayed on the farm all these years. In four days, he gave me a lifetime, a universe, and made the separate parts of me into a whole. I have never stopped thinking of him, not for a moment. Even when he was not in my conscious mind, I could feel him somewhere, always he was there. ... I'm sure you found my burial request incomprehensible; thinking perhaps it was the product of a confused old woman. After reading the 1982 Seattle attorney's letter and my

notebooks, you'll understand why I made that request. I gave my family my life,
I gave Robert Kincaid what was left of me. (Waller 1992: 154–155)

The enormity of their mother's decision is not lost on her children. As
daughter Carolyn exclaims: "four days together, just four," followed by a
"lifetime" of desperate wanting: while their "innocent" family life had carried on in routine ways for years, "all the time … the images she [Francesca]
must have seen" (Waller 1992: 159–160).

What do I say, as an anthropologist, about Waller's fiction? That his perception rings true to me ethnographically (Rapport 1993). Individuals meet
in social interaction only on the surface of their selves. The ambiguities of
symbolic discourse serve to effect misprision of possibly limitless degree;
the very symbolic resources that enable individuals to meet and perform
social roles of mutual engagement, such as husband and wife or parent and
child, also enable individuals to develop world-views and fulfill life-projects
that draw those individuals further apart. Francesca's secret meeting with
Robert Kincaid and her secret decision regarding its consequences for her
social life enable her to play her part as wife and mother for the remaining
years of her life. The images of Robert that occupy her mind as she engages
with her husband and children and that give her strength are absolutely unknown and unknowable by anyone else unless she attempts to convey them.
Yet it is to such hidden individual intentionality that *all* social order owes its
nature: a private individual consciousness projects itself through all social
institutions (a marriage, for example) and animates all cultural forms (being
an attentive mother, for example). The social owes its continuing structuration and the cultural owes its reproduction to the intentioning practice of
individual world-views and life-projects.

More than this, however, I find Waller's treatment of his perception
inspiring. His story of Francesca comprises a truth concerning human social life, its constitution and its operation, to which, as an anthropologist, I
would wish to lend *scientific credibility* and *moral recognition*. It is the nature of
our human condition that private individual consciousness has this public
consequence and bears this public responsibility, I say. The individual is the
site where life is lived. A person is social insofar as they are individual, and
we are social for private individual purposes: there is no social life except
that there is personal individual life. I would write an anthropology that
provides the existence of such individual interiority and its workings with an
ontological basis (Rapport 2008); I would write an anthropology that recognizes the role of individual imagination in social life, how every relationship
is first and foremost an imagined relationship (Rapport 2015).

I would also write an anthropology that affords such individual interiority and imagination moral recognition and legitimation. Social life is a beneficent state; what makes that social life more than mere role-playing or oppression is the authenticity of its enactment by individual members who are true to themselves. Social life is an ethical state insofar as individuals inhabit their own truth, enacting roles in accordance with their own intentionality. Francesca willingly plays her parts as wife and mother because it is in doing so that she determines she is most able to be herself to herself. I am committed anthropologically to the moral project of fashioning a code, a set of procedures and manners, whereby the authenticity and the propriety of individual interiority and imagination are safeguarded. Meeting on the surfaces of themselves and by virtue of ambiguous symbolic forms also means that that very superficiality and ambiguity can afford the private space of a personal preserve. One envisages a code of conventional politeness through which individuals may be both liberal with one another and true to themselves (Rapport 2012).

A cosmopolitan anthropology deals in fictional truths that are recognized as being vital both ontologically and morally.

Nigel Rapport is Professor of Anthropological and Philosophical Studies at the University of St. Andrews, Scotland, where he is founding director of the St Andrews Centre for Cosmopolitan Studies. He has also held the Canada Research Chair in Globalization, Citizenship and Justice at Concordia University of Montreal. His research interests include: social theory, phenomenology, identity and individuality, community, conversation analysis, and links between anthropology and literature and philosophy. Among his books are: *The Prose and the Passion: Anthropology, Literature and the Writing of E. M. Forster* (Manchester University Press), *Transcendent Individual: Towards a Literary and Liberal Anthropology* (Routledge), and *Distortion and Love: An Anthropological Reading of the Art and Life of Stanley Spencer* (Ashgate).

REFERENCES

Amit, Vered, and Nigel Rapport. 2012. *Community, Cosmopolitanism and the Problem of Human Commonality.* London: Pluto.
Auerbach, Erich. 1974. *Mimesis.* Princeton: Princeton University Press.
Baert, Patrick. 2005. "Towards a Pragmatist-inspired Philosophy of Social Science." *Acta Sociologica* 48, no. 3: 191–203.
Barber, Karin. 2003. *The Generation of Plays.* Bloomington: Indiana University Press.

Bateson, Gregory. 1959. "Anthropological Theories." *Science* 129: 294–298.

Boon, James. 1973. *From Symbolism to Structuralism.* New York: Harper and Row.

Bowen, Elenore (alias for Laura Bohannon). 1954. *Return to Laughter: An Anthropological Novel.* London: Gollancz.

Briggs, Jean. 1970. *Never in Anger.* Cambridge, MA: Harvard University Press.

Brodsky, James. 1988, "The Politics of Poetry." *The Sunday Times,* January 10.

Cohen, Anthony. 1994. *Self Consciousness.* London: Routledge.

Cohen, Anthony, and Nigel Rapport, eds. 1995. *Questions of Consciousness.* London: Routledge.

Crapanzano, Vincent. 2003. *Imaginative Horizons.* Chicago: University of Chicago Press.

Devereux, George. 1978. *Ethnopsychoanalysis.* Berkeley: University of California Press.

Eliot, Thomas Stearns. 1917. "Eeldrop and Appleplex (Part I)." *The Little Review* 4, no. 1: 7–11.

Finnegan, Ruth. 1967. *Limba Stories and Story-Telling.* Oxford: Oxford University Press.

Forster, EM. 1972. *Two Cheers for Democracy.* Harmondsworth: Penguin.

———. 1984. *Aspects of the Novel.* Harmondsworth: Penguin.

Geertz, Clifford. 1983. *Local Knowledge.* New York: Basic.

———. 1988. *Works and Lives.* Cambridge: Polity.

Golding, William. 1962. *Free Fall.* New York: Harbinger.

Handler, Richard, and Daniel Segal. 1990. *Jane Austen and the Fiction of Culture.* Tucson: University of Arizona Press.

Herzfeld, Michael. 1997. *Portrait of a Greek Imagination.* Chicago: University of Chicago Press.

Jackson, Michael. 1996. "Introduction: Phenomenology, Radical Empiricism, and Anthropological Critique." In *Things As They Are,* ed. Michael Jackson. Bloomington: Indiana University Press.

———. 2004. *In Sierra Leone.* Durham, NC: Duke University Press.

———. 2013. *The Other Shore: Essays on Writers and Writing.* Berkeley: University of California Press.

Kierkegaard, Soren. 1941. *Concluding Unscientific Postscript.* Princeton: Princeton University Press.

La Farge, Oliver. 1929. *Laughing Boy: A Navajo Love-Story.* Boston: Houghton Mifflin.

Leach, Edmund. 1976. *Culture and Communication.* Cambridge: Cambridge University Press.

———. 1982. *Social Anthropology.* London: Fontana.

Lodge, David. 1977. *The Modes of Modern Writing.* London: Arnold.

Mill, John Stuart. 1963. *The Six Great Humanistic Essays of John Stuart Mill.* New York: Washington Square.

Narayan, Kirin. 2012. *Alive in the Writing: Crafting Ethnography in the Company of Chekhov.* Chicago: University of Chicago Press.

Needham, Rodney. 1978. *Primordial Characters.* Charlottesville: Virginia University Press.

Nussbaum, Martha. 1996. "Patriotism and Cosmopolitanism." In *Love of Country,* ed. Joshua Cohen. Boston: Beacon.

Pratt, Mary. 1992. *Imperial Eyes*. London: Routledge.

Rabinow, Paul. 1977. *Reflections on Fieldwork in Morocco*. California: University of California Press.

Rapport, Nigel. 1993. *Diverse World-Views in an English Village*. Edinburgh: Edinburgh University Press.

——. 1994. *The Prose and the Passion: Anthropology, Literature and the Writing of E. M. Forster*. Manchester: Manchester University Press.

——. 1997. *Transcendent Individual: Towards a Literary and Liberal Anthropology*. London: Routledge.

——. 2003. *I Am Dynamite: An Alternative Anthropology of Power*. London: Routledge.

——. 2008. "Gratuitousness: Notes towards an Anthropology of Interiority." *The Australian Journal of Anthropology* 19, no. 3: 331–349.

——. 2010a. "Apprehending *Anyone*: The Non-Indexical, Post-Cultural and Cosmopolitan Human Actor." *Journal of the Royal Anthropological Institute* (N.S.) 16, no. 1: 84–101.

——. 2010b. "Cosmopolitanism and Liberty," *Social Anthropology* 18, no. 4: 464–470.

——. 2010c. "Human Capacity as an Exceeding, a Going Beyond." In *Human Nature as Capacity: Transcending Discourse and Classification,* ed. Nigel Rapport. Oxford: Berghahn.

——. 2012. *Anyone, The Cosmopolitan Subject of Anthropology*. Oxford: Berghahn.

——. 2015. "'Imagination is in the Barest Reality': On the Universal Human Imagining of the World." In *Reflections on Imagination: Human Capacity and Ethnographic Method,* ed. Nigel Rapport and Mark Harris. Farnham: Ashgate.

Street, Brian. 1975. *The Savage in Literature*. London: Routledge and Kegan Paul.

Turner, Victor. 1976. "African Ritual and Western Literature." In *The Literature of Fact,* ed. Angus Fletcher. New York: Columbia University Press.

Waller, Robert. 1992. *The Bridges of Madison County*. New York: Warner.

Watt, Ian. 1964. "Literature and Society." In *The Arts in Society,* ed. Robert Wilson. Englewood Cliffs, NJ: Prentice-Hall.

Watson, Bill. 1995. "The Novelist's Consciousness." In *Questions of Consciousness,* ed. Anthony Cohen and Nigel Rapport. London: Routledge.

Wilmsen, Edwin. 1999. *Journeys with Flies*. Chicago: University of Chicago Press.

Wulff, Helena. 2002. "Aesthetics at the Ballet: Looking at 'National' Style, Body and Clothing in the London Dance World." In *British Subjects,* ed. Nigel Rapport. London: Berg/Bloomsbury.

——. 2012. "An Anthropological Perspective on Literary Arts in Ireland. " In *Blackwell Companion to the Anthropology of Europe,* ed. Ulrich Kockel, Máiréad Craith, and Jonas Frykman. Oxford: Wiley-Blackwell.

Chapter 14

On Timely Appearances
Literature, Art, Anthropology

Mattias Viktorin

One of the short stories of Andrei Volos's widely acclaimed book *Hurramabad* (2005) includes a few intriguing paragraphs about a woman who sometimes feels unable to express her thoughts. Even ideas that to her seem both clear and convincing invariably appear unfounded and without persuasive power the moment she attempts to share them with her husband or son. Persistently they refuse her attempts to "wrap them into words," as Volos phrases it. Her thoughts, not entirely unlike luminescent fish of the deep sea, seem able to survive only by virtue of the pressure of a bottomless abyss. As soon as they surface, they die. And once they lie there, with bulging lifeless eyes, she too immediately finds them both dull and empty. It makes no difference if time would ultimately prove her right, because with time, novel thoughts, the one more significant than the other, are liable to succeed her previous ones. Words, Volos concludes, seem only to complicate things. They fail her.

And yet, without communication, no idea will appear as real. "Each time we talk about things that can be experienced only in privacy or intimacy," according to Hannah Arendt, "we bring them out into a sphere where they will assume a kind of reality which, their intensity notwithstanding, they never could have had before." Thus in a sense, one might say that appearance—"something that is being seen and heard by others as well as by ourselves"—constitutes reality (Arendt 1998: 50). More specifically, Arendt maintains that the "whole factual world of human affairs depends for its reality and its continued existence, first, upon the presence of others who have seen and heard and will remember, and, second, on the transformation of the intangible into the tangibility of things" (Arendt 1998: 95).

Anthropology has traditionally focused on how society or culture reproduces itself. By conducting participant observation within a cultural setting for an extended period of time, anthropologists have been able to represent a particular way of life from "the native's point of view" through written ethnographies. In addition to this mode of anthropological research, the discipline has in recent years also increasingly become oriented toward the emergent, empirically and analytically (see, e.g., Fischer 2009; Rabinow 2008, 2011; Viktorin 2008, 2013). To focus on something that has not yet assumed a stable form is challenging. First, what participant observation might mean is far from obvious. How could we observe the emergent? Second, "representation" does not seem to be the right term. Since "the emergent" is still in the process of becoming, it has not yet been fully presented, which means it cannot be "re-presented." Instead, one of the tasks for an anthropology centered on the emergent is to give form to that which is in the process of coming into being. And finally, the fact that there is no *ethnos,* whose perspective we could observe, understand, and represent through writing, makes ethnography, too, problematic. Experimentation with other forms of writing becomes necessary.

In this chapter, I discuss the differences between these modes of inquiry—"reproduction" and "emergence"—by placing anthropology in the context of literature and art. Not entirely unlike several contemporary anthropologists, such modernist writers as Robert Musil or Robert Walser sought to develop an approach to literature that focused on giving form to what was in the process of becoming. And as my example from Volos intimates, there is indeed a difference between giving form to what is in a process of coming into being and representing what exists already. If, like the woman in Volos's story, we try to wrap the emergent into already existing forms, it inevitably evades us.

Literature, art, and anthropology actually tend to intersect precisely on the problem of innovative form-giving. To explore such convergences, and what we might learn from them, I emphasize the notion of appearance. "Appearance" and "representation" are not synonymous terms, but signify two different modes of putting anthropology to work. Following Arendt, "appearance" connotes a process of coming into being as in emergence, of becoming visible or noticeable. To speak of appearance in this sense thus brings into focus questions about how something appears or is made to appear, and how it assumes or is given a particular appearance. Also, examples from literature and art show that "appearance" does not necessarily imply a construction that veils or conceals reality, but rather an *actualization* that brings distinct facets of the real into view.

PAYING ATTENTION TO ART

In May 1908, three years after their resignation from the Vienna Secession, the new artists' association opened its first art show in the city. Gustav Klimt (1862–1918), the most prominent member of the group, had been intimately involved in the planning of the *Kunstschau 1908,* which, along with a remarkable variety of contemporary Austrian art, exhibited no less than sixteen of his own paintings (including *Der Kuss,* purchased instantly by the Ministry of Education). It was also an event of extraordinary proportions in other respects. Josef Hoffmann, perhaps the most important among Vienna's *fin de siècle* architects, had been commissioned to design the exhibition complex especially for the occasion. That an entire room of the building was devoted exclusively to *Der Kuss* tells us something about the level of ambition involved. Hinting at grandiosity, too, gilded letters above the main entrance stated, *Der Zeit ihre Kunst, Der Kunst ihre Freiheit* ("To the age its art, to art its freedom"). This had been the Secessionist motto. The "Klimt Group" had retained this dictum, however, when they left the organization—quite literally, in fact, by removing the actual sign from the Secession building (Bisanz 2006: 112–119; Schorske 1981: 267–273; Whitford 1990: 111–129).

Most critics unequivocally praised the *1908 Kunstschau,* which is still considered "the most important exhibition held in Vienna before the First World War" (Dube 1998: 181), and a "crucial turning point in Viennese artistic life" (Bassie 2005: 71). Nevertheless, according to Frank Whitford the exhibition in one sense also intimated a limit to Klimt's artistic reputation. "In the midst of all the critical enthusiasm, all the full-throated songs of praise to Vienna's greatest painter," he writes, "one voice hinted that Klimt's art was so much part of its time that it would die with it" (Whitford 1990: 126). When the "Klimt Group" insisted on *Der Zeit ihre Kunst,* this was probably not what they had in mind. Yet more than a hundred years later *Der Kuss,* although decidedly dated, seems to remain at least equally popular. Timeliness, however, is important—not only the timeliness intrinsic to a work of art itself, but also that of particular ways of presenting, approaching, and appreciating art.

If Klimt was accused of being too much in accord with his time, then perhaps the opposite could be said of the American modernist Charles Sheeler (1883–1965). Several different media—including photography, film, drawing, printmaking, and painting—were central to Sheeler's art. During most of his career, however, photography was not generally accepted as art. Thus, in the early 1930s, Sheeler's dealer, Edith Halpert, the founder of the Downtown Gallery in New York City, advised him to avoid all references to his photography, and to exhibit only paintings (Brock 2006: 109). And during the nine single-artist exhibitions she organized for Sheeler, not a single photograph was included. (So much for *Der Kunst ihre Freiheit.*) Despite the fact that influential figures like Alfred Barr, at the MoMA in New York, had praised Sheeler as "one of the greatest American photographers" (quoted in Elderfield 2004: 215), Halpert and Sheeler's patron, William Lane, even made sure after Sheeler's death to acquire all his photographic prints and negatives—only to conceal them. And at that point in time, their strategy to promote Sheeler as primarily a painter continued to prove highly successful.

When in 2007 the de Young Museum in San Francisco opened a new exhibition on Sheeler's art, the approach was remarkably different. "Across Media" was not a traditional retrospective. Instead, it focused explicitly on the relationships between the different media that Sheeler worked with. Timothy Anglin Burgard, curator at the Fine Arts Museums of San Francisco, claimed in a talk on Sheeler that thinking "across" media is the key to understanding his development as an artist, and to appreciating his art (cf. Brock 2006; Rawlinson 2007: 44–76).[1] Sheeler himself seems indeed to have been concerned with creating relationships across media—both within an individual image, and between series of works. His 1943 painting *The Artist Looks at Nature* is a case in point. It is based on a 1932 photograph (*Self-Portrait at Easel*) that portrays Sheeler in the process of making a conté crayon drawing (*Interior with Stove*), which was in turn based on a 1917 photograph (*The Stove*). Although the drawing Sheeler is working on shows a dark interior, the painting has him seated outdoors in a somewhat peculiar landscape. It does not depict one particular location, but is forged together of a set of diverse scenes that Sheeler had carried out in previous drawings (see Brock 2006: 108–117).

In some sense, we must engage actively with art in order to appreciate it. This is perhaps particularly true when approaching an artist like Sheeler, who, as Burgard put it in his talk, "shows everything but reveals nothing." Of course, no artist steps out of his or her time; and no critic does either. Actually, "Across Media" conveyed a perspective that is decidedly timely. Like Halpert's concealment of Sheeler's photographs, the current method through which his works become available and appear as art is itself informative. I agree that instead of approaching *The Artist Looks at Nature* as a display of already existing significances—in the motifs represented in it, or of the media used to produce it—it seems more productive to consider how, by bringing them together, Sheeler reconfigures and literally remediates the meaning of motifs and media alike. Perhaps especially since "Across Media" really does seem to make sense, I think it offers an intriguing invitation for thinking about the contemporary, and the actual forms through which it appears. It is interesting in this context to recall once again the *Kunstschau 1908*. In his opening address, Klimt explained his and his co-exhibitors' view on who is an artist. "We construe the concept of artist just as generously as we do that of the artwork," he declared. "Not only those who create, but also those who enjoy are in our view artists, people who are able to experience and to appreciate what has been created" (quoted in Brandstätter 2006: 184).

The anthropologist, too, pays attention in particular ways that enable the contemporary to emerge as an object about which knowledge is possible. Indeed, since the emergent by definition has not yet assumed "tangibility" in Arendt's sense, we must engage analytically and conceptually with such a phenomenon in particular ways in order for it to appear. I find it helpful here to recall Merleau-Ponty's definition of "attention" as "the active constitution of a new object which makes explicit and articulate what was until then presented as no more than an indeterminate horizon" (Merleau-Ponty 2002: 35). "There are no arbitrary data which set about combining into a thing because *de facto* proximities or likenesses cause them to associate," he writes. On the contrary, it is "because we perceive a grouping as a thing that the analytical attitude can then discern likenesses or proximities. This does not mean simply that without any perception of the whole we would not think of *noticing* the resemblance or the contiguity of its elements, but literally that they would not be part of the same world and would not exist at all" (Merleau-Ponty 2002: 19, emphasis in original).

To explore such analytical engagements, I continue to discuss anthropology by way of art and literature. A difference in focus between Impressionism and Expressionism, in particular, helps illuminate challenges and possibilities for contemporary anthropology.

IMPRESSIONISM, EXPRESSIONISM—AND ANTHROPOLOGY

Realist painters such as Gustave Courbet worked in the second half of the nineteenth century on landscape motifs in their studios according to strict aesthetic conventions. In contrast, Impressionists advocated *en plein air* painting: they left their studios, brought their easels outdoors, and painted what they saw. Typically they carried out their works in light colors applied to the canvas in hasty brush strokes, because whenever possible the Impressionists preferred also to finish their paintings on location. Claude Monet (1840–1926) played a decisive part in the development of this mode of art.

"The young [Monet] felt dissatisfied with the useless, conventional form of teaching he received at the studio of Gleyre in 1863. He therefore rounded up three like-minded fellow pupils, [Pierre-August] Renoir, [Jean Frédéric] Bazille and [Alfred] Sisley and announced—'there is no sincerity here: the atmosphere is unhealthy: let's escape.' Instead of taking them to another studio, they set out for the forest of Fontainebleau where they began to paint in the open air" (Taillandier 1982: 16).

The techniques and aesthetics associated with Impressionism instigated a major break with academic art. "Courbet knew that grass was green, and that was an end to it," as Alan Bowness puts it. "But Monet and Renoir saw that grass could look grey, or yellow, or blue, depending on the light, and this observation revolutionized their painting" (Bowness 2003: 26). Essentially, however, Impressionism shared with Realism the aim to record reality. How to properly represent an outer object remained its dominating concern. "The essential difference between Realism and Impressionism," according to one commentator, "is that Impressionism recognized and, in a sense, fetishized the subjectivity of the act of representational transcription" (Brettell 1999: 16). Thus Impressionism still belonged to a representational art that ultimately left unproblematized the idea of the artist as a subject who copies an outside object.

Reminiscent of Impressionists, anthropologists, too, have engaged directly with the world. Introduced through early enterprises such as the Torres Straits expedition of 1898 and, of course, through Malinowski's subsequent work in the Trobriand Islands, the practice of fieldwork became essential to the emergent twentieth-century anthropology. Like *en plein air* painting revolutionized academic art, the instigation of fieldwork revolutionized anthropology. It was no longer adequate, as Anna Grimshaw points out, "to sit like Sir James Frazer in a college study, and interpret or speculate on the basis of information supplied by an array of missionaries, explorers and colonial officials. It was important to go and see for oneself, to collect one's own data in the field and to build theories around such first-hand information" (Grimshaw 2001: 20). Yet anthropologists nevertheless mostly remained, again in a way reminiscent of the Impressionists, within the category of the "representational." While now increasingly based on firsthand observations, the aim was still to record reality and to build—or reproduce—theory.

Fieldwork-based anthropology, however, also contributed to transcending the idea within contemporary art that artistic merit was assessed primarily by its ability to imitate. This came about somewhat epiphenomenally. Several painters whose approach to art deviated from Impressionism began at the turn of the century to accompany anthropologists on their ethnographic expeditions to "exotic countries." Notable such figures were Emil

Nolde, Max Pechstein, and Wassily Kandinsky (see Selz 1974: 288–297; Weiss 1995). These and other artists—including Paula Modersohn-Becker, Ernst Ludwig Kirchner, Franz Marc, Gabriele Münter, and Paul Klee—soon became known as Expressionists.

"Primitive art" was an important source of inspiration for Expressionist painters. Many felt a strong affinity with the "art of the savages." Nolde, for instance—who frequently in his work used grotesque expressions to convey a directness that would "shake the observer into a new state of emotional awareness" (Selz 1974: 129)—found the power and immediacy of much exotic art deeply fascinating. He eulogized "its absolute primitiveness," as he put it: "its intense, often grotesque expression of strength and life in the very simplest form" (quoted in Goldwater 1986: 105). In 1910, Nolde had begun drawing objects in Berlin's Ethnology Museum; and a few years later, although he had to pay for his own trip, he accepted an offer to take part in the Külz-Leber expedition to the German possessions in the South Seas. Nolde was interested in primordial forms, and among the "primitive peoples" of the Pacific Islands he hoped to find nothing less than the very sources of art. Thus in the fall of 1913—precisely one year before Malinowski's seminal trip to the tropics—Nolde, accompanied by his wife, left for New Guinea (King 2013: 81–89; Reuther 2008; Ring 2015: 22–24). A common area of interest, then, seems to have existed between Expressionism and the emergent discipline of anthropology. "The science of ethnography, however," as Nolde noted in his autobiography, "considers us still as troublesome intruders, because we love sense perception more than sole knowledge" (quoted in Selz 1974: 289).

Unlike Impressionism (or modernist anthropology), Expressionism was not, in other words, concerned primarily with reproducing an outer world aesthetically (or scientifically). Instead, guided by the pleasure of design, these artists sought to invent aesthetic forms for expressing individual emotional states. Klee, in a review of a 1912 exhibition, provided one of the earliest definitions of the term: "a form of artistic expression in which a long period can elapse between the moment of perception and the actual painting, in which several impressions can be combined or rejected in the final composition, and in which the constructive element of art is heightened and emphasized" (quoted in Selz 1974: 214). Klee outlines here a mode of art astoundingly deviant from Impressionism. Expressionism, as he defined it, introduces a shift in temporality, a new orientation toward composition, and an enhanced emphasis on the creative act.

The term "Expressionist" had in fact originated as a label for art that was self-consciously anti-Impressionistic. Kandinsky and Marc of the *Blaue Reiter* group in Munich, for instance, considered themselves "to be primitives of a new art and to be part of a loosely defined, radical European Post-Impressionist tradition that rejected nineteenth century Realism" (Rhodes 1994: 21). Far from merely a new style of painting, Expressionism became a broad cultural movement—proclaiming an altogether new mode of living—that emerged from Germany and Austria in the early twentieth century. The Expressionists pointed out that Impressionism, despite its alleged break with the norms of academic art, nevertheless remained firmly within its constitutive logic. Expressionism, they argued, went further. By problematizing the relationship between subject (the artist) and object (the world), it abandoned the idea of mimesis and focused instead on what appeared in the process of creating art—not only the work of art itself, but also the painter as subject. The result was not abstract art—abstractions of something already known—but a nonrepresentational art that offered new ways of seeing (Bassie 2005; Dube 1998; Friedel & Hoberg 2000). Expressionist art, then, in the words of Oskar Kokoschka, was "form-giving to the experience, thus mediator and message from the self to fellow humans" (quoted in Selz 1997: 115).

Yet as a revolutionary movement, Expressionism was transitory in nature. As it gained wider popularity epigones began increasingly to mimic its aesthetic forms, and many artists found it problematic, or even offensive, that Expressionism transformed in this way into an accepted style of mainstream art. Thus a proliferating sense of innovative exhaustion paralleled its gradual popularization, and at least partly because of its own increasing fashionability the Expressionist movement eventually dissolved. In 1919, the theorist and art historian Wilhelm Hausenstein, who had been one of its passionate supporters, declared that Expressionism was dead.

> We, who at one time expected everything from it, are not spared the admission that we are sinking back into bankruptcy after tremendous efforts. Ten or fifteen years ago, earlier for some areas, we were correct in noting the bankruptcy of Impressionism. After a passionately extended effort we have no choice but to confirm the collapse of Expressionism. We have moved from one ending into another. ... Today Expressionism has its crystal palace. It has its salon. No cigarette advertisement, no bar can get along without Expressionism. It is revolting. ... We, after having consciously experienced Expressionism, after having loved and fought for it, live today with the nagging feeling of having come face to face with nothing. (Hausenstein 1995: 281–282)

Perhaps, although I do not want to push this comparison too far, we might think of the mode of anthropology advocated by Boas and his students as Expressionistic in character. Through a detour via the "primitive," these anthropologists sought, not entirely unlike Nolde, to shake the observer into a new state of awareness in order to achieve a defamiliarization of the taken-for-granted. But while a book such as Margaret Mead's *Coming of Age in Samoa* really did "speak" when it first came out in 1928, duplications of this mode of anthropological inquiry today—no matter how eloquent or accomplished—arguably seem as epigonic as postwar Expressionism. The death of Expressionism illustrates how a proliferation of concepts or rhetorical tropes might lead to analytical exhaustion: the "repetition of expressionist forms in the postwar period," as Selz (1974: 217) points out, "had little but popular value."

RENDERING VISIBLE

Expressionism also captures one significant aspect of art that I find promising for contemporary anthropology—its concern, as Kokoschka had it, with form-giving. One artist who took up this dimension in extremely productive ways was Paul Klee (1879–1940). He shared with the Expressionists an obsession with the creative act in art, and remained immensely productive throughout his career. Indeed, with a catalogue of works encompassing close to ten thousand items, Klee hardly suffered from any severe innovative exhaustion. Featured in many of the most significant exhibitions and journals of the period, Klee was an important member of the Expressionist milieu. Significantly, however, he never entirely adopted the Expressionist idiom. "Unlike most of the expressionist painters, Klee was not occupied merely with the state of his own mind, nor did he express an explosive image of an unresolved conflict with society. ... [He] was concerned with the world itself—not merely with the world as his senses perceived it. He considered the present state of things as only a momentary and accidental arrangement, and occupied himself with a visual formulation of the world as it might once have been or as though it were *in the process of becoming* something quite different" (Selz 1974: 296–297, emphasis added). To Klee, the mere "thought of having to live in an epigonic age," as he wrote in his diary, was "almost unbearable" (Klee 1968: 125). Rather than embracing a single aesthetic model he sought persistently in his work to give form to that which was in the process of becoming. "Art," as he famously put it, "does not reproduce the visible; it renders visible" (quoted in San Lazzaro 1957: 105).

This orientation toward the possible and the "not yet" is not restricted to the visual arts. In this regard, Klee seemed for instance to share common ground with several modernist writers, including Robert Walser (1878–1956)—whom Susan Sontag (2001: vii) has characterized as "[a] Paul Klee in prose"—and Robert Musil (1880–1942), whose approach to literature was continuously sustained by an "attitude that treats the given, the reality of facts, as merely one actualized option of countless nonrealized possibilities" (McBride 2006: 15; cf. Jonsson 2000: 213). The artist, according to Musil, is "concerned with expanding the range of what is inwardly still possible" (Musil 1990: 7). Thus in his own way, Musil, too, emphasized art's ability to render visible: "To love something as an artist," he wrote, "means to be shaken not by its ultimate value or lack of value, but by a side of it that suddenly opens up. Where art has value it shows things that few have seen. It is conquering, not pacifying" (Musil 1990: 7). At this point, I want to return for a moment to the woman in Volos's story, whose "fishlike" thoughts no words seemed able to convey. Perhaps one might think of her predicament in relation to the problem of form-giving. What Musil has called the *tertium separationis* is precisely "the condition that one cannot express what ought to be said directly as pure conceptualizing; otherwise," he added, "everything except precise exposition would be inferior" (Musil 1990: 16). Coincidentally, what appears in one of Klee's most popular paintings, *Der goldene Fisch* of 1925, is precisely a "luminescent fish [that] glows brightly in suspension in an aquatic netherworld" (Bassie 2005: 239).

Anthropologists who take seriously the primacy of inquiry in attempts to engage analytically with the emergent could no doubt find inspiration in artists and writers such as Klee and Musil, and in their persistent focus on giving form to what is in the process of becoming (see, e.g., Carrithers 2005; Rabinow 2003: 68–75; 2008: 101–103). And anthropologists who are concerned with the emergent must also, like these artists, be creative. "That which one is trying to understand … must be made into an object of study," as Paul Rabinow reminds us. "And, as any minimally coherent philosophical or social scientific understanding of *Wissenschaft* holds, that means it must be constructed" (Rabinow 2008: 34).

Klee never fully adopted the Expressionist idiom. He felt a "distaste for theorizing" and, as he declared in his diary, "protested forcefully against the notion of theory in itself." Yet he also always remained "willing to exchange ideas, but healthy ideas arising from concrete cases" (Klee 1968: 318, 323–324). Musil, too, persistently opposed the doctrinal. In similar fashion, anthropologists should not, I think, adhere to one particular theory and apply it. Instead, as we engage with concrete empirical cases we must always be prepared to change our forms of inquiry and styles of writing. Anthropology, like literature and art, has the potential to give form to that which cannot, in the words of Musil, "be said directly as pure conceptualizing." What arguably makes anthropological concepts analytically productive, then, is precisely the way in which they make things appear. Anthropology, to paraphrase Klee, does not reproduce the visible; it renders visible.

Mattias Viktorin received his B.A. (2001) and Ph.D. (2008) degrees in Social Anthropology from Stockholm University, and is currently Senior Lecturer in the Department of Cultural Anthropology and Ethnology at Uppsala University. He has previously been a Fulbright visiting scholar at UC Berkeley (2006–2007); the secretary of the Swedish Society for Anthropology and Geography (2009–2011); a research fellow at the Stockholm Center for Organizational Research (2009–2011); and lecturer in the Department of Social Anthropology at Stockholm University (2011–2013). He is the author of *Exercising Peace: Conflict Preventionism, Neoliberalism, and the New Military* (2008), and the co-editor of *Antropologi och tid* (2013).

NOTES

1. Timothy Anglin Burgard, "Charles Sheeler: Across Media," lecture at the de Young Museum, San Francisco, 10 February 2007.

REFERENCES

Arendt, Hanna. 1998. *The Human Condition.* Chicago: University of Chicago Press.

Bassie, Ashley. 2005. *Expressionism.* London: Sirrocco.

Bisanz, Hans. 2006. "The Klimt Group." In *Vienna 1900: Art, Life, and Culture,* ed. Christian Brandstätter. New York: Vendome Press.

Bowness, Alan. 2003. *Modern European Art: From Impressionism to Abstraction.* Revised edition. London: Thames and Hudson.

Brandstätter, Christian. 2006 "The Wiener Werkstätte." In *Vienna 1900: Art, Life, and Culture,* ed. Christian Branstätter. New York: The Vendome Press.

Brettell, Richard R. 1999. *Modern Art 1851–1929: Capitalism and Representation.* Oxford: Oxford University Press.

Brock, Charles. 2006. *Charles Sheeler: Across Media.* Berkeley: The University of California Press.

Carrithers, Michael. 2005. "Anthropology as a Moral Science of Possibilities," *Current Anthropology*, 46(3): 433–456.

Dube, Wolf-Dieter. 1998. *The Expressionists.* London: Thames and Hudson.

Elderfield, John, ed. 2004. *Modern Painting and Sculpture: 1880 to the Present at the Museum of Modern Art.* New York: The Museum of Modern Art.

Fischer, Michael MJ. 2009. *Anthropological Futures.* Durham: Duke University Press.

Friedel, Helmut and Annegret Hoberg. 2000. *The Blue Rider in the Lenbachhaus, Munich.* London: Prestel.

Goldwater, Robert. 1986. *Primitivism in Modern Art.* Enlarged edition. Cambridge, MA: The Belknap Press of Harvard University Press.

Grimshaw, Anna. 2001. *The Ethnographer's Eye: Ways of Seeing in Modern Anthropology*. Cambridge: Cambridge University Press.

Hausenstein, Wilhelm. 1995. "Art of this Moment." Reprinted in *German Expressionism: Documents from the End of the Wilhelmine Empire to the Rise of National Socialism*, ed. Rose-Carol Washton Long. Berkeley: University of California Press.

Jonsson, Stefan. 2000. *Subject without Nation: Robert Musil and the History of Modern Identity*. Durham: Duke University Press.

King, Averil. 2013. *Emil Nolde: Artist of the Elements*. London: Philip Wilson Publishers.

Klee, Paul. 1968. *The Diaries of Paul Klee, 1898–1918*, ed. and Intr. Felix Klee. Berkeley: University of California Press.

———. 1995. "Exhibition of the Modern League in the Zurich Kunsthaus." Reprinted in *German Expressionism: Documents from the End of the Wilhelmine Empire to the Rise of National Socialism*, ed. Rose-Carol Washton Long. Berkeley: University of California Press.

McBride, Patrizia C. 2006. *The Void of Ethics: Robert Musil and the Experience of Modernity*. Evanston: Northwestern University Press.

Merleau-Ponty, Maurice. 2002. *Phenomenology of Perception*. Translated by Colin Smith. New York: Routledge.

Musil, Robert. 1990. *Precision and Soul: Essays and Addresses*, ed. and trans. Burton Pike and David S. Luft. Chicago: University of Chicago Press.

Rabinow, Paul. 2003. *Anthropos Today: Reflections on Modern Equipment*. Princeton: Princeton University Press.

———. 2008. *Marking Time: On the Anthropology of the Contemporary*. Princeton: Princeton University Press.

———. 2011. *The Accompaniment: Assembling the Contemporary*. Chicago: University of Chicago Press.

Rawlinson, Mark. 2007. *Charles Sheeler: Modernism, Precisionism and the Borders of Abstraction*. London: IB Tauris.

Reuther, Manfred, ed. 2008. *Emil Nolde: The Journey to the South Seas 1913-1914*. Köln: DuMont Buchverlag.

Rhodes, Colin. 1994. *Primitivism and Modern Art*. London: Thames and Hudson.

Ring, Christian. 2015. "Art itself is my language." In *Emil Nolde: The Great Colour Wizard*, by Christian Ring and Hans-Joachim Throl. München: Hirmer Verlag.

San Lazzaro, Gualtieri di. 1957. *Paul Klee: His Life and Work*. London: Thames and Hudson.

Schorske, Carl E. 1981. *Fin-de-siècle Vienna: Politics and Culture*. New York: Vintage Books.

Selz, Peter. 1974. *German Expressionist Painting*. Berkeley: University of California Press.

———. 1997. *Beyond the Mainstream: Essays on Modern and Contemporary Art*. Cambridge: Cambridge University Press.

Sontag, Susan. 2001. "Foreword: Walser's Voice." In Robert Walser, *Selected Stories*. New York: New York Review Books.

Taillandier, Yvon. 1982. *Claude Monet*. New Revised Edition. Trans. from French, APH Hamilton. Naefels, Switzerland: Bonfini Press.

Viktorin, Mattias. 2008. *Exercising Peace: Conflict Preventionism, Neoliberalism, and the New Military.* Stockholm Studies in Social Anthropology, 63. Stockholm: Stockholm University.

——. 2013. "Antropologi och tid—en inledning" ("Anthropology and Time—An Introduction"). In *Ymer: Antropologi och tid,* Vol. 133, ed. Mattias Viktorin and Charlotta Widmark. The Swedish Society for Anthropology and Geography.

Volos, Andrei. 2005. *Hurramabad.* Trans. into Swedish, Nils Håkansson. Uppsala: Ruin.

Weiss, Peg. 1995. *Kandinsky and Old Russia: The Artist as Ethnographer and Shaman.* New Haven: Yale University Press.

Whitford, Frank. 1990. *Klimt.* London: Thames and Hudson.

Chapter 15

Digital Narratives in Anthropology

Paula Uimonen

Imagine a book series that breaks away from conventional genres, combining artistic styles of writing with multimedia forms of publication. A book series that offers the best of two worlds, a well-renowned publisher and creative writing in innovative online formats:

> The new Routledge Innovative Ethnographies book series publishes fieldwork that appeals to new and traditional audiences of scholarly research through the use of new media and new genres. Combining the book and multimedia material hosted on the series website, this series challenges the boundaries between ethnography and documentary journalism, between the scholarly essay and the novel, between academia and drama. From the use of narrative and drama to the use of reflexivity and pathos, from the contextualization of ethnographic documentation in felt textures of place to the employment of artistic conventions for the sake of good writing, this series entertains, enlightens, and educates. (http://innovativeethnographies.net/about)

While doing fieldwork at an arts college in Tanzania, I learned of the Innovative Ethnographies series through the mailing list of the Media Anthropology Network of the European Association of Social Anthropologists. I quickly expressed my interest to the series editor, Phillip Vannini, and the more I learned about the series, the more inspired I got. As we continued exchanging emails, I realized that the series afforded me a rare opportunity to present my research material in a befitting style. Not only would the series help me do justice to the subject of the arts, but it would also allow me to explore my own creativity in writing, while making good use of all the visual material I had gathered. In June 2011, only eighteen months after completing my fieldwork, I submitted the final manuscript to Routledge, and two months later, I resubmitted a hyperlinked version of the book, which interacted with a website that I had created together with the editor's web team.

In this chapter I will share the experience of writing ethnography in three interrelated formats: a printed book, a website, and a hyperlinked e-book. These different genres can be conceptualized in terms of textual, visual, and hyperlinked narratives. The leitmotif is digital: the development of a website to accompany a printed book, the adjustment of a manuscript for hyperlinked e-book format, and last but not least, a subject matter that I define in terms of digital anthropology, as suggested in the very title of the book: *Digital Drama* (Uimonen 2012). Digital media offer new opportunities for writing ethnography, but how can anthropologists navigate the brave new world of digital narratives in a way that makes sense to us? I hope that by sharing my experiences with you, we can all learn something in the process. I have no doubt that books with accompanying websites and hyperlinked e-books will become more common in anthropological writing, and hope that this will strengthen the production and presentation of anthropological knowledge. The writing and publication of *Digital Drama* is an experiment in this direction.

DIGITAL DRAMA AS TEXTUAL NARRATIVE

"You can assess the number of people inside the Internet room from the amount of shoes scattered outside the entrance door." This is how I introduce digital anthropology in *Digital Drama* (Uimonen 2012: 34). The Internet room has been the primary site for my ethnographic engagements at Taasisi ya Sanaa na Utamaduni Bagamoyo (TaSUBa), a national institute for arts and culture in Tanzania, formerly known as Chuo Cha Sanaa Bagamoyo or Bagamoyo College of Arts (BCA) (Uimonen 2009, 2011). From my early engagements as an information and communication technology (ICT) Consultant in 2004 to 2007 to my fieldwork in 2009, I have paid attention to the shoes outside the Internet room. Occasionally I have taken photos of the shoes, sometimes prompted by my research interlocutors, and to my great delight, when Nina filmed the Internet room, she also filmed the shoes. Nina Stanley, a young student at the college, was one of my research interlocutors, and helped me explore video as a research method during fieldwork. In her visual art class, she had painted the Internet room, and when we filmed campus, she made sure to film the room, along with the shoes outside.

I like the contrasts and symbolism of the shoes outside the Internet room, and the way it may surprise the reader. Who would expect to read about shoes under the heading of digital anthropology? But then again, one of the roles of anthropology is to surprise, by bringing new knowledge to bear on seemingly mundane details of everyday life. And what better way to surprise than to use shoes as an introduction to a discussion of digital media in the peripheries of our interconnected world, to underline an analysis of Internet access in terms of partial inclusion in the global network society, or to illustrate user patterns of hybrid media engagement? Naturally, it takes thousands of words to make that kind of analytical leap from one simple image. And that is why I had to write a book (cf. Hastrup 1992).

To capture the complex interlinkages between shoes and digital media, I tried to explore a more creative form of writing, a challenge in its own right. The target market for the book was graduate students, along with scholars from various disciplines, so the monograph had to maintain academic standards. In this sense, it was a piece of scholarly writing, with abstract theorizing and stringent referencing. But as I wrote the book, I had a different audience in mind, not least my research interlocutors. I wanted to tell their stories as vividly as I could; capturing their life stories as creative artists in a social context full of drama. But I also wanted to offer them a book that could serve as a mirror of their everyday life, just like they had taught me that art serves as a mirror of society. From my perspective, their lives intersected with historically shaped social forces that were inseparable from global patterns of cultural dependency and social inequality. And this was the message I wanted to convey to them, as well as to other readers of the book.

I picked a title for the book that would evoke some of the drama I tried to capture in the text, while building on the scholarly work of earlier anthropologists. The title *Digital Drama* draws on Victor Turner's (1987) concept "social drama," which I found to be a suitable structure for my analysis of digital media and institutional transformation. I structured the text into three parts, with the first part, "mise-en-scène," serving as an introduction, situating the text ethnographically as well as theoretically. Throughout the monograph, I tried to create dramatic effects, using vibrant characters and spectacular events to introduce and explain an unfolding social drama of cultural change and conflict. I thought I had managed to write in an accessible and engaging manner, until I received comments from my reviewers, who kindly urged me to get on with the action much earlier in the text and to sharpen my analytical focus. They wanted to hear the drums, they explained to me. It was only then that I realized that I had followed the standard format of academic writing, focusing more on scholarly than creative aspects of writing, a style so deeply ingrained in my work since the writing of my dissertation a decade earlier. Inspired and encouraged by one of my reviewers, I made a greater effort to bring out the senses in the book (Stoller 1989, 1997, 2009).

It took another visit to the fieldsite to reach a more creative flow in the textual narrative. I revisited TaSUBa in December 2010 to go through the draft manuscript with my research interlocutors. By then I had written a complete manuscript, sufficiently well structured and substantiated to share with people at the college. During this period, some staff at the college organized a spectacular cultural event, *tuwaenzi wakongwe* (let us honor the legends). It was the first time the college organized an event to commemorate teachers who had passed away and it was a huge success: skillful performances combined with a creative use of digital media and attentive audiences interacting with the performers on stage. This is how I should conclude the book, I thought to myself, as I documented the manifestation of cultural creativity with my video camera. This event is bringing back the spirit of the arts to the college, I reflected. Later on I realized that maybe the reader should not have to wait until the end of the book to get a taste of the spirit of the arts. So, I chose to start the book with this dramatic event, using the rest of the book to explain why the college lost the spirit of the arts in the first place. A creative twist that made for a much more interesting read, starting with the sound of drums and sense of drama that I wished to convey.

ONLINE VISUAL NARRATIVES

In the research field of digital anthropology, scholars have combined monographs and online forms of expression in creative ways. The earliest ethnographies of the Internet had websites with complementary information, although the sites were discontinued after some time (Miller and Slater 2000; Uimonen 2001). More recently, anthropologists have explored new forms of online publication. True to his subject matter of free and open source software, Kelty (2008) shared a digital version of his entire monograph online, where readers can also modulate the text (see http://twobits .net/). While Boellstorff's (2008) monograph on virtual culture follows a rather standard form of academic writing and publishing, he maintains his avatar Tom Bukowski and gives occasional seminars for students in the virtual world Second Life, where he did fieldwork for two years. Wesch has presented his work on digital culture through YouTube, where his short video *The Machine is Us/ing Us* (2007) has received over 1.6 million views.

I used visual narratives for the website accompanying *Digital Drama,* thus taking advantage of visual material gathered during fieldwork. Throughout my years of ethnographic engagement at TaSUBa, I had documented various activities with photo and video. During fieldwork, I made a more concerted effort to collect visual and audiovisual material. Inspired by the concept of social aesthetic fields (MacDougall 1999, 2006), I was keen to document the sensory dimensions of campus life, especially visual cultural forms (Banks 2001; Banks and Morphy 1997). In most cases, I used my camera to document what was going on, as visual and audiovisual field notes. But my interest in visual and sensory anthropology led me to explore more creative forms of photography and video. While writing the book, I kept browsing through my photos and videos, to jog my memory, to note down details, and to keep myself semi-immersed in the field. This was the empirical material that spoke to me, the visuals and audiovisuals told me stories that I could weave together into a textual narrative. And it was through sounds and images that I reached some of my most far-flung theoretical extrapolations. Like the shoes outside the Internet room. Or the poster at the campus entrance. Or the sound of *marimba* (xylophone), *ngoma* (drum), and trumpets.

"The accompanying web site will host multimedia material for each chapter, with photos, videos, sound clips and multimedia productions gathered during fieldwork, combined with material specifically developed for the site, in collaboration with TaSUBa artists." Alas, the planned website I had presented in my book proposal to Routledge in June 2010 was indeed ambitious. When I submitted the book manuscript two years later, the website still remained undeveloped, but the series editor promised that a team would help me out at his end. We agreed I would complete the site by mid July.

A website has to tell a story of its own, I quickly realized when I set out to develop it. As much as the site was meant to accompany the book, it would be visited by people who had not read the book. So the site needed to tell its own story, in a style that suited the medium: lots of visuals, very little text, and some hyperlinks to other online material. This was a great opportunity to bring existing and potential readers closer to the realities described and analyzed in the book. Through the online material, I could offer the reader a mediated form of sensory immersion: colors, forms, movement, and sounds. The material would serve as some form of evidence, but more importantly, it would bridge the contextual gap between the reader and the empirical underpinnings of the ethnography, bringing the reader closer to the sights and sounds of TaSUBa.

The only way I could build the site was by temporarily discarding the manuscript, creating a visual narrative instead of a textual one. At first I had tried to reread some book chapters and design web sections accordingly. But I got lost in the process. The website had to be more than just photo illustrations of text, my editor, Phillip, and I agreed. So I focused on photos and videos, ignoring the text. I carefully went through my collection of almost four thousand photos, selecting photos that told stories, were of publishable quality, and could work on their own. By the time I was done, I had selected around 180 photos. And based on these photos, I developed the website. I had some ideas of metanarratives, sections reflecting the main components of the book. But the actual structure only became clear once I had selected the photos; they dictated the content of the website.

When selecting the photos, I encountered several ethical considerations. Before I started developing the website, I had considered posting material on the main characters in *Digital Drama,* so that readers would get better acquainted with the personalities described in the book. I started in this vain, but I soon realized that the narrative of the book required a different approach, capturing more general and abstract angles. I also felt uncomfortable about exposing my research interlocutors to such an extent. In the book, all characters appear with their real names and identities. But the story reaches well beyond these individuals, while the great majority of research interlocutors do not appear in the book at all. To emphasize a select number of ethnographic characters through the website would not only overexpose them, but it would do so disproportionately. So I only picked a few photos of individuals, while most of the photos showed groups of people or places where no people appeared at all. I also had to strike a balance in exposing some of the more politically sensitive visual material. In my folders I had plenty of images that illustrated the contradictions between vision and reality that I analyzed at great length, but I kept this to a minimum on the website. After all, to fully understand the power dynamics at play, viewers would have to read the book.

While it was easy enough to select photos depicting people, places, and activities, I also tried to create visual narratives that captured more abstract aspects of the book, especially the key concepts of liminality and creolization (Hannerz 1987, 1996, 2006; Turner 1969, 1987). As mentioned earlier, it was through visual images that I reached some of the more abstract theoretical insights of my analysis. I had used certain images in lectures and presentations, so I decided to use these on the website. I also found complementary images that visualized these concepts, so I posted those as well. In the end, I created a whole section on liminality and creolization, with an introductory text that summarized my theoretical argument. Somehow I think it works, at least I hope it does.

VIDEO AND VIMEO

Preparing videos for the site took me in yet another direction, as I joined the online community Vimeo. The web team explained that the videos would not be hosted on the same server as the site. Instead, I should host them elsewhere and they would embed them in the book site. I had YouTube in mind, but the web team recommended Vimeo, which they called "a classier version of YouTube." A quick Google search for comparative reviews proved the web team right in their assessment. So I joined Vimeo, which describes itself as "a respectful community of creative people who are passionate about sharing the videos they make" (www.vimeo.com). I felt thrilled by the prospect of being a member of such a distinguished community of creative people. In one hectic day I went from never having heard of Vimeo to becoming a Plus-member (paid service with extra benefits) with my own channel, album, and even address: www.vimeo.com/paulauimonen.

Through Vimeo I produced yet another visual narrative. Not only would my *Digital Drama* album and channel have to work on its own, but it would have to do so within a community of video professionals. My video clips could hardly be labeled documentaries, or ethnographic films. What I had was raw footage from the field, recordings of various places and events that formed part of the greater narrative of *Digital Drama*. Joining Vimeo compelled me to make an effort to produce more professional audiovisual material. I spent a few days going through eight DVDs of video material, selecting clips worth putting online. Some clips were publishable as they were; others needed editing.

Anyone who has done video editing knows how time consuming it is, and when the medium of distribution is the Internet, you want to make the video clips short. Luckily enough my Tanzanian "brother," Sixmund Begashe, was visiting Stockholm and could help me out. Sixmund had been one of my research interlocutors at TaSUBa and he was also quite skilled in recording and editing video. What I knew of video editing I had learned from Sixmund, sitting next to him when he was working at TaSUBa. Now we worked in tandem; I selected videos and he edited them. All in all, Sixmund helped me produce seven videos, edited compilations of clips. Three of them were based on reflexive video narratives, produced by research interlocutors filming and commenting on their surroundings when walking around campus with me, as exemplified by Nina's video mentioned above. It was a new method I had tested during fieldwork, combining walking with video (Pink 2007) with participatory video production (Banks 2001). Nina had filmed the campus and its surroundings on two different occasions, and Sixmund edited the material into three videos, one showing the campus, another one the town of Bagamoyo. The third one focused on the Internet room, and for the book site we decided to use Nina's video instead of the material I had recorded. Nina's video was interesting in its own right, providing an insider's narrative on central arguments in the book. And as I mentioned earlier, she even filmed the shoes.

The Vimeo site required me to produce yet another set of written narratives to accompany the video clips: titles, descriptive text, and tags. I tried to make short captivating titles, while contextualizing the clips through brief descriptions. Similarly to the photos, I tried to strike a balance: enough information to explain the clips, while pointing to the book for greater depth, thus also encouraging people to read the book. The tagging process was a bit cumbersome. To facilitate online searches, I could tag each video through keywords. Identifying suitable keywords was not all that easy, but I tried to use tags for two interrelated audiences, the Vimeo community and Internet users at large.

THE # AND [X] OF HYPERLINKED NARRATIVES

"Please use the same style I've used to denote a hyperlink. See attached file. I sent you this before but you must not have received it. On page 2 of my book there is a legend. You can use those symbols to identify the kind of hyperlinks you display. Each hyperlink must also be spelled out in a footnote or endnote for those readers who access only the print version." The series editor Phillip sends me these instructions as I am trying to figure out a way of hyperlinking the manuscript, thus prodding me to use the method he used for his book, the first in our series (Vannini 2012). We are extremely pressed for time, and I had thought of an alternative to the editor's original concept, to save some time. Luckily, the web editor informs us that he can comply with Philip's instructions by simply "anchoring" each photo and video on the website, with a "#" followed by a number. This way, the hyperlinks can point directly to a photo/video. What I have to do is identify the passages in the book that I want to link to the site and insert the anchored hyperlink. Since the manuscript has to work for both print and e-book, Phillip has devised a system of symbols for the e-book, which I have to denote through callouts: [photo], [video], [web link], etc., accompanied by an endnote where the exact web address is spelled out. In other words, to link to Nina's video, I mark the text in the book where I want the link to appear as hyperlink, adding [video] and an endnote with the same hyperlink, http://innovativeeth nographies.net/digitaldrama/digital-anthropology#1. In the printed book, the callout appears as a symbol with an endnote.

In preparing the manuscript for the print/e-book combination, I produce yet another version of Digital Drama: a hyperlinked narrative. By now time is running out and the publisher expects the manuscript within days, yet I have only prepared about half of the manuscript. I spend a few hectic evenings completing the process, marking suitable passages in the text, inserting hyperlinks, callouts, and endnotes. Yet another balancing act: enough hyperlinks to point readers to photos and videos on the website, or external websites for more information, but not so many hyperlinks that the reading process gets interrupted. In some cases I hyperlink entire sections, marking the heading as a link, while adding more specific links in the ensuing text. By the time I am done, I have inserted 127 hyperlinks. In some cases I have adjusted the text in the manuscript to accommodate the hyperlink, but most of the time I have simply marked existing text.

As I hyperlink passages in the text I realize that by doing so, I am also highlighting certain parts. The hyperlinks bring more attention to certain narratives, emphasizing them by underlining them, literally through the hyperlinks, figuratively through the added online material. This will clearly be more obvious in the e-book than in the printed version, but it makes me realize that the hyperlinks add more significance to the text than I had envisaged, the complementary digital narratives serving as tags in the text itself, calling out for attention.

The hyperlinks transform the text from a unidirectional narrative to an interactive one, thus integrating visual and textual narratives in interesting ways. The hyperlinks in the text point to specific parts of the website, while many of the sections on the website point to specific sections in the book. So people can read the same section online as well as in the book, or switch between the two. This is indeed an experiment in the direction of interactive digital narratives.

CONCLUDING REFLECTIONS

Time will tell how future readers of *Digital Drama* will experience the interlinkages of textual, visual, and hyperlinked narratives. But I hope it will be an exciting and illuminating experiment in digitally mediated anthropological writing. If it works, *Digital Drama* will bring us one step closer to what I envisage for anthropology in general and digital anthropology in particular. To paraphrase MacDougall (1997: 283), *digital anthropology should be concerned with the study of digital cultural forms as well as the use of digital media to describe and analyze culture.*

Yet I am also painfully aware of the digital discrepancies that this experiment brings forth. In certain ways, the website for *Digital Drama* will be more accessible to my research interlocutors in Tanzania than the book itself will be. Most of them cannot afford to buy the book, but they can browse the website for free, or almost free, depending on where they access it. Even so, the videos on the site will not be as accessible. Bandwidth limitations in Tanzania make it difficult to watch videos online. I have tried to keep the videos short, so that they will be easier to download, but I know that the online sights and sounds of *Digital Drama* will be far more accessible to people in the centers of the global network society than for people in the peripheries, even when they take off their shoes to enter the Internet room at TaSUBa.

It was to capture these patterns of digital stratification that I spent over a year writing a book, weeks to develop a website, and days to prepare a hyperlinked e-book about digital media and intercultural interaction at an arts college in Tanzania. I wanted to tell a story of the complexities of cultural digitization and global interconnectedness. I started off with cultural creativity, ending up with chaos, confusion, and crisis. It is the most challenging ethnography I have written so far. Hopefully the website and e-book can help get the message across and show the continued significance of anthropological writing in the age of digital mediation.

Paula Uimonen is Associate Professor in the Department of Social Anthropology, Stockholm University. She is specialized in digital anthropology and the anthropology of art, media, visual culture, and globalization. Her recent publications focus on mobile photography in Tanzania, mobile infrastructure in Africa, and visual identity in Facebook. Paula has done research on digital media at an arts college in Tanzania, published in the monograph *Digital Drama: Teaching and Learning Art and Media in Tanzania* (Uimonen 2012); see www.innovativeethnographies.net/digitaldrama. In another project, she focused on an anti-corruption campaign by Tanzanian musicians, presented in an ethnographic road movie *Chanjo ya Rushwa* (2013), freely available online at https://vimeo.com/paulauimonen.

REFERENCES

Banks, Marcus. 2001. *Visual Methods in Social Research.* London: SAGE.

Banks, Marcus, and Howard Morphy, eds. 1997. *Rethinking Visual Anthropology.* New Haven: Yale University Press.

Boellstorff, Tom. 2008. *Coming of Age in Second Life: An Anthropologist Explores the Virtually Human.* Princeton: Princeton University Press

Hannerz, Ulf. 1987. "The World in Creolisation." *Africa* 57: 546–560.

———. 1996. *Transnational Connections: Culture, People, Places.* New York: Routledge.

———. 2006. "Theorizing Through the New World? Not Really." *American Ethnologist* 33, no. 4: 563–565.

Hastrup, Kirsten. 1992. "Anthropological Visions: Some Notes on Visual and Textual Authority." In *Film as Ethnography,* ed. Peter Ian Crawford and David Turton. Manchester: Manchester University Press.

Kelty, Christopher M. 2008. *Two Bits: The Cultural Significance of Free Software.* Durham: Duke University Press.

MacDougall, David. 1997. "The Visual in Anthropology." In *Rethinking Visual Anthropology,* ed. Marcus Banks and Howard Morphy. New Haven: Yale University Press.

———. 1999. "Social Aesthetics and the Doon School." *Visual Anthropology Review* 15, no. 1: 3–20.

———. 2006. *The Corporeal Image: Film, Ethnography, and The Senses.* Princeton: Princeton University Press.

Miller, Daniel, and Slater, Don. 2000. *The Internet: An Ethnographic Approach.* Oxford: Berg.

Pink, Sarah. 2007. "Walking with Video." *Visual Studies* 22, no. 3: 240–252.

Stoller, Paul. 1989. *The Taste of Ethnographic Things: The Senses in Anthropology.* Philadelphia: University of Pennsylvania Press

———. 1997. *Sensuous Scholarship.* Philadelphia: University of Pennsylvania Press.

———. 2009. *The Power of the Between: An Anthropological Odyssey.* Chicago: University of Chicago Press.

Turner, Victor Witter. 1969. *The Ritual Process: Structure and Anti-structure.* London: Routledge & Kegan Paul.

———. 1987. *The Anthropology of Performance.* New York: PAJ.

Uimonen, Paula. 2001. *Transnational.dynamics@ development.net: Internet, Modernization and Globalization.* Stockholm: Stockholm Studies in Social Anthropology, 49. Stockholm University.

———. 2009. "Internet, Arts and Translocality in Tanzania." *Social Anthropology* 17, no. 3: 276–290.

———. 2011. "African Art Students and Digital Learning." In *Interactive Media Use and Youth: Learning, Knowledge Exchange and Behavior,* ed. Elza Dunkels, Gun-Marie Frånberg, and Camilla Hällgren. Hershey, PA: Information Science Reference.

———. 2012. *Digital Drama: Teaching and Learning Art and Media in Tanzania.* Innovative Ethnographies Series. New York: Routledge. http://www.innovativeethnographies.net/digitaldrama.

Vannini, Philip. 2012. *Ferry Tales: Mobility, Place, and Time on Canada's West Coast.* Innovative Ethnographies Series. New York: Routledge. http://ferrytales.innovativeethnographies.net/.

Wesch, Michael. 2007. Web 2.0…the machine is us/ing us. http://www.youtube.com/watch?v=6gmP4nk0EOE&feature=channel.

Chapter 16

Writing Otherwise

Ulf Hannerz

I remember a conversation I had, many years ago, with one well-known anthropologist, quite senior, but still very active. He had taken an interest in the varieties of scholarly careers, and had been struck by the contrast between anthropologists and historians. The anthropologists, he said, tended to establish their reputation quite quickly, but then perhaps did not accomplish so much in their later years. With the historians it was rather the opposite: they worked and worked, wrote and wrote, and reached the top of their career and their greatest reputation when they approached retirement, or were well beyond it—except that they might keep going.

I do not know if this colleague ever wrote up his comparative careers study.[1] In any case, we can probably rather easily see what would lie behind such a difference between anthropologists and historians. The former do fieldwork, and in the classical mode the best time to do it is when you are young. You may be unattached, and you have hardly any competing obligations, so you can immerse yourself in some foreign field, and then come home and write up. And if you are successful in this, your career is launched, and your first book is a must read for your peers, for those who are coming up behind you, and perhaps even for discipline elders. Meanwhile, the historians work away in the archives, learn more and more over the years, gaining in both depth and breadth, and earning the respect or even admiration of others for both insight and overview.

We may take this contrast between types of careers—which, as often when one delineates types, is very likely a bit exaggerated—as a fact of life, recognized and basically accepted. The anthropologist may have more materials to write up from that early, comprehensive field study. After the successful monograph has been launched, later pieces may perhaps draw more attention than if they had been the work of some largely unknown writer. But then there may also be other things to do, and writing could become less important. Those who remain in Academia may be deeply involved in their teaching, and find satisfaction in that. Some take on administrative and organizational tasks, perhaps one after another. Those whose lines of work take them away from university life may have job descriptions not including much writing—or including writing of other kinds, such as reports.

Yet there are those who insist on looking for ways of keeping on doing research, continuing writing—even as those practical conditions of immersion in research are no longer there. It might also be the dark truth that with the growth of late-twentieth-, early-twenty-first-century academic audit society, the question whether to write or not to write, and to publish, is not just a matter of intrinsic personal pleasure, an intellectual challenge. It may become to a degree a bread-and-butter issue, on an individual as well as collective basis. It would be unfortunate if your president/rector/provost/dean concluded that his/her anthropological employee is typically a has-been, a scholarly lightweight, someone who seems not to have lived up to the promise that seemed at one time to be there. The anthropologists, and their departments, may appear less productive than they ought to be, in terms of publications—perhaps with certain fairly junior scholars as shining exceptions—and consequently less visible in the citation indexes as well.

So if there is in fact that kind of scholarly career pattern in anthropology that my distinguished colleague described—early rise, then stagnation—we should perhaps ask if we can do something about it. The possibilities would seem to be at two levels.

One of them is a matter of finding ways of continuing to do field research. At times this may indeed entail a return to conditions more or less similar to those that characterized that first study: going on full-time research leave, taking time out from domestic obligations as well, or bringing them along.[2] That, however, is not always possible—and it could just be that as exhilarating a personal experience as that first study may well have been, perhaps with a full, almost overwhelming engagement with an alien way of life, going through another equally demanding experience of the same kind could just seem to be a bit too much of a good thing.

Consequently, later field research may have to be of another kind: in a field more readily accessible, perhaps something that can be handled on a part-time basis, in bits and pieces, off and on over time. Obviously much anthropological work is carried out in this way, although that fact is given rather little explicit attention compared to the celebration of fieldwork in the classic style. Probably first field studies, such as for doctoral dissertations, are actually often conducted in similar ways as well; partly because the re-searchers even then may work under personal and material constraints that allow no alternatives, partly because some fields under the circumstances of modernity simply do not lend themselves to a more complete immersion. Much more could be said about this, but it is not my concern here.[3]

The other level of possibilities involves kinds of writing rather than kinds of fieldwork, and this is what I wish to explore in this chapter. I want to enter a plea for experimenting with a greater diversity in styles of writing, more ways of using anthropological ideas and materials, perhaps developing new genres. It seems that much of the soul searching and debate about writing anthropology has continued to be about "me and my fieldwork," "me and my ethnography." What can we do about writing otherwise?

COMPARISONS AND SYNTHESES

For one thing, I would suggest that we can do more with ethnography as a shared resource, built up collectively over time. One may indeed think it is rather odd that so much ethnographic knowledge, materials gathered and analyzed with a great deal of effort, is basically put to work only once, in a fieldworker's own publications. Colleagues working on related topics or in the same region may refer to it, in large part in passing and to contextualize their own work, but quite possibly it is not really *used* again.

"Comparison" is obviously a keyword here. Comparative work has had a checkered history in anthropology. Cross-cultural surveys, for a mid-twentieth-century period with an institutional base in the Human Relations Area Files, were held by some to lead the way to a really scientific anthro-pology—but then critics identified the epistemological weaknesses of exist-ing approaches, and furthermore their abstract correlation-seeking formal-ism was probably of little appeal to many of the people drawn to anthro-pology.[4] I suspect that for an extended period this was what "comparative method" came to stand for, and later generations who really had not been much exposed to it mostly absorbed a vague notion that this was not the thing to do.

Then, however, we have had some attempts to reconsider the varieties of comparison, their possibilities as well as the issues to remain wary about (see, e.g., Holy 1987; Fox and Gingrich 2002).[5] I would argue that there can be many anthropological writing styles that can draw creatively on the wealth of both ethnography and anthropological ideas, pointing to parallels and showing contrasts, demonstrating both variations and common themes. This is less likely to be a matter of trying to establish truths about universals or regularities. It has more to do with using an anthropological imagination, with human diversity in thinking, practices, social relations, and living conditions as its major resource. And this imagination is also what we can at times effectively turn into cultural critique.

What is there to be compared? No doubt a great many things, large and small, but let me point to a couple of the things that have entered my mind.[6] Recently we have been hearing again and again about the greying of a large part of the human population—in much of Europe, not so much in North America, certainly not in Africa or the Arab world, but clearly in Japan, and when one realizes the consequences of the one-child policy, in China as well. Before that, for several decades in "the West," we followed the passage of the "baby boomers" through the stages of life, from the shaping of youth cultures and rebellions through powerful consumer habits to the present when these are the people who are indeed involved in greying. It seems to me that a kind of cultural demography that offers an organized picture of generational changes in interests and experiences, of the implications of differing generation sizes, and of demographic policies and manipulations, could be of great general interest—and I do not see that we have that, as a large-scale comparative enterprise, in anthropology yet.

Or take, as another topic, disasters. Fairly long ago now, I was impressed by the historical sociologist Kai Erikson's book *Everything in Its Path* (1976), about the destruction of the way of life of the people of Buffalo Creek, West Virginia, as a dam burst, and their habitat was laid waste. Since then, we have learned, increasingly rapidly and extensively through global media, about a great many other and often larger catastrophes: to remember just some, Bhopal in 1984, 9/11 in New York, the Southeast Asian tsunami of 2004, the hurricane Katrina in New Orleans, the earthquake and tsunami in Japan in 2011, and more. Some have been human-made, some natural, and then in some cases what is what has been a matter of controversy. Certain of them have indeed been the subjects of extensive ethnographic study.[7] Beyond that, I could imagine a kind of comparative treatment of what might be recurrent themes: the immediate shock of the disaster; the collective, more or less long-term trauma that follows; spontaneous and organized actions to help victims and deal with conditions; world responses; rebuilding lives; the political and legal aftermath. There would be a challenge here in combining narrative with comparison, but it would seem well worth trying.

These would be instances of comparison, in an intellectually creative mode. There would be other potential projects of retrieving existing ethnography that I would think of rather as syntheses. Take one example here: in recent years, there has been much public interest in the global rise of the BRIC countries, Brazil, Russia, India, China, or BRICS, if South Africa

is also to be included. On each of these, there exists a great deal of ethnographic writing. Synthesizing some of it, on one or other of these countries,
could be a way of offering a sense of diversity and time depth that is frequently lacking in other accounts—including some of the journalism that is
inclined to dwell on some single story line and be mostly presentist.

An attempt at such synthesis, however, probably had better not take the
shape of a hermetically sealed anthropological enterprise. Rather, it would
need to connect to the ways in which the country in question, or whatever
other kind of topic is involved, is in the news, or in public discourse in other
channels, or in shared memory. It would be a synthesis that opens up to
what is in the headlines, or in the movies, or on the bestseller lists of global
fiction. If you write about Brazil, you may be writing in a kind of dialogue
with Jorge Amado, and certainly Gilberto Freyre; if you write about India,
do not forget Arundhati Roy, Salman Rushdie, or *Slumdog Millionaire.*

Trying out comparisons and syntheses, you may come close to the ways
of some historians. In their later work, anthropologists like Eric Wolf and
Jack Goody have indeed become more like historians along such lines—or
critics of some work by historians, or by historical sociologists. But then
there is also a question of audiences. On the whole, I believe, Goody's and
Wolf's writings may have remained largely with a circle of, if not anthropological, then at least academic readers. The kinds of work I envisage should
have a potential, if the writing is right, of bringing some portions of the
wealth of anthropological knowledge also to wider publics. Look at the footnotes and the references of most of the journalists, and many of the academics from other disciplines, currently writing about one region or other of the
world, and you will not come across much evidence of an awareness of anthropological research. Most historians certainly likewise write monographs
in large part to be read by their peers in history departments—but then you
also have people like Simon Schama, Timothy Garton Ash, the late Tony
Judt, and (in a somewhat different mode) Peter Burke, who reach out much
more widely. Anthropology could do with some writing more comparable
to theirs.[8]

WHOSE ETHNOGRAPHY?

The suggestion that we should make more use of the body of accumulated
anthropological knowledge, that you or I should feel free to use other people's ethnography, raises various questions. One of them is about data quality, not least comparability. Past critiques of work drawing for example on

the Human Relations Area Files often focused on the way that such studies built on uneven sources of highly diverse origins, with the consequence that methodological demands were not really met. More recently, the point has often been made that ethnographic fieldwork and writing has a very personal quality, that it is perhaps rather more art than science.[9]

What are the implications of this for the kinds of comparison and synthesis I have suggested? I think they are manageable, with a measure of professional common sense and critical ability. Some ethnography may be "very personal," other ethnography in fact less so. The materials assembled for writing of these kinds need, certainly, to be critically assessed in each instance for their suitability as sources and illustrative instances. But it could even be that writings acknowledged to have a strong personal quality become powerful ingredients in a more synthesizing work precisely because of this.

Then there is the question of how we may feel about using other people's ethnography, or having ours used by others. Ethnographies may not be quite in a textual commons. What, if any, probably informal rather than formal, are our rules of intellectual property? We may be mostly flattered if a colleague draws on our work as an example in an introductory textbook, but would we be uneasy about using large portions of someone else's ethnography for some synthesis of our own, or would we be upset if a colleague, somewhere in the world, draws extensively on what we have written and published ourselves? When Ruth Benedict (1934) recycled other writers' ethnography in *Patterns of Culture,* perhaps it was less problematic because she could draw on people in her own circle—her mentor Franz Boas on the Kwakiutl; Reo Fortune, the husband of one of her closest friends, on the Dobu—as well as on her own (rather limited) work on the Zuni, but in this latter case on that of other associates as well. When at advanced stages in their careers Mary Douglas and Edmund Leach turned to the Bible for materials, they were presumably on safe grounds. No text could be more clearly in the public domain; only God could possibly claim this one as his own intellectual property (and we cannot know if He might eventually take revenge on any infringements).

Perhaps there will be a need to identify some practical rules of conduct here. On the whole, I would think that we must recognize that what has been written and published is available for new uses. Of course, as in any scholarly writing, sources must be properly acknowledged. If one's interpretation of materials is notably different from, or even contrary to, that of the original author, that probably ought to be made clear. But more issues may arise that require further discussion.

WRITING OTHERWISE: THREE EXAMPLES

One might think that the preoccupation among anthropologists with a pattern of authorship that involves an unbroken line from intensive fieldwork to a monograph based on and dominated by the ethnographic materials one has thus collected and organized is just a little puzzling. Consider the fact that a fair amount of the most successful writing has been of another kind, and that a number of prominent anthropologists are really best known for other sorts of work. Who now connects Mary Douglas first of all with *The Lele of the Kasai* (1963), or Sidney Mintz primarily with *Worker in the Cane* (1960)? There are indeed many ways of contributing to the written corpus of anthropology. A few examples from the work of currently active colleagues may be illustrative.

The first is Michael Herzfeld's *Cultural Intimacy* (1997).[10] Herzfeld is someone who has certainly not given up on fieldwork, even in new locales, but he does other kinds of writing as well. In *Cultural Intimacy* he may never distance himself very much from the Greek ethnography that he knows so expertly, but basically this is a work of theory and critique. His newly minted notion of "cultural intimacy" refers to those well-known modes of thought and conduct in a group (mostly understood at the national level) that are nevertheless taken to be a little embarrassing, should therefore not be observed or commented on by outsiders, and may be denied, attributed minimum importance, or explained away. So in the case of Greece, festive porcelain crushing and rural sheep thefts show up again in this book, but as topics of debate and stereotyping. And overall, the focus of attention here is on the inherent complexities of the tension between the actual practices and strategies of ordinary people and the essentializing, politically correct cultural claims set forth by elites and state machineries—which are, in the end, only another kind of ordinary people.

My intention here is not to try and summarize or review Herzfeld's subtle and wide-ranging argument in this book, the chapters of which actually draw extensively on articles and chapters published elsewhere (including places that for many anthropologists would be a bit out of the way), although they have been reworked to offer aspects of a coherent, integrated point of view. I want rather to draw attention to a style of work, continuously intellectually expansive. Herzfeld draws on his own previous studies as well as those of other ethnographers of Greece, but also, through comparisons-in-passing and in other ways, on a much wider knowledge of world ethnography, classic and more recent: the Nuer show up, and creolization. For his theoretical repertoire he draws not only on his own discipline but also on philosophy, linguistics, and semiotics, and enters into brief exchanges with scholars from other disciplines as well. In this way, he manages to offer a more general perspective toward the handling of meaning in relationships of state and society, and by extension also toward the meaning of Europe, with its relations of dominance—where we can see Greece again and again finding itself in problematic positions of marginality. Through this work, "cultural intimacy" may have succeeded in establishing a foothold not just as a book title but as a concept more widely used in anthropology, and perhaps beyond. (Possibly as in other such instances of successful, collectivized concepts, one should only be aware of a danger that if in other hands, it could become overextended and misunderstood.)

And then Herzfeld ends his book with an afterword, proposing a "militant middle ground," a field of scrutiny between established polarities. There is a defence of the work of anthropologists here, pointing to its ability to gain significant insights from inside, backstage observations of what to outsiders (not least from other disciplines) may seem like quaint trivia. But there is also an admonition to the anthropologists themselves not to give in to the polarities, not to accept rules of etiquette that would land them in bland cultural relativism, but to exercise the critical capacity that can come out of their special social and cultural positioning.

In some ways, at least, it would seem reasonable to take my second example as a case of such critical work; in other ways perhaps not. Aihwa Ong's *Neoliberalism as Exception* (2006) is a set of essays, anchored in the Asia-Pacific region, with its North American extensions. Ong grew up in Malaysia, obviously has an especially deep understanding of that country but an excellent overview of Southeast Asia generally, and has had a long-term academic base at one of California's leading universities; this offers her the opportunity to keep an eye on, and stay involved with, what goes on in the San Francisco Bay area, a hub of Asian economic, cultural, and other activities in North America.

Her emphasis in this book, however, is rather on theory, broadening into social commentary. "Neoliberalism" is a term that has entered anthropology with some force since the late twentieth century, but unlike "cultural intimacy" it did not originate there but has seemed to be all over the place, in a variety of academic disciplines as well as in the political vocabulary generally. And this is a term that has come to stand for many things, at the same time as it may have been reified as One Big Thing. Generally, it may be taken to refer to a triumph of the market, and the retreat of the state; but as one looks a little closer, one can see that state machineries have often been among the frequent and enthusiastic users of what are taken to be neoliberal principles.

Ong's theme throughout these essays, then, is the study of neoliberalism as "mobile calculative techniques of governing that can be decontextualized from their original sources and recontextualized in constellations of mutually constitutive and contingent relationships" (2006: 13). It is a matter of "midrange theorizing," drawing prominently also on classic and current thinking about sovereignty and governmentality but still remaining rather close to the terrain of facts. Neoliberalism turns out to be a rather protean entity, shifting shapes as it migrates between sites. Ong can discuss the creation of new economic zones in China, an emergent Chinese diaspora cyberpublic, the governmental response to Islamic feminism in Malaysia, the refashioning of Singapore as a "global city" characterized by high-tech knowledge enterprises, and the exploitation of transnational migrant maids and nannies as an Asian form of neoslavery; on the other side of the Pacific, she can comment critically on the consequences of the globalization of American universities, and on "body shopping" in Silicon Valley, where skilled Asian workers come to do contract labor for information technology industries.

Ong's account of the penetration of the Asia-Pacific region by neoliberalism, however, tends to stay rather consistently at an institutional and organizational level. It can be seen as a pioneering contribution to an anthropology of the large-scale, a contemporary macroanthropology. As one reviewer of the book (Choy 2008) has pointed out, there is on the other hand rather little here of people's own words and experiences, of interpersonal relationships, of thick accounts of face-to-face contacts. Perhaps, then, this is not ethnography in the strictest sense. The political scientists and economists who might be consternated by some of the ethnographer Herzfeld's enthusiasms will probably feel more at home with Ong's description of the social landscape.

Where Ong comes closest to a more conventional ethnographer's craft, I think, is in the final chapter, on "Reengineering the 'Chinese Soul' in Shanghai." The nature of Ong's field engagement with Shanghai does not become particularly clear; endnotes refer to dates when certain interviews took place. One senses that the chapter is based on a brief stay, and it involves a kind of sophisticated reporting, with some local personal color, not entirely different from what a good journalist—a *good* journalist—might do. More generally, *Neoliberalism as Exception* can perhaps be characterized as a work with a strong intention of contributing to a theoretical debate, drawing for the purpose on a kind of continuous low-intensity fieldwork, and sometimes fieldwork at a distance, rather than fieldwork by immersion. For that purpose, too, Ong shows her skills of synthesis. She cites a variety of academic sources for theory as well as empirical materials, but she is clearly a well-organized consumer of other media as well: among the references one finds the *New York Times, Wall Street Journal, South China Morning Post, San*

Francisco Chronicle, Metro: Silicon Valley's Weekly Newspaper, Manila Times, and *Straits Times,* as well as Mao's *Little Red Book.*

The anthropologist as a writer is usually a lone wolf, just as he or she tends to be as a fieldworker. My third example of "writing otherwise," in contrast, is a collaborative effort. The authors are an anthropologist and a sociologist; however, this divide between disciplines matters much less than the fact that of these two Israeli academics, one is Jewish and the other Arab. As *Coffins on Our Shoulders,* by Dan Rabinowitz and Khawla Abu-Baker, appeared in English, published by a major American university press, in 2005, it had already been through two editions, in Hebrew and in Arabic. To show that it was the work of equals, the authors' names appeared in different orders on the covers of these editions.

This is not a purely academic work, intended for consumption only by peers on campuses. It is a personal inquiry into the development of the nation of Israel, and the situation of its Arab minority. Social and political history is interwoven with the authors' family histories. Abu-Baker's begins as her maternal grandfather, born at the beginning of the twentieth century in a West Bank village in what was still an undivided Ottoman Palestine, migrates to the growing coastal city of Haifa. Her family remains there, through a couple of generations, until with the war of 1948 it is forced to relocate a little further north, in the ancient town of Acre, where a stronger Arab community remained. After some years, however, at least parts of the family could return to Haifa, and Khawla Abu-Baker was born and grew up there. Both of Dan Rabinowitz's parents had their family roots in East Central Europe. His mother's family came directly from there to Palestine in the years between the world wars. His father's family had moved from there to South Africa, where his father was born and lived until his Zionist commitment took him as a young adult to Palestine. The Rabinowitz family made its home in Haifa, where Dan was born. So he and his co-author grew up in the same city, and they are the same age; later both had academic training abroad. A substantial part of the book involves switching back and forth between these parallel family lives, into the present, where they have each formed families, and where they themselves have children who travel outside Israel, and whose perspectives toward the home country are shaped partly by such experiences.[11] But especially the latter part of the book focuses more on the period after 2000, the period after what became known to the outside world mostly as "the second intifada," the Israeli political response to it, and the situation and the points of view of the "Stand-Tall Generation" of young Palestinian citizens of Israel, born in the last quarter of the twentieth century, the third generation since Israel became an independent state. As the label suggests, and as the authors portray this age category, it is a generation with self-confidence, disillusioned with the Israeli national project, and with a strong sense of collective identity.

Throughout the book, to the extent that there is a sense of local settings, these are in Haifa, Acre, and the Galilee, central to the authors' personal lives and to their own research experiences. If much writing on Israel centers on Jerusalem, Tel Aviv, and the contrast between them, this book thus contributes to a wider perspective. But as it also takes on an interpretation of wider tendencies particularly in recent Israeli life; it becomes a matter of more general, incisive political reporting. Here it undoubtedly matters that especially Rabinowitz has for some time been a practicing public intellectual, recognized not least for his contributions to *Haaretz,* the most intellectually inclined Israeli daily newspaper. Yet one should note that while the parts of the text dealing with family and personal histories can obviously be identified with one author or the other, it is not otherwise dialogical in character. Abu-Baker and Rabinowitz seem to agree on overall narrative and analysis. As they end their book with fundamentally post-Zionist suggestions for a reconstruction of Israeli society that would allow a better, more equal incorporation of its Arab citizens in societal life, it becomes politically rather daring.

These are three quite different books, involving anthropologists with reputations already established on the basis of field studies of a more classic type, who have gone on to writings along other lines. Certainly they can draw on their field experiences, but they also reach beyond them, in various directions. And they tend to suggest that in the field studies early in anthropologists' careers, there are very possibly not only single completed projects, but also the seeds for new projects, continued explorations in writing.

CULTURAL BROKERAGE IN THE SHADOW
OF THE TOWER OF BABEL

Finally, let me report briefly on a writing experiment of my own. A great many members of the global anthropological community, including presumably readers of this book (and, in fact, a number of its contributors, including myself), are not native speakers of English, and they live and work in countries where English is not the national language. This is the context for my recent book *Café du Monde* (2011b). The main title happens to be in French, or seems to be in French, but quite possibly many will recognize that it is the name of a well-known establishment in New Orleans. The book starts out there, but above all this is taken as a metaphor for a point of view toward the world. The subtitle, something like "Places, roads and people in the global swirl" suggests that more directly, although it comes out a bit more idiomatically in Swedish—and the book is in that language.

It is a book of essays, not easily placed in a genre. There is an autobiographical element in it, but as one of my early commentators pointed out, it is personal but not private—not about me, but about various things that have interested me. I may confess that one of the reasons I got around to writing it was that I had, in quick succession, two exciting sojourns as an academic visitor, in Tokyo and in Tel Aviv.[12] I learned a lot about Japan, and about Israel and Palestine, through observations, talking to colleagues and other people, and reading. In the end I felt that there were things that I wanted to write about—but then I could not claim any real expertise on these countries and regions. So my solution was to try and find a kind of reportage that would be some sort of hybrid between anthropology and journalism, aiming at an audience that might well have some general academic background (after all, a great many book readers do), but who would most likely, even preferably, not be anthropologists.

And again, it is a book in my Swedish mother tongue. Very little of my academic writing has been in that language, and most of my writing has been aimed largely at anthropologists and people in adjacent fields. This, then, was part of my reason for doing this book: to let any interested compatriots know what the life of an anthropologist might be like these days, but also because it might serve as an excuse for reporting on things where my expertise was limited, but where "nobody had really written on these topics in quite the same way in Swedish before."

The essays thus draw on three of my field studies; in a black neighborhood in Washington, DC, in a Nigerian town, and among news media foreign correspondents. There are also those that come out of my stays in Tokyo and Tel Aviv. Another chapter, on the recently popular notion of "soft power" as a kind of international politics of culture, moves between the United States and Japan. Some use mostly historical materials: one summarizes the life history of a Japanese renaissance figure of the Meiji era (whose portrait is now on ten-thousand-yen notes); another is based on colonial archival materials where young British district officers report to their superiors about my Nigerian field site as it once was. A chapter on some ships in history suggests how at one time a vessel could have a captain who may just possibly have been taken to be a god; and how at present, on the other hand, ships may carry as passengers the wretched of the earth, refugees who risk their lives and are unwanted at the point of arrival. There is a sort of narrative thread here, but it also allows me for one thing to report on the anthropological controversy over the reception of Captain Cook in Hawaii, and for another, to view the 1948 journey of the steamer *Empire Windrush* from Jamaica to London as a starting point of colonial and postcolonial migration to Europe, and the transformation of the receiving society.

As several chapters are attempts at journalism and synthesis, I take pleasure in bringing together rather diverse materials. A chapter on the Brazilian city of Salvador, to which I was once fortunate to make a kind of brief pilgrimage, dwells on its contacts across the Atlantic with West Africa, and the history of scholars' and other visitors' encounters with it. Here I could draw on the studies by anthropologists from Ruth Landes (1947) to Lorand Matory (2005), but also on other writers, from Daniel Defoe by way of Stefan Zweig, Simone de Beauvoir, and Bruce Chatwin to Wole Soyinka. And for a portrayal of Jerusalem, from Ottoman times to the present, I could draw on the travel reporting by a leading nineteenth-century Swedish feminist and by an early-twentieth-century Swedish cultural and literary critic, both still well known to audiences in what had been their home country.

Generally I seize opportunities to show connections, particularly more surprising ones, between places. Lafcadio Hearn, Greek-Irish writer, shows up in New Orleans as well as Japan. A Nigerian novelist, who turns out to be born in the town where I did fieldwork, writes on the basis of his father's reminiscences, about the African soldiers fighting for the British against the Japanese in Burma, in World War II. I come to that as I report on the Yasukuni shrine in Tokyo, devoted to honoring fallen Japanese soldiers but also, more controversially, a number of convicted war criminals. But then another African serving with the British in Burma was Barack Obama's Kenyan grandfather—and I get to that fact when, as an extension of my Salvador chapter, I visit a Yoruba temple in the American South, a few days after Obama's 2008 election victory. That chapter in fact becomes rather multi-sited: it allows me also to reminisce about my road journey, several decades earlier, along the West African coast, and past the ruins of an old Portuguese fortress that had overstayed its welcome in independent Africa, as a mini-colony and reminder of the days of the slave trade.

You may sense that it is a book I enjoyed doing. But it is a book I do not want to have translated into English; it is written for a Swedish audience and not really for anybody else. Again, partly this would be simply because a fair amount of the materials I draw on are already accessible enough in English, so there is no need. At least as importantly, however, I have tried to anchor the writing in understandings shared with a specifically Swedish audience. When we do more purely academic texts, we may write in a style that fits everywhere but nowhere in particular, one that we try not to make intellectually parochial by belonging too narrowly in some particular cultural context. In *Café du Monde,* in contrast, there can be another kind of cultural density, as at least here and there I seize opportunities to connect precisely to what is familiar to a Swedish reader: places in the Swedish geography, an old Swedish children's game, stars of Swedish intellectual history. When I describe the ups and downs of a local ruling dynasty in nineteenth-century Nigeria (if I may be allowed an anachronism—in that century there was not yet a Nigeria), I can allude to the similarities with a certain American television serial once shown world-wide, but I can also remind the reader of the Vasa royal dynasty in Sweden in the sixteenth century, with its own heroes and fools.

How can my *Café du Monde* experiment point to ways of "writing otherwise" for other anthropologists situated in the borderlands between an international academic language (nowadays mostly but not always English) and some national language with its own reading publics? I would argue that in the shadow of the Tower of Babel, still globally powerful, colleagues in such locations can serve usefully as cultural brokers and gatekeepers.[13] In most countries, even highly literate citizens are usually not entirely at ease reading long texts such as books in any foreign language. And even if they are, it is a practical fact that they are unlikely to stumble onto foreign-language anthropology in the bookstores they frequent. Usually there will not be many straight translations of such work either. Consequently, the scholars who are at home in the national language can draw on the entire library of international anthropology, in a more or less personal and creative fashion, to introduce parts of it to audiences otherwise out of reach, and thus draw on it to give a view of what anthropology is about. And who knows, perhaps such probably brief glimpses can even stimulate an occasional reader to go the library, or to www.amazon.com, and seek out the original text?

Ulf Hannerz is Professor Emeritus of Social Anthropology, Stockholm University, and a member of the Royal Swedish Academy of Sciences, the American Academy of Arts and Sciences, and the Austrian Academy of Sciences. A former Chair of the European Association of Social Anthropologists, he has taught at American, European, Asian, and Australian universities and conducted field studies in West Africa, the Caribbean, and the United States, as well as a multi-site study of the work of news media foreign correspondents. Among his books are *Soulside* (1969), *Exploring the City* (1980), *Cultural Complexity* (1992), *Transnational Connections* (1996), *Foreign News* (2004), and *Anthropology's World* (2010).

NOTES

1. He touched on the theme briefly, with a contrast between historians and mathematicians, in another connection (Geertz 1983: 159).

2. Alma Gottlieb's edited volume *The Restless Anthropologist* (2012) brings together the accounts of a number of anthropologists who have moved on to new fields; they do not conceal the fact that there are sometimes obstacles to be faced, of both personal and institutional nature, as one chooses to do so.

3. I give the contemporary varieties of fieldwork a little more attention elsewhere (Hannerz 2010: 59–86).

4. For a review of early comparative method in anthropology, and criticisms directed against it, see Köbben (1970).

5. See also Gingrich (2012) for a current view of the place of comparison in the context of anthropological methodology generally.

6. If one or both these projects have indeed already been carried out, my apologies for not knowing about it, and my congratulations to the achievement.

7. Although the floodings in Argentina that she has studied may not have the same status as globally known events as those just mentioned, let me also point to Ullberg's (2013) rich work on the memoryscapes of victims in a flood-prone city.

8. Eriksen has discussed the possibilities of "reaching out" with anthropological writing more extensively, and my views of the issue would be much like his. See also particularly chapter 3 of my book *Anthropology's World* (2010) on the need to build a more accurate and up-to-date public understanding of anthropology, and Hannerz (2011a) for further suggestions. Not all attempts to write in academically unconventional genres may contribute much to individual or institutional rankings in acknowledged indexes of scientific achievement—but perhaps we can hope that they can function, and be acknowledged, as public service (what in Swedish academia is described as "the third task," after research and teaching).

9. The discussion of these two faces of anthropology actually goes back at least to Kroeber (1952, 1963) and Redfield (1962); see also Leslie (1960: 79–91). I am grateful to Adamson Hoebel for drawing my attention to Leslie's book in a conversation as I visited the University of Minnesota in April 1968. See also Kloos (1990).

10. A later edition of *Cultural Intimacy* (2004) is expanded to include later developments, and responses to the key concept.

11. What the book actually does not say much about is how the authors came to know each other, and how their joint book project actually came about. There are, on the other hand, a few illuminating passages about later working interactions over the project, including questions of language.

12. I remain grateful particularly to Shinji Yamashita and Moshe Shokeid for making those stays both possible and very enjoyable.

13. I devote Chapter 6 of *Anthropology's World* (2010) entirely to issues connected to the linguistic diversity of world anthropology.

REFERENCES

Benedict, Ruth. 1934. *Patterns of Culture.* Boston: Houghton Mifflin.

Choy, Timothy K. 2008. "Review of Aihwa Ong, Neoliberalism as Exception." *Political and Legal Anthropology Review* 31: 338–342.

Douglas, Mary. 1963. *The Lele of the Kasai.* London: Oxford University Press.

Eriksen, Thomas Hylland. 2006. *Engaging Anthropology: The Case of a Public Presence.* Oxford: Berg.

Erikson, Kai T. 1976. *Everything in Its Path: Destruction of Community in the Buffalo Creek Flood.* New York: Simon & Schuster.

Fox, Richard G., and Andre Gingrich, eds. 2002. *Anthropology, by Comparison.* London: Routledge.

Geertz, Clifford. 1983. *Local Knowledge: Further Essays in Interpretive Anthropology.* New York: Basic Books.

Gingrich, Andre. 2012. "Methodology." In *Handbook of Sociocultural Anthropology,* ed. James G. Carrier and Deborah B. Gewertz. London: Berg.

Gottlieb, Alma. ed. 2012. *The Restless Anthropologist; New Fieldsites, New Visions.* Chicago: University of Chicago Press.

Hannerz, Ulf. 2010. *Anthropology's World: Life in a Twenty-First-Century Discipline.* London: Pluto.

———. 2011a. "Operation Outreach: Anthropology and the Public in a World of Information Crowding." *Archivio Antropologico Mediterraneo* 13, no. 1: 11–17.

———. 2011b. *Café du Monde: platser, vägar och människor i världsvimlet.* Stockholm: Carlssons.

Herzfeld, Michael. 1997. *Cultural Intimacy: Social Poetics in the Nation-State.* London: Routledge.

Holy, Ladislav, ed. 1987 *Comparative Anthropology.* Oxford: Blackwell.

Kloos, Peter, ed. 1990. *True Fiction: Artistic and Scientific Representations of Reality.* Amsterdam: VU University Press.

Köbben, André JF. 1970. "Comparativists and Non-Comparativists in Anthropology." In R. Naroll and R. Cohen, eds. *A Handbook of Method in Cultural Anthropology.* Garden City, NY: Natural History Press.

Kroeber, AL. 1952. *The Nature of Culture.* Chicago: University of Chicago Press.

———. 1963. *An Anthropologist Looks at History.* Berkeley: University of California Press.

Landes, Ruth. 1947. *The City of Women.* New York: Macmillan.

Leslie, Charles. 1960. *Now We Are Civilized: A Study of the World View of the Zapotec Indians of Mitla, Oaxaca.* Detroit: Wayne State University Press.

Matory, J. Lorand. 2005. *Black Atlantic Religion: Tradition, Transnationalism, and Matriarchy in the Afro-Brazilian Candomblé.* Princeton, NJ: Princeton University Press.

Mintz, Sidney W. 1960. *Worker in the Cane: A Puerto Rican Life History.* New Haven, CT: Yale University Press.

Ong, Aihwa. 2006. *Neoliberalism as Exception: Mutations in Citizenship and Sovereignty.* Durham, NC: Duke University Press.

Rabinowitz, Dan, and Khawla Abu-Baker. 2005. *Coffins on Our Shoulders: The Experience of the Palestinian Citizens of Israel.* Berkeley: University of California Press.

Redfield, Robert. 1962. *Human Nature and the Study of Society.* Chicago: University of Chicago Press.

Ullberg, Susann. 2013. *Watermarks: Urban Flooding and Memory Scape in Argentina.* Stockholm: Stockholm Studies in Social Anthropology, n.s. 8. Stockholm University.

Index